AESTHETIC DEMOCRACY

AESTHETIC DEMOCRACY

Thomas Docherty

STANFORD UNIVERSITY PRESS

STANFORD, CALIFORNIA

2006

Stanford University Press
Stanford, California

Printed in the United States of America on acid-free, archival-quality paper

Library of Congress Cataloging-in-Publication Data

Docherty, Thomas.
    Aesthetic democracy / Thomas Docherty.
        p.   cm.
    Includes bibliographical references and index.
    ISBN 0-8047-5188-9 (cloth : alk. paper)
    ISBN 0-8047-5189-7 (pbk. : alk. paper)
    1. Democracy—Philosophy.   2. Critical theory.   I. Title.

JC423.D667 2006
321.8—DC22

2005025801

Original Printing 2006

Last figure below indicates year of this printing:
15   14   13   12   11   10   09   08   07   06

For Bridie May Sullivan and Hamish J. S. Docherty

Contents

Preface

This book starts from the premise that there is an intimate link between aesthetics and democracy. That, in itself, is not new: indeed, much of the history of twentieth-century criticism and theory consists in an argument about the extent to which art has been politically determined. Some thinkers have seen the link as being so intimate that they will claim that art is political through and through, whereas for others the relation is more attenuated, although still there. The debate is given its most urgent point and clearest articulation in the work of Walter Benjamin, especially in his response to the great question of what we should do when confronted with a state of affairs in which the political has become aestheticised: we should politicise the aesthetic. Yet the title of this book is *Aesthetic Democracy*, and the suggestion here, in my qualifying of the concept of democracy with the adjective 'aesthetic', is meant to indicate that the link between aesthetics and democracy is indeed so intimate as to suggest that democracy is entirely *conditioned* by aesthetics as such.

In the present book, I argue what might seem at first to be a counterintuitive proposition. Instead of accepting that a political state of affairs determines the shape and nature of our art, I propose that the relation is effectively reversed, and that it is the aesthetic determinants of a given social formation that enable us to be political beings at all, to be members of, participants in, or even citizens in a polity. In short, we might see that there is a certain inflection in our living of 'democracy' that is dependent on aesthetics. It is important to see this not as some homage to Oscar Wilde, however thought-provoking his habitual counterintuitive pronouncements might have been; rather, my argument is that we do not fully understand democracy unless and until we have an understanding of how much it depends on what is at stake in any given moment of the aesthetic.

What is at stake is that there be established a social relation among subjects of perception. How might we think of this? First, subjects of perception here are those entities who will constitute themselves as 'I' or as 'we'—and thus become identities—precisely by virtue of the act of perception in which they can propose themselves as a community that shares, at least for the purposes of their mutual engagement, an object. They do not yet 'own' the object except as a conceptual other against which they can identify themselves precisely as subjects of perception, locations of a point of view. Second, that establishment of a relation that constitutes an opening to the social is also a *moment* of perception. It is important for this argument that such a moment be seen precisely as a matter *of moment*, an 'event' that carries with it the physically kinetic energy of a momentum. Third, the nature of that event may or may not establish a relation among the subjects of perception that could truly be said to be democratic; and, for this, we might have recourse to a specific understanding of the stakes of democracy itself.

In all of this, I have to face up to the fact that for many, democracy is consonant with, indeed identified with, a certain freedom; and, further, that what I propose here might seem to be at odds with such ideas. There is a reason for this. Freedom has been reduced in most common discussions of democracy to a matter of choice: where there is choice (between political parties, between consumables) there is also thereby freedom, and such freedom is identified with a political system that calls itself democratic. My argument here goes completely against this view. I try to deepen the idea and the fact of freedom by seeing it not as a matter of choice but as a matter of the event, and most significantly, of the event that I call cultural. The cultural event is that moment in our relations, in our perceptions or in the aesthetic, in which we see the possibility or potential for freedom; and the location for that, most often, is in what we call art: literature, poetry, painting, music, dance, sculpture. A democracy that is intent on establishing and furthering the freedom of subjects—subjects who know themselves always to be conditioned by the alterity to which art opens them—is the most fundamental form of democracy that we might have. A polity that degrades or ignores the aesthetic, or sees it as an arithmetical add-on to a social formation rather than a fundamental geometry that shapes the very possibility of our being sociable and free at all, entirely misses the point; and the consequence of that is not only a degradation of the concept of freedom, but also a reduction in actual freedom.

〜

I have had the pleasure of trying out many of the ideas in the pages that follow before many audiences who provided most welcome feedback. I thank my audiences in Bergen, Canterbury (University of Kent), Cairo, Edinburgh, Ghent, Grahamstown (Rhodes University), Harvard, Leeds, London, Reims, Rosario, and Utrecht. Parts of some of the chapters have appeared in different form in the following journals or volumes: chapter 2 in Martin McQuillan, ed., *Emergencies: Deconstruction, Politics, Cultural Studies* (London: Routledge, 2006); chapter 4 in John Joughin and Simon Malpas, eds., *The New Aestheticism* (Manchester: Manchester University Press, 2003); chapter 6 in *Paragraph* 25, no. 2 (2002), special number on Agamben, ed. Brian Dillon; and chapter 8 in the journal *Shakespeare in Southern Africa*, vol. 13 (2001). I thank the editors and publishers for permission to reuse some materials here.

Many others have contributed to my thinking on the issues here, and I have in particular benefited from discussions, dialogues, or correspondence with Wolfgang Iser, J. Hillis Miller, Andrew Gibson, Hoda Gindi, Daniel Thomières, Wendy Jacobson, Malvern Van Wyck Smyth, Brian Dillon, Stefania Ciocia, David Herd, Randall Stevenson, Jürgen Pieters, Ann Rigney, Paolo de Medeiros, and Stuart Sillars. Colleagues at my previous institution, the University of Kent, provided a strong, supportive, and congenial intellectual environment. Needless to say, none of these can be held responsible for the infelicities that may lie in these pages: those, at least, I can claim as my own. Let me here also thank two people whose life and thought sustain me, the two without whom nothing would matter at all: Bridie Sullivan and Hamish Docherty. The book and the work in it, like everything I do, are dedicated to them and to their freedom.

Warwick, September 2005

Introduction

Culture is extraordinary.

Let us begin from this statement. Culture, I shall argue here, is not a state of affairs, not a mode or manner of living; rather, 'culture' names an event in which the ordinary—a manner of living—discovers or reveals a foundation that is extraordinary, and whose extraordinariness makes possible a different manner of living. Culture can be defined as that event of perception—the root sense of 'aesthetic' (*aisthanomai*)—that calls a human subject to differ from itself, and to find or to constitute its very identity precisely through the specific mode of that differing. It therefore names the possibility of a transformation, a change in our ordinariness that is occasioned by aesthetics or art. The name that we give to that change is history: our historical becoming and our becoming historical.

Democracy is extraordinary.

By this second statement, I mean to suggest that democracy, like culture, is not a constant, not a state of affairs, not a political mode of being; rather, democracy—episodic and rare—names those moments in which the possibility of an ethical respect for selfhood, a selfhood that is marked by cultural change, discovers or reveals itself to be conditioned by alterity, or by our condition of being-with-otherness. The name that we give to this, usually, is 'becoming'. Democracy, we might say, is the condition of our becoming human; and a democracy that finds its episodic roots in the event that we call cultural is the condition of our becoming humanly and socially historical.

∽

This book begins from these two statements and explores the logic of taking them seriously. The argument is that democracy depends on a prior aesthetic event; or, to phrase it differently, democracy is impossible in a polity that degrades the arts. We might call this a 'new aestheticism', and there are many who would support such a position, from diverse political perspectives. I prefer here to call it 'aesthetic democracy'.

Democracy is confused in our commonplace speech today with the idea of a so-called free market, in which consumers, not citizens, celebrate themselves and their freedom in the choices that they allegedly make in an unregulated marketplace or *agora*. It is important to note that in this state of affairs, the subject as *consumer* has usurped the subject as *citizen*. Freedom is thereby reduced to a matter of 'choice', the entire content of freedom being evacuated and replaced by an activity that supposedly demonstrates a 'freedom of choice'. This debased version of freedom is demonstrated through the enactments of choice in a supposedly 'free' or unregulated market. Although we may not quite be 'nations of shopkeepers' (Napoleon's famous scornful description of England), we are nations of shoppers.

In such a polity, there is no possibility of substantive change, no possibility of history; and such a society is therefore precisely anathema to the very democracy that it vaunts as its allegedly founding condition. Baudrillard's early work is useful here. In his analyses of consumer culture, made especially in his 1970 study of *La Société de consommation*, Baudrillard was able to demonstrate that the logic and structures of consumer society have an effect that goes well beyond the merely mercantile economy. It is in this work that Baudrillard begins the trajectory in his thought that leads him towards what appears as an ostensible pessimism and nihilism. In consumer society, there is established a particular condition in which human subjects start to define themselves not in terms of their relations with other subjects, but rather in terms of their relations with objects. Those objects thus start to exert a dramatic force over human subjects: we start off thinking we are empowering ourselves through our objects, enhancing our identity through them; but little by little, the relation is subverted and we become the victims of our objects, such that we feel ourselves to be not fully ourselves unless and until we possess the specific objects in which we have invested the image of our identity.

A new logic of *seduction* operates here, in which humans lose the very subjectivity that would enable them to become free and autonomous. Seduction works as a play of forces in which seducers gain power by ostensibly giving up their subjective power: they pretend, in fact, to be an object in order to exert a force of attraction that will force the other into taking the first step in the seduction. Crudely put, and in an analogy with erotic seduction, I seduce you precisely by making myself into an object for your desires, such that you initiate the action that will bring us together; and at that moment, precisely when you believe yourself to be acting freely in what you imagine to be your seduction of me, you are in fact already in my power. As in erotic relations, so also in consumer relations. The logic here is clear: consumer society is one in which we believe ourselves to be free subjects precisely at the moment when we have lost all subjective autonomy and have instead become simply those objects that are the instruments of the desires of others.[1] In this state of affairs, any 'change' that we might feel that we initiate as a demonstration or enactment of our 'autonomy' turns out to have been already programmed and decided for us in advance by others who hold a firm power over us. Further, such a condition precludes the possibility of our acting as citizens in any meaningful sense of the word.

It is not entirely surprising, then, to find, within such polities, that Lyotard's diagnosis of 1979 has some persistent validity. Knowledge itself, he wrote then, 'is and will be produced in order to be sold', in what is essentially the mercantilisation of the university as institution, and especially, within that institution, the mercantilisation of the aesthetic disciplines of the arts and humanities, where our practices are construed and legitimised in almost entirely instrumentalist terms. It is indeed the case that today, 'knowledge is a matter for TV games',[2] in that our social norms increasingly assume that knowledge—including humanistic knowledge—leads to monetary gain, and that that is its point.

The corollary of this is that knowledge no longer disrupts or disturbs the subject of learning, the student. Hans Blumenberg, in his magisterial study of *The Legitimacy of the Modern Age*, describes how, for the ancient world, knowledge was eudemonic. It was taken for granted that knowledge, being better than ignorance, made the subject happy. However, something happens to this notion in the eighteenth century, argued Blumenberg, and it becomes a measure of truth's absoluteness that, instead of giving pleasure, it gives pain: truth becomes 'harsh', unaccommodating, disturbing.[3] The situation that I describe above is one where we have lost such austerity once more in relation to truth and knowledge, certainly;

yet we have not returned to the ancient condition either. Rather, we have tended first to relativise all knowledge such that it becomes 'situated'; and, second, we have thus replaced epistemological value with financial value, quality with quantity. 'Situated' knowledge (I borrow the term from David Simpson[4]) is that form of knowledge that eschews any possibility of 'absolute knowing' or of a truth that transcends the position from which the knowledge is claimed. However, the point of such situatedness is always to call into doubt the knowledge that is claimed from any position that is different from one's own: in this mode of thinking, 'my' knowledge remains absolute 'for me', whereas 'yours' is always dubious (also 'for me', and therefore dubious *tout court*). In short, dialogue and debate—and with these the very possibility of a social formulation of truth or of knowledge—disappears. Such a disappearance allows subjects to continue in the solace of their ignorance of a knowledge that might require subjects to think themselves differently.

Truth or knowledge cannot be evaluated in such a condition, for there are simply no grounds that can be shared between two or more 'situations': by its very definition, the situations are situated differently from each other, their respective 'knowledges' incommensurable. Instead, what gives value here is simply the (literal) *currency* of truth. At its meagre best, this means that what passes for truth is simply what used to be called ideology: the 'what is taken for granted' by a majority within a community; and at worst, it means that what passes for truth is what most people will buy in a populist market (again, often literally, as in the paid-for subscription to certain 'news' discourses that are but the medium for advertising).

For those condemned to live and work within such a polity, knowledge indeed becomes a celebration of the ordinary as such, a celebration of the preexisting identities of its students. Made financially richer by their knowledge, they can enact more choices, and thereby come more fully into themselves, actualise more fully their real identities, or realise themselves 'freely' ('I can choose what to do or buy') and 'democratically' ('if I can do it, so can anyone'; 'everyone's doing it'; *così fan tutti e tutte*). It follows that there can be no culture—no event such as I described it above, in my opening gambit—and, further, no one is ever called on to change, to extend or to expand the self into something different. Finally, it also follows from this that the very ethical demand of the cultural event—the requirement that we can be attentive to alterity and to otherness as such—is also threatened.

Against all this, I will contend that the university and its once central disciplines of humanistic criticism ought to be a site of fantasy, in the genuine sense of that term—not Disneyland, which would not know magic if it suddenly appeared in a puff of smoke; but fantasy, as in imagining the impossible, and in then establishing or actualising the impossible, the unforeseeable. The activity of criticism ought to be a site for the exploration of the unpredictable and of the unspoken. Such an engagement is only possible, I contend, within a formation that is 'democratic' in the sense that I have given to that term above: conditioned by a 'becoming alterity', by our changing our very situatedness or our shared situation.

∼

Aesthetic democracy, as I term it here, would be that which places a rather austere and difficult set of demands upon the critic, the teacher, the student, the reader. The fundamental task of criticism would be, quite simply, to make culture happen, to bring about the event that reveals the extraordinary by making us step out of that which is ordinary for us. This is what is at the root of the long history of the fraught relations between aesthetics and politics. The truism has it that in *The Republic*, Plato banished the poets from the ideal republic essentially on political grounds. However, this is not entirely precise. Plato has Socrates make a fundamental distinction between two kinds or modes of literature. There is the diegetic, in which a narrative may be recited in the third person; and there is the mimetic, in which I assume the character of one of the persons in the narrative and portray her or his words dramatically and in the first person. It is only the latter that is to be banished:

if we are visited in our state by someone who has the skill to transform himself into all sorts of characters and represent all sorts of things, and he wants to show off himself and his poems to us, we shall treat him with all the reverence due to a priest and giver of rare pleasure, but shall tell him that he and his kind have no place in our city.[5]

In this argument, Socrates has it that mimesis, or adopting the voice of someone other than the self, is a fundamental threat to identity as such; and, further, if our educative practices are grounded in such mimesis (learning by heart; reciting dramatically), then there is the danger that we will be seduced away from our own identity and be too given over to alterity. Yet, as always in Plato, this cannot be the full story; for this is asserted precisely by Plato speaking mimetically in the figure and voice of Socrates. It follows that, if we banish mimesis, we must also banish the very text that argues for the banishing of mimesis; and thus mimesis can be repermitted, in an endless cycle of what we have learned to call undecidability. In this book, as the reader will see in due course, I prefer to think of this as a 'passion of the possible' or a 'potentiality'. Culture, I shall argue, forces us to inhabit potentiality in this unsettling way in which, for example, we cannot simply 'situate' an identity for ourselves in our reading of *The Republic*. The formulation that says that 'Plato banishes the poets' is, as it were, knowledge for the TV show: definite, fixed, reassuring in that it requires no thinking and is thus, in all essentials, wrong; on the other hand, the formulation 'Plato dramatically banishes the dramatic' is a knowledge that troubles in that it is unsettling to the self who speaks it, even as it constitutes knowing as such. This latter knowledge requires a democratic attitude, as I outlined it above, for its reading and understanding.

This earliest example demonstrates that the question of culture is traversed by the political. What I have tried to do in this book is to articulate the grounds and conditions on which a specifically 'democratic' politics might be possible. At the root of this is the problem of the status of aesthetic (or indeed of any) experience. The task, as so amply dramatised by Plato, is to find a mode of intimacy with art that does not preclude an intimacy with those others that form the condition of our being social. The logic of this, of course, is that 'my' experience of reading disappears, replaced by 'our' experience of reading. Democracy, properly understood, is not just something that allows the self to come to full fruition; it is also, and simultaneously, a threat to the very self that demands the democratic fulfilment of itself. My claim in this book is that it is in art and in aesthetics that we find a privileged site or a paradigm of the very *potentiality* of selfhood that establishes this democratic condition.

~

Aesthetic Democracy begins with an exploration of the foundations of a critical consciousness. From where, I ask, does criticism or the critical act and the critical consciousness emerge? I take it as read that a certain deconstruction is intrinsic to the critical consciousness as such; and accordingly, one first requirement of the book is to find an at least hypothetical *fons et origo* of deconstruction. In my opening section, I identify a grounding condition of criticism in what is essentially a classic encounter with otherness as such: the colonial and postcolonial context of modernity. I am able also here to relate the urgencies of reading critically to the always emergent awareness of the imminence and immanence of death, against which criticism might be construed as a form of apotropoeia, that warding off of a final closure through which we become, once dead, *only* figures in and through alterity, through the memory that others may have of us, and the traces that we may leave as remains. The name that we have often given to those remains, of course, is literature itself; and thus criticism becomes imbued with the eschatological demands that themselves figure an absolute alterity. I bring this to a head through an exploration of what constitutes 'the west', and especially a west that might always be seen as the scene of a decline.

That colonial condition of criticism raises the question of how we can ever constitute the 'we' that experiences art or that makes culture come about. This requires an exploration of how experience relates to a new aestheticism, an aestheticism that I claim to be radical in the sense that it opens us to the very possibility of experience through the perception (*aisthanomai*) of alterity. Further, that experience is defined in terms of the potential for experience (and thus again an apotropaic warding off of death or of the end of experience as such), and in terms of the inhabiting of an uncertainty that I call, after Kierkegaard, a 'passion of the possible'. Through an exploration of Agamben, I am able to tie this directly to political issues, and to what we can see as the potential for and of democracy.

My final section follows the logic of the work in such a way as to argue that the concept of autonomy on which modern democracy rests is limiting and limited. I argue that we replace it with a notion of 'sovereignty', in which I can expose and explore the logic of exceptionality that shapes our 'multiculturalist relativities', whereby all beliefs become relative except our own. I argue that, through the kinds of radical aestheticism that I propound in the book, we can formulate a 'sovereign' subject that is always already multiple, always already conditioned by alterity, always already democratic.

The Colonial Condition of Criticism

CHAPTER I

On Prejudice and Foretelling

An opening chapter ought to give some sense of what is to come. It is thus written in a mode of foretelling, and, in some senses, it exists to prejudge what follows. My argument here will be that there are fundamentally two different ways in which we have understood the term 'criticism'. In the first way, criticism has been understood as an activity related intrinsically to *evaluation*; and my claim here will be that evaluative criticism is implicated precisely in a structure of prejudice and foretelling. In the second mode, criticism is understood as a mode of *analysis*; and my claim here will be that it is the task of critical analysis to escape the structure of prejudice and foretelling that haunts it. It is only this second mode that can authentically be called 'critical'.[1]

Not only does such criticism face the problem of where to begin—and in this it is exactly like all writing, facing the old Heideggerian question of why there should be something rather than nothing at all; criticism also faces the problem of how to escape from its beginnings. By this I mean to suggest that criticism, if it is genuinely critical, must not be entirely determined—predetermined, that is—by its origins or sources. This is another way of saying that criticism should not be prescribed by dogma, or by the Self or by the subject. If criticism is to respond adequately to its object, then the critic must be prepared to be changed by that object, to allow herself or himself to become other in the face of the object; and thus to place the object at the source or origin of a new and changed subjectivity. The word that we give to this is *aesthetics*.

The present chapter explores the nature of a critical aesthetics. It takes deconstruction, in its fundamental figure as a mode of *analysis* (the setting free of the constituents of a whole), as at once the most developed and yet the most basic mode of critical practice. Its question thus becomes, 'where does deconstruction—criticism—come from?'

Beginnings

And should I then presume?
And how should I begin?

—T. S. ELIOT, 'THE LOVE SONG OF J. ALFRED PRUFROCK' (1917)

Let us begin by going back to a beginning, in which the question of going back to a beginning is posed (but not for the first time). In 1967, Derrida wrote this: 'The displacing of the relationship with the mother, with nature, with being as the fundamental signified, such indeed is the origin of society and languages. But can one speak of origins after that? Is the concept of origin . . . anything but a fiction'?[2] There is thus an original point—an origin of society and languages—identified as 'the displacing of the relationship with the mother', even if this point, once alluded to, destroys the very possibility of its own conceptualisation in anything other than the terms of a necessary fiction. Yet the point stands that talk of origins remains possible. Thus it remains possible seriously to ask the question of 'how to begin', to ask 'where does a deconstruction come from?', or even 'where does deconstruction begin?' It is not satisfactory, in response to such questions, to offer the glib warning that deconstruction will always already have demonstrated that origins are inhabited by the derivations that owe their status to the origin as such, and that derivations in turn are marked by originality. Derrida's own gloss on the situation remains clear:

There is a point in the system where the signifier can no longer be replaced by its signified, so that in consequence no signifier can be so replaced, purely and simply. For the point of nonreplacement is also the point of orientation for the entire system of signification. . . . That point does not exist, it is always elusive or, what comes to the same thing, always already inscribed in what it ought to escape or ought to have escaped. . . . If culture is thus broached within its point of origin, then it is not possible to recognize any linear order, whether logical or chronological. In this broaching, what is initiated is already corrupted, thus returning to a place before the origin.[3]

The 'displacing of the relation with the mother' that is the origin of society and languages, thus, is an event that disrupts the purity of a logical/chronological order in which the present moment can be simply aligned with a 'prior' moment whose essential content determines—*predetermines*—the possibilities of the present.

Far from being a 'nonquestion', the question of the origins of deconstruction, and within that, the question of how a beginning might be possible, remains a significant problem and issue. Yet in literary or cultural criticism, one does not simply 'decide' to 'do a deconstruction' with respect to any particular text or concept; one does not 'initiate' a deconstructive manoeuvre in a simple act of decision making. As has been repeatedly pointed out by Derrida and others (but every repetition implies an origin that is being reiterated), deconstruction is not a 'method' to be 'applied'. In the relatively early days of the controversies surrounding deconstruction, Jonathan Culler pointed out that even after we might deconstruct the ostensibly temporal logic of cause and effect, in which we disturb the neat linearity in which effects are thought to follow from causes (or, as I'll put it here—and this will become more significant—sons from mothers), this 'does not lead to the conclusion that the principle of causality is illegitimate and should be scrapped'.[4] Deconstructions must have their beginnings in some sense of that term; and it is this that will be the concern of this opening chapter; but put in the manner in which I raise the question above: 'where does deconstruction come from?'

For de Man, deconstruction was, in a sense, always already there. When he briefly works on a passage from Proust's *A la recherche du temps perdu* by way of introduction to *Allegories of Reading*, he is able to argue that 'The deconstruction [in this instance of the relation between metaphor and metonymy] is not something we have added to the text but it constituted the text in the first place'.[5] In this sense, deconstruction involves an 'unveiling', an *aletheia*, whose point is to effect an intimacy between the act of reading and the consciousness that was required to make • the text as a written document in the first place. As de Man glosses his argument: 'A literary text simultaneously asserts and denies the authority of its own rhetorical mode, and by reading the text [of Proust] as we did we were only trying to come closer to being as rigorous a reader as the author had to be in order to write the sentence in the first place'.[6] The criticism at work in deconstruction, then, is not a simple *aletheia*—a hermeneutic tearing away of veils—but also an act involving a temporal unveiling, a revelation of the *reading* carried out by the author *prior* to her or his *writing*. That temporal unveiling, with its seeming disturbance of chronological linearity, opens the necessary relation of noncoincidence between writer and reader, between writing and reading. In short, it opens the text to time itself, which, in de Man's words, 'can be defined as precisely truth's inability to coincide with itself'.[7]

It can be seen, thus, that we have both *aletheia* and a temporality in which difference as such is established as the very condition of the revelation of a truth. These, combined, give a hint at what is at the core of deconstructive activity. That core, we might say in this beginning, can be characterised as a *failed confessing*. Confession promises revelation, and it strives for a revelation that stems from the kernel of whatever we might identify as 'the self'; further, it invokes a temporal predicament, for it confesses, in the present moment, now, a past, doing so in such a way as to establish not only a coincidental identity between past and present (I, who stole the ribbon, am the same I who now narrates the tale of that theft), but also a difference between the present and the past (in now revealing my self, I am different from the self who preferred to occlude the fact of my theft in the past: I am now more honest, more truthful, more giving). Confession, in this regard, is marked by the kinds of temporal predicament explored by de Man in his famous 'Rhetoric of Temporality' essay, where he argues that 'irony divides the flow of temporal experience into a past that is pure mystification and a future that remains harassed forever by a relapse within the inauthentic. It can know this inauthenticity but can never overcome it'.[8]

Confession, put in these terms, is related directly to the presiding problem governing modernity: autonomy. To ask 'where does a deconstruction come from?' is thus rather like asking 'where does a confession come from?' Both are tantamount to asking whether it is possible ever to be *authentic*. Both confession and autonomy involve the question of origination, beginning; both involve finding some motivating or determining agency that initiates the act as such. Lyotard, in his posthumously published work in progress on Augustine's *Confessions*, indicates the double temporality of the confessional order:

Les *Confessions* s'écrivent sous le signe temporel de l'attente. L'attente, c'est le nom de la conscience du futur. Mais ici, parce qu'il s'agit non seulement de confesser la foi dans une fin 'en souffrance', mais de *se* confesser, d'exhiber la souffrance de ce qui a été fait, l'attente doit repasser par le passé, remonter vers sa source, vers la vie malheureuse, vers l'oeuvre qu'elle fut.[9]

The Confessions unfold under the temporal sign of anticipation. Anticipation is the name for a consciousness of the future. But here, because it's a question not only of confessing faith in an ending that is 'in abeyance', but also of confessing *one's sins*, of exhibiting the pain of what has been done, anticipation must pass again through the past, return to its origin, back to the unhappy life, to the work that it was.

Waiting here is a waiting oriented at once towards the future and towards the past, thereby making the present moment a moment of a specific *conversion*. Confession is ostensibly the revelation of a truth that preexists the act of confessing; and yet, that truth *is* not unless and until it has been narrated or unless and until it *has the potential that it will be* narrated and revealed. The condition of autonomy is extremely similar: autonomy rests on the presumption that there is an originating, motivating self or a self as agent, while, simultaneously, the self is given only after the autonomous act identifiable as acts motivated from that self, originating in that self, will have been carried out.[10]

Given this abiding problem of origination, it is perhaps not surprising that Derrida eventually made the turn towards a kind of confessing in his 'Circonfession'.[11] In what follows, I shall explore two related questions: what is at stake in deconstruction as a confession or *aletheia* (and this will be related to a complex meditation on suicide)? And can we be precise in finding a motivating instance for deconstruction, even dating it (and this will involve a question concerning politics, coloniality, and theology)? The result will be one that allows me to relate deconstruction directly to foretelling and to prejudice, to 'telling' the future and judging it *in advance*.

On Suicide

Who himself beginning knew?

—MILTON, *Paradise Lost*

Lurking behind Milton's question here is another, perhaps simpler, question: 'who knows his own mother?'

Derrida's 'Circonfession' is, through all its fifty-nine 'periods', in some ways, the chronicle of a death foretold. The abiding concern all the way through it is the coming—foretold—death of Georgette Derrida, Jackie's mother; and the text is punctuated by a further concern about whether Jackie (who has just been diagnosed, at age fifty-nine, with Lyme disease, a condition whose symptoms approximate in some respects to those of a stroke) might predecease his mother.[12] 'Circonfession' takes its place in a text whose pedagogical purpose is the conventional one, whereby Geoffrey Bennington will describe 'sinon la totalité de la pensée de J.D., du moins le système général de cette pensée' (if not the totality of the thought of J.D., then at least the general system of that thought).[13] The task of 'Circonfession' is to escape such systematicity, to 'surprise' Bennington (and all other readers). Paradoxically, thus, 'Circonfession' aims to contribute to the elucidation of 'Jacques Derrida' (and, by synecdochic extension, of deconstruction) while simultaneously obfuscating such elucidation: it will reveal and conceal at once, the concealment thereby requiring further elucidation in turn.

The 'confessional', elucidatory aspect of 'Circonfession' is driven by a tacit presumption that somehow, in the living self of Derrida—in the autobiography, the self-life-writing, the life that writes itself, the self that is lived as writing—we might find a source or origin for deconstruction, an explanatory 'cause' back to which the sophisticated work can all be referred, as a son might refer his identity back to his mother and to his formation at her hands; and yet, simultaneously, such a view is called into question by the text's relation to the 'Derridabase' of Bennington, circling above it, striving to be able to 'foretell' all that Derrida might ever write. Confession is here yoked to autobiography as a form of *aletheia*; but, simultaneously, there is nothing to be revealed, for nothing can surprise 'G.', sometimes 'Geo', ambiguously Geoffrey and Georgette, who, like blind Tiresias in whom two sexes meet, knows and foresuffers all.[14]

Derrida models his own beginnings here on those of his Algerian compatriot, St Augustine. For both men, the mother-son relation is determining and the death of the mother is felt as a crucial event, a turning point, or a 'conversion'. Further, Augustine (rather belatedly in his text) opens his famous meditations on time by asking why he should confess to God when God already knows in advance the entire content of the confession; and when Derrida begins his own text with an explicit allusion to this *cur confiteor* passage, the jocular analogy here is with the 'predictability' of deconstruction, as G., whose system (or 'programme' / *logiciel*) will reveal the predeterminability of all that Derrida can write, circles over and above Derrida's confessional text.

For Augustine, the confession is to stem from the core of his being, and it is to be truthful and communicable, but this raises problems:

When [men] hear me speak about myself, how do they know whether I am telling the truth, since no one *knows a man's thoughts, except the man's own spirit that is within him?* . . . what does it profit me, I ask, also to make known to men in your sight, through this book, not what I once was, but what I am now? I know what profit I gain by confessing my past. . . . But many people who know me, and others who do not know me but have heard of me or read my books, wish to hear what I am now, at this moment, as I set down my confessions. They cannot lay their ears to my heart, and yet it is in my heart that I am whatever I am.[15]

For Derrida, the confession stems not from the heart but rather from the mutilated penis: it is as if the foreskin, and most especially its cut, is what will foretell; or as if the core of the self—and indeed, the very motivating force or animating force of Derrida and his work—is in this mutilating cut, this attack on the very forefront of Derrida's infant body.

This cut is, of course, at the centre of the text of *Jacques Derrida*, as it is in many of Derrida's doubled/doubling texts (most famously and perhaps most extremely in *Glas*, the earlier text that already sounds a death knell). Derrida 'privé d'avenir' (denied a future) as he puts it,[16] ponders why it is that one might write 'quand on ne croit pas a sa propre survie . . . quand on écrit pour le présent mais un présent qui n'est *fait* . . . que du retour sur soi de cette survie refusée' (when one no longer believes in one's own survival . . . when one writes for the present but a present that is comprised only of this return to oneself of that refused survival).[17] Such a writing might be called 'une création sans lendemain' (a creation without tomorrow); and, indeed, it was so called by another Algerian writer, whose presence haunts 'Circonfession': Camus.

The menacing, circumcising cut, carried out by a knife that was unseen by Derrida but graphically presented in the cut text of *Jacques Derrida*,[18] echoes the presence of a knife seen elsewhere, when Meursault, his eyes blinded by tears and salt, confronts the Arab whom he is about to kill. There are numerous parallels linking Derrida's text and that of Camus available in these pages, but two are most important.[19] Meursault describes the day's heat: 'C'était le même soleil que le jour où j'avais enterré maman' (It was the same sun as on the day that I buried Mama); and, further, when the Arab takes the knife from his pocket as Meursault advances, 'La lumière a giclé sur l'acier et c'était comme une longue lame étincellante qui m'atteignait au front' (The light flashed on the steel and it was like a long sparkling blade striking my forehead).[20] The decisive moment of the murder is the moment when 'tout a commencé', according to Meursault, when 'la mer a charrié un souffle épais et ardent' (when 'everything began', when 'the sea carried a thick, ardent breath').

It is difficult to ignore this kind of parallel, given that Derrida himself puns in his text between *mer* and *mère*, and when he wonders about the propriety of his being 'capable de publier sa fin, d'en exhiber les derniers souffles' (capable of publishing one's end, of showing the last breaths), publishing these last breaths for rather literary reasons, as if he is adding to the literary series of texts on '"l'écrivain et sa mère", sous-série "la mort de la mère"' ('the writer and his mother', subseries 'the death of the mother').[21]

Camus, who opens *L'Etranger* with the death of a mother 'aujourd-hui . . . ou peut-être hier' (today . . . or was it yesterday),[22] knew, like Augustine and Derrida, the importance attaching to the death of the mother. Whereas for Augustine that moment reverberates with theological significance, for Camus it was always political. Rather reverentially disposed towards his mother, he always feared the fact that she remained in Algeria at times of crisis when there was the constant possibility of her being killed in the midst of the political battles at any time between the passionate communist struggles of the 1930s and the moment of decolonisation for which Algeria was preparing when Camus died. Derrida's anxieties about prede-

ceasing his mother were misplaced; Camus was the son who died, absurd-
ly, before his own mother, with the unpublished confessional text of his
beginnings, *The First Man*, in his briefcase.

To know one's own beginning is to know one's mother, but it is also
to distance oneself from one's mother, to assert an autonomous identity,
and thus, crucially, it is to know the death of the mother. Distancing such
as this can be achieved, for Derrida, either through the death of the mother
or through writing (broadly equivalent, as we should recall from the citation from *Of Grammatology* with which I opened the present chapter):

j'attends l'interruption d'une course contre la montre entre l'écriture et sa vie, la
sienne, la sienne seule, celle dont je m'éloigne à mesure que j'en parle, pour la tra-
hir ou calomnier à chaque mot.[23]

I await the interruption of a race against the clock between writing and living,
hers, hers alone, that from which I distance myself insofar as I speak of it, to be-
tray or slander it with every word.

That writing of a distance is a mode of asserting autonomy; and in it, Derrida demands pardon, as in a restorative or 'holy' confessional act. The
question of excuses and pardon permeates the text of Camus, as it does
that of Augustine. All three of these writers are thus linked, structurally
and geopolitically.

Interestingly, all three have interesting things to say regarding suicide. For Augustine, it was unforgivable, 'monstrous'. It is not to be permitted even as a means of escaping from the commission of sins.[24] Camus,
famously, describes suicide as the only serious philosophical problem, be-
side which everything else is mere frippery: 'Juger que la vie vaut ou ne
vaut pas la peine d'être vécue, c'est répondre à la question fondamentale
de la philosophie' (to judge that life does or does not warrant the pain of
being lived is to answer the fundamental question of philosophy).[25] And
here, also, in 'Circonfession', that spontaneous (*sua sponte*), responsible,
self-confessing and self-denying (suicidal) text, Derrida writes that 'je me
donne la mort' (I give death to myself).[26]

This last case requires a further gloss. In 'period' 34 of 'Circonfession', Derrida describes the 'conversation' between him and Georgette 'this
30 December 1989' in which his questions or conversational gambits to his
mother are as words spoken to himself, for he knows that he will get no

response from his mother. It is this situation, of course, that allows him to present the confession as a 'confession of/for others' ('je ne me confesse pas, je confesse plutôt les autres' [I don't confess myself, rather I confess others][27]). This confession is not a straightforward *aletheia* in this sense; the self that is confessed is not the self who speaks the confessional discourse. As argued above, that self is not only temporalised, but also displaced. More importantly here, though, this situation provokes an extremely telling response, in every sense of that phrase. When Derrida responds himself in the place of his mother, in period 34, he writes an intriguing phrase: 'nous nous euthanasions à demander ce qu'une vivante penserait *si* elle voyait la mort arriver' (we give ourselves a happy death in asking what a living woman would think *if* she saw death arriving).[28] This is Derrida and his mother, then, finding a happy death together, in this very writing or failed confession. The mother cannot confess (she is silent); the son cannot confess himself; yet the writing unites them in an initiating act of writing that both distances Derrida from his mother and, paradoxically, offers a most personal portrait of their extremely intimate relation at once.

When 'nous nous euthanasions' (we euthanise ourselves) returns, as 'je me donne la mort' (I give death to myself) in period 53, it does so in a fashion that explicitly politicises this happy death. In 53, Derrida considers the concept of heritage or inheritance, in the logic of which, citing Augustine, we have a paradoxical inversion of chronological time: '*ut* maior *seruiret* minori', 'that the elder will serve the younger'. This is taken from book 7, chapter 9 of Augustine's *Confessions*, and in that text, it is lifted directly from Paul's Epistle to the Romans (Romans 9:12). In this chapter, Paul expresses pity for the Jews, but he does so in terms that call to mind the question of knowing one's own beginning. Paul argues here that salvation depends on God's mercy: 'it is not of him that willeth, nor of him that runneth, but of God that sheweth mercy' (Romans 9:16); and, in this situation, who are we to question God?

18 Therefore hath he mercy on whom he will have mercy, and whom he will he hardeneth.

19 Thou wilt say then unto me, Why doth he yet find fault? For who hath resisted his will?

20 Nay but, O man, who art thou that repliest against God? Shall the thing formed say to him that formed it, Why hast thou made me thus?

21 Hath not the potter power over the clay, of the same lump to make one vessel unto honour, and another unto dishonour?

Paul goes on to discuss the *conversion* of the Jews, which, according to Paul, will bring salvation, *survie*. Conversion, linked to the relation with the mother, is of the essence of Augustine's text; but in Derrida, the issue is not so explicitly theological. The relation between Jews and Christians is, in some ways, already integral to Derrida's biography, for he is, after all, a kind of *marrano* or 'Catholic Jew':

si je suis une sorte de marrane de la culture catholique française, et j'ai aussi mon corps chrétien, hérité de sA en ligne plus ou moins tordue . . . je suis de ces marranes qui ne se disent même pas juifs dans le secret de leur coeur, non pour être des marranes authentifiés de part ou d'autre de la frontière publique, mais parce qu'ils doutent de tout.[29]

if I am a kind of marrano of French catholic culture, and I also have my christian body, inherited from sA in a more or less twisted line . . . I am among those marranos who don't even call themselves jews in their innermost heart, not in order to be maranos authenticated by a public frontier somewhere or other, but rather because they doubt everything.

In Derrida, the question becomes more explicitly a political question of inheritance, and specifically of his Algerian inheritance. In period 53, where he considers why one writes solely for the present, 'quand on ne croit pas à sa propre survie ni à la survie de quoi que ce soit' (when one neither believes in one's own survival, nor in the survival of whatever it may be), he remarks that his writing is necessarily in an inherited tongue:

je me donne ici la mort ne se dit qu'en une langue dont la colonisation de l'Algérie en 1830, un siècle avant moi, m'aura fait présent, *I don't take my life*, mais je me donne la mort.[30]

I give death to myself here is spoken only in a tongue that the colonisation of Algeria, a century before me, gave me as a present, *I don't take my life*, but I give death to myself.

Thus, giving oneself death, giving death to oneself, is explicitly related to a question of geopolitical inheritance. Its origin lies exactly one century before Derrida's birth, in the colonisation by France of Algeria.

Confession, we might say, requires sovereignty over the self. How can there be such sovereignty in a colonial situation and its legacies? This may well be the reason why 'une confession n'a rien à voir avec la vérité' (a confession has nothing to do with truth).[31] Derrida is frequently at pains in 'Circonfession' to claim a confession that is not *aletheia* at all, but rather a 'making' true, a *faire la vérité*. That is an important distinction, whose politics I shall now try to reveal more explicitly, for it relates directly to the fraught fundamental Camusian question that is haunting 'Circonfession'. Is life worth being lived? Should one attend to survival, to a 'living on', as Derrida expressed it in his contribution to Yale's *Deconstruction and Criticism*?

On Prejudice

When Milton opened *Paradise Lost*, he was already blind; and when Derrida opened 'Circonfession', written while he was frequently blinded by tears, he had just prepared the exhibition entitled 'Mémoires d'aveugle' for the Louvre. Milton will write 'Of Man's First disobedience, and the Fruit/Of that Forbidden Tree, whose mortal taste/Brought Death into the World'; and, in doing so, he will write (perhaps involuntarily) the narrative of how humanity can attain to a condition of sovereignty. Derrida is also writing a 'paradise lost' in a mode of *nostalgérie*, a painful return homewards to Algeria. The fundamental question in both writings regards freedom and how it is that humanity can assert sovereignty over life itself, over a living on. Both are related to vision, but to vision in the sense of the possibility not just of seeing with the eyes, nor of de Manian 'insight', but also of vision in the sense of what can be 'envisioned', or what can be foreseen, foretold.

Agamben has also recently considered this question in relation to his fundamental thesis that modernity is marked by the politicisation of what he calls 'bare life'. Agamben's contention is that in modernity, the distinction available between *zoe* (biological existing) and *bios* (the mode of living) has been effectively elided, and that politics (properly the domain of a *bios* distinguished from *zoe*) has fully entered 'bare life' itself. In a certain sense, we are all as Poor Tom in *King Lear*, a 'poor, bare, forked animal' (3.4), but an animal whose 'unaccommodated' condition is not just a biological but also a political condition. In Agamben, this situation is one that begins to allow us to address what has happened to the Jews during the twentieth century.[32]

One particular aspect of Agamben's case is relevant for my present argument. In *Homo Sacer*, he considers the question of suicide and its unpunishability in law. To do so, he begins from a 1920 text, *Die Freigabe der Vernichtung lebensunwerten Lebens* (*Authorization for the Annihilation of Life Unworthy of Being Lived*), by Karl Binding and Alfred Hoche, both eminent professors of medicine. Agamben points out that 'in order to explain the unpunishability of suicide, Binding is led to conceive of suicide as the expression of man's sovereignty over his own existence'.[33] Such a conception, ostensibly one that dignifies the suicide and gives a (paradoxical) freedom to beings who kill themselves, brings problems in its wake, however. The explication of suicide in this manner allows for a similar conceptualisation of the stakes of euthanasia, as an act that annihilates a 'life unworthy of being lived'. It is not difficult to see, from this ostensibly well-intentioned 1920 medical text, the gradual shift into the position of Nazism, just over a decade later, where Jews and other refugees were deemed to be living 'a life unworthy of being lived' and therefore killed, but killed in accordance with a philosophy that could not conceive of such killing as a 'crime' or as a homicide in the normal sense. Suicide, seen as a limit-case of autonomy, becomes complicit with its opposite; in this instance, the assertion of a freedom becomes complicit with the Holocaust.

This has its counterpart in Derrida's text. The confessional text is not concerned with crime, but with its theological counterpart, sin; or, as Derrida puts it, Augustine's *Confessions* are 'une forme de théologie comme autobiographie' (a form of theology as autobiography).[34]

When Augustine considers—and prohibits—suicide, in *City of God*, he does so in terms that are explicitly concerned with sin; but also, and more importantly for my present purposes, in terms that relate to the issue of sovereign control over one's own body and life. He asks whether it might be permissible to kill oneself if the aim is to *forestall* sin. In particular, he thinks of those who have been or may become victims of sexual assault or rape during imperial wars. The argument is a sophisticated one, in which Augustine makes the point that if the victim is not party to the sin or violation, then she remains chaste: 'virtue, the condition of right living, holds command over the parts of the body from her throne in the mind, and . . . the consecrated body is the instrument of the consecrated will; and if that will continues unshaken and steadfast, whatever anyone else does with the body or to the body, provided that it cannot be avoided without committing sin, involves no blame to the sufferer'.[35] Augustine then further agues that this holds good in all cases, so that there is no excuse for those women who kill themselves *in advance* of being violated, in order to try to *prevent* the very possibility of their becoming complicit with the rape and thus complicit with sin. The key question here, for our understanding of Derrida, is not just that pertaining to forestalling future sin, but also that pertaining to what might be done, or has been done, to the body (and particularly to its sexual parts) *without consent* or *complicity*. Such is Derrida's circumcision. By analogy with the Augustinian argument, circumcision thus does not 'identify' Derrida, does not bind him, does not determine or predetermine what he is and does. In short, deconstruction cannot be seen to derive from a Judaic mentality or psychology.

The foreskin, cut from the body, is described as a wedding ring, *une alliance*. Such a ring, such an alliance, ties Derrida to his mother in a most intimate fashion; but the text also plays explicitly on the multiple meanings of the *alliance*. In the first place, in 1943 and since, 'L'alliance' was above all the name not of a wedding ring, but rather of the school that Derrida was supposed to attend, having been expelled from his previous school in El-Biar on account of his Jewishness. Derrida, however, confesses to playing truant from this school, going instead to watch the file of allied soldiers (soldiers in an *alliance*) going into the brothels, in an ostensibly legitimised form of that imperial sexual violation discussed by Augustine.[36] Thus the foreskin—and more particularly its violation—links sex to war and both to the position of the schoolboy (the 'petit juif très noir, tres arabe' ['little jewish boy, very black, very arab']) expelled.

For Augustine, then, suicide is forbidden even if its aim is to control one's final theological destiny, by preventing a future of sin and thus enabling the regaining of paradise. For Derrida, suicide is impossible, for there is no self to be killed in the first place. Yet suicide is still related to the question of sovereignty and futurity. The eradication of the self that is 'Circonfession', confession as the *privation de soi*, is a theological 'suicide' directed at trying to open the possibility of a futurity that is not predetermined. Derrida's wager, after all, is that he will be able to surprise Geoffrey, that he will take Geoffrey by surprise, that he will escape identification in Geoffrey's 'Derridabase'.

It is this that the confession fails to do; and it is in this respect that it is a failed confession. Bennington, in the 'Actes' section of *Jacques Derrida*, is able to write, in parentheses, that he is less surprised than Derrida might suppose by this exhibiting of Derrida's circumcision: 'depuis longtemps, il ne parle que d'elle, je pourrais le montrer citations à l'appui' (for a long time now, he has been speaking of nothing but that, which I could show and back up with quotations).[37]

It is thus the case that deconstruction, as a failed confessing, also fails to produce the possibility of surprise. That is to say, deconstruction fails to enable the possibility of a nonpredetermined future; in other words, it fails to produce a freedom in the form of an autonomous sovereignty. To rephrase that yet again, deconstruction is tied to predetermination, which calls into question the relation between deconstruction and foretelling a future, between deconstruction and prophecy (especially, of course, the prophet Elijah in particular), between deconstruction and prejudgements or prejudice.

When I opened this section with my allusion to Milton, it was not simply to allow the alignments of various blindnesses. Milton struggles in *Paradise Lost* to maintain the claim that humanity is free with the Augustinian question of 'why confess'/ *cur confiteor*. Milton's God knows that the first man and woman will fall, but Milton claims that such foreknowledge is not in itself prejudicial, for man was made 'Sufficient to have stood, though free to fall', as God says:

> Freely they stood who stood, and fell who fell . . .
> . . . They therefore as to right belong'd
> So were created, nor can justly accuse
> Their maker, or their making, or their Fate;
> As if Predestination over-rul'd
> Their will, dispos'd by absolute Decree
> Or high foreknowledge; they themselves decreed
> Their own revolt, not I: if I foreknew,
> Foreknowledge had no influence on their fault,
> Which had no less prov'd certain unforeknown.[38]

This passage tries to reconcile freedom with prejudice, and the consequence is the rather shocking suggestion that God is no more or less in control of things than humanity itself. The choice of Adam and Eve would have been as it was, would have been 'certain', whether God knew it or not.

Likewise, deconstruction is prejudicial. Its practice is a constant struggle to reconcile *aletheia* (the confessing or revelation of what has been done: the past in all its necessity) with the prophetic (the 'making' of truth in all its contingency). The name for this struggle is nothing other than prejudice itself. Deconstruction's origin lies in a certain prejudice that bars Derrida from his schooling, certainly; but the originary and motivating source of deconstruction lies in this problematic issue of free autonomy, an autonomy whose enactments will always already have been foreseen once they have been carried out. Predetermination is the stake.

For Derrida, that is also a political question. 'Qui suis-je?' (Who am I?) he asks his mother on many occasions; but, because his mother remains silent, he is also asking himself. He is Jew, he is Arab, he is Catholic; he is Algerian, he is French. How can these be reconciled in J.D. (the initials, pronounced in French, approximate to the enunciation of another author whose ties to Algeria were profound and whose writings played a formative role in Derrida's literary education, Gide)? 'Qui suis-je' is also a question that must not predetermine 'qui serai-je' (who will I be?), nor can it itself have been predetermined by the question 'qui étais-je' (who was I?). Fore-skinning is not foretelling; and, it follows, one's inheritance or tradition (one's Jewishness or Christianity, say) can neither explain nor forgive/excuse one's actions: the subject is, of necessity, an ethical being whose freedom is determined in the act and after the fact. That is to say, freedom is not to be characterised as it would be in existentialism, say, by the subject making choices; rather, freedom is seen only after the fact or after the act has been committed.

This would align deconstruction with the politics of the absurd, that near-indigenous Algerian philosophy. The absurd is that point, in mathematics, it makes no sense to go beyond: it is the origin of deconstruction.

CHAPTER 2

On Urgency and Emergency, or
Deconstruction Not Reading Politics

In Chapter 1, I described deconstruction as being marked, in its very origin, by something that could only properly be described as 'political'. The origin of deconstruction, as I described it, lies in a complex relation involving Algeria (in the mode of *nostalgérie*), maternity, and the kinds of 'adoption' or adaptation that are inscribed in the consciousness of those who live in and through a postcolonial moment. From this, it would seem inevitable that I should stake a claim for a deconstruction that is fundamentally political, or for a criticism that is always essentially a political act or gesture. However, what I aim to show here is that, just as the critical (as analysis) must escape the critical (as evaluation) in order to be most fully itself, so likewise the political (as something related to culture or to reading) must escape the political (as something related to power) in order to be most fully itself. In short, I shall argue for a deconstruction that allows politics to *emerge*, rather than a deconstruction that reads the issues and problems of politics as something *urgent*, and which claims to be able to do something about those problems or issues precisely by its (prejudicial) readings.

The relation of deconstruction to politics has long been fraught with difficulties and uncertainties. Even among Derrida's closest and most intimate—most 'friendly' or 'hospitable'—readers, an unease persists over the questions concerning politics, especially insofar as one's politics might be 'read off' from the philosophical substrata of acts of literary or cultural criticism. Critchley would be one such friend, yet he finds it important to raise the question of politics at the close of his fine *Ethics of Deconstruction*:

It would not be inaccurate to say that political questions have come to dominate Derrida's thinking in recent years: one has only to look at his recent work on democracy and European identity, his responses to de Man's and Heidegger's political engagement, his work on friendship, on apartheid and Nelson Mandela, on law, on nationalism and philosophical nationality, on *Geschlecht*, on the university, on nuclear criticism, on the teaching of philosophy (and the list could be continued). Further, it would be absurd to look to Derrida's biography to confirm any thesis claiming political quietism. . . .

So . . . why raise the question of politics?[1]

Despite this impressive demonstration for the prima facie engagement of Derrida (and, by extension, of deconstruction as such) with politics, Critchley still feels the need to raise this question; and his response, effectively, is that there is a question mark over the manner in which the political is engaged: 'it is not so much the avoidance of the question of politics that characterizes Derrida's work, but the way in which politics is discussed, which itself needs to be questioned'; and Derrida's work 'results in a certain *impasse* of the political',[2] a road from which there is—and here, one hears an echo of a different kind of political thinker, one whose engagements could never have been called oblique: that is, Sartre—no exit.

For another friend, Geoffrey Bennington, this would already be a rather imprecise way of considering the question of politics in Derrida. Bennington (and in this, he follows Derrida quite strictly) consistently entertains the possibility of an impossibility of 'achieving certain knowledge'; and he phrases the position in which this places him well in his professorial lecture delivered in Sussex in June 1996. There, he reflects on his own position, now 'professing' French, and wonders

who will be able to tell what sort of professing the professor professes in professing to know, and to profess, the true sense of the profession of professing?. . . . who, if not the professor, will profess the professor's true profession? I tend to call situations of this kind, where a formal impossibility lives with, and probably generates, even inaugurates, a practical urgency, by that rather tired old epithet 'political'.[3]

Thinking such as this allows Bennington to argue the case for a Derrida whose work, in a certain and very specific sense, has always been political. For Bennington (and in this I concur fully), it is the event of making a decision that would be of the essence of the political as such; and, insofar as deciding is of the nature of an event, a decision cannot have been pre-programmed, nor can it gain its legitimacy through the fact that it measures up as an answer (to the crisis requiring the decision in the first place) whose adequacy is determined by its consistency with any already given set of rules.[4] It simply must engage with the paradox outlined above. There is, therefore, always a question of temporality inscribed in the politics that is deconstruction: on the one hand, there is the urgency, as Bennington describes it, of a practical instant; on the other, there is the delay occasioned by the necessity of meditating on/as a formal impossibility.

Responses to Derrida such as these, however, have typically failed to respond to the intent behind the question, emanating as it usually has from the political left in literary and cultural criticism: what can deconstruction do, or what can it effect politically in the way of decisions made for emancipatory change?[5] For this 'left', it is precisely what is perceived as this enclosedness, this ostensible 'closure' of the political within a hermetic thinking, that causes the typical anxiety of the literary or cultural critic faced with the seeming inevitabilities of deconstruction. Seeing that critical thinking worth the name is always inherently an effect of deconstruction, however weakly construed, the left can acknowledge the power and purchase of Derrida's work; but seeking an urgent effect of its critical practice, the left in question requires an immediate result, which deconstruction, as a practice marked by a necessary delay, simply cannot yield. As a consequence, the left typically rejects deconstruction, remaining silent and uneasy about its power as an intellectual engagement.[6] That is to say, while deconstruction might be asking always the question *Was ist Denken?*, the left has preferred to see what it construes as direct and material historical action, thereby effecting (despite itself) a split and opposition between philosophy and politics.

I shall argue here a case that I expect might be regarded, in the current university climate and (specifically) institution of English and/or cultural studies, as tendentious, even (politically) objectionable. My claim will be that deconstruction does not—cannot—read politics, and, further, that this should give us (whether we consider ourselves to be deconstructors or not) no cause for concern at all, for the simple reason that the cultural and the political are two separate orders. To clarify this opening gambit further: we might say that cultures exist within political situations, and that political states of affairs exist within cultural situations; yet this is no reason to expect—much less demand or require—that criticism (in this instance, specifically deconstructive criticism) should engage the political as such or at all as an explicit or primary part of its agenda.[7] This, of course, is explicitly not to say that critics, insofar as they are citizens, should not have political commitments, nor is it to suggest that criticism should not be concerned about the political states of affairs in relation to which cultural practices happen, nor is it fundamentally to disagree with Bennington's description of the status of deconstruction as at once the most and least political of philosophies; rather, it is to say that we have no fundamental reasons for expecting that deconstruction should do that which it cannot do, which is to 'read' politics.

In the first part of this chapter, I outline, in an admittedly sketchy form, the critical situation in which it has become normative to expect that the 'question concerning politics' might be raised of deconstruction. Following this, in the second part I explore the relation of literary criticism and of politics to questions of emancipation, freedom, or autonomy; and here, I argue the case for a certain necessary 'hypocrisy' in criticism, one inimical to notions of 'authenticity' that the 'left' sees as basic to political commitment. This section will also require a meditation on the relation of criticism and politics to death. Third, in my brief concluding section, I propose a mode of reading based on certain 'hospitalities' or 'friendships', the purpose of which is to raise questions concerning the purpose of criticism within pedagogical and institutional frameworks such as that of 'the university', or 'cultural studies', or 'literature'. Friendship and hypocrisy are the emergent issues here; and I will show that they have their own kinds of urgency.

Political Criticism as the Demise of Politics

Many of those engaged in or formed by deconstruction are products of a broadly post-1970s epoch that saw the attempt to resuscitate the notion of the politically effective and engaged literary critic within Europe.[8] In many ways, of course, we might expect to find a model for this available in the figures of Sartre, de Beauvoir, Camus; yet the moment is one that seems, in true 'modernising' fashion, to want to make a break with these immediate precursors. The somewhat neo-Romantic—organicist—dream of the period around 1968, in which worker and intellectual stood side by side, as, famously, they did (however briefly) at the gates of the Renault factory in Boulogne-Billancourt, offered an image and an icon of the power—indeed, the 'reality'—of the Gramscian organic intellectual. In this conjuncture, it appeared that intellectuals were no longer on the margins of revolutionary political practice, but rather that their engagements were every bit as active and 'material' as those of workers-by-hand.[9] Yet this is also the moment at which we witness (not the triumph but rather) the demise of the Sartrean intellectual. When Sartre came to address the students in the *grand amphi'* in the Sorbonne in 1968, he found (as is well known) a note on the lectern: 'Sartre, be brief'. I take this as a symptomatic incident: on the one hand, political action needs philosophy for its legitimisation; but at the same time and on the other hand, the urgency of a political situation leaves no time for philosophy. It is on this paradox that the urgency of the literary critic to find a response to her marginal position is based. At the core of the paradox is the question of time, speeds, or rates of change: the intellectual requires time—and specifically an opening to futurity—in which to allow the events that we call 'thinking' to take place, to find a place; yet the political is marked by the instantaneity of urgency itself, a *Jetztzeit* to be 'shot through' or blasted into something called 'history' understood as a present packed with and characterised by its fullness of action, praxis. Here, in fact, we find the first condition effectively separating the critical from the political: they operate in different orders—indeed, in incommensurable orders—of temporality: on one side, we have the urgent/present/practical/identical set against the mediate/delayed/theoretical/differential on the other.

Although Derrida certainly was present as a part of the marches and so on in 1968, he nonetheless remained somewhat detached[10]; and the philosophical reason (as opposed to the biographical reason) for this might lie in his intervention, just two years previously, in the celebrated Johns Hopkins symposium where his work made its first major impression on an anglophone audience. 'Structure, Sign and Play', it should be recalled, was a major intervention in this conference for the simple reason that it fundamentally attacked the structuralist ethos around which the conference had taken its polemical position. Where structuralism, armed with its semiotic apparatus, felt entirely able to weave together the practices of literary criticism and politics into a seamless continuum, this newly emerging deconstruction found a major fault in such an ostensible continuity. The question, for Derrida, was (as he would put it in that essay, the understanding of which is axiomatic for those who would engage with early deconstruction, 'Force et signification') whether we had a way of addressing 'force' that would not reduce the content of such force to merely 'form', or to the forms and signs of force. To put this in relevant terms for the present argument: is politics (a domain appropriate to the regulation of force and with due attention to its urgencies) amenable to 'reading' (a domain appropriate to formal conceptualisations) at all? Here, we have a second ground for scepticism regarding the seamless confusion or confounding of politics with criticism.

Although, in these crafting hands of Derrida, deconstruction might have a source that was not in the first instance political, the political situation in which it began—not instantaneously—to make its mark was precisely that one in which the political position, efficacy—even relevance—of the intellectual was in question. The anglophone academic community in this period, it is now clear, effectively failed to follow the logic of Derrida's case (despite its tendency to laud his work) and tried to read it as part of a more general set of cultural phenomena, in which it was taken for granted (taken 'as read', we might say) that the intellectual was undoubtedly effective politically, that reading/criticism/teaching as a nexus of the intellectual's activity was fundamentally politically constructed. The consequence of this is the emergence of a truism (which has, of course, no solid epistemological basis) that deconstructors—like the structuralist/semiotician—see their work as being fully imbricated with a politics, and that the purpose of the work is, among other things but often primarily (which really means instantaneously), political. There is, as it were, no time allowed as a differentiating factor between the orders of the critical and of the political; to make a critical gesture is—in that very instance—also to make a political gesture. That this makes a form out of force—or that Derrida had been carefully attenuating the relations between deconstruction and politics—was, for the most part, overlooked.

However, as deconstruction began to take firmer hold, certain hesitancies became increasingly apparent. Thus, Barbara Johnson, in interview with Imre Salusinszky in 1986, effectively evades (short-circuits/begs) the question when she argues that 'I think that Marx was as close to deconstruction as a lot of deconstructors are'; and shortly before this, in 1982, Michael Ryan finds it necessary to ask the question of whether deconstruction can be effectively 'articulated' with Marxism.[11] Such political questions were yet more insistent in Britain. That 'theory' was effectively inhabited by a *soi-disant* leftist criticism in Britain meant that the important debates there were conducted within a fundamentally Marxist or neo-Marxist set of circumstances. For as long as the effort was to see, either in Gramscian fashion or (more usually) in Althusserian fashion, that there was effectively a seamless continuity—what I referred to above as an instantaneity or what we might now call a cotemporality or coincidence—between what one did within the classroom and the conduct of all other aspects of one's life, it remained impossible to see that deconstruction, at least as Derrida's work crafts it, was fundamentally inimical to such an evasion of the fine discriminations and attenuations of the 'question concerning politics'. Deconstruction has a different relation to time, as Derrida's later work (most obviously in *Donner le temps*) makes explicit. Only gradually did the most prominent anglophone leftist critics of the 1970s and 1980s begin to attend more fully to the kinds of complications regarding the relation of deconstruction with politics to which Derrida had been long adverting. Yet the response became almost equally simplistic: deconstruction, insofar as it leads to undecidability, gives no immediate grounds for choosing a leftist political stance over any other; and therefore, it is suspect.[12]

Thus, we are left with a situation in which *either* deconstruction can be seen as a logical development of what is fundamentally a formalist American New Criticism (suspect politically precisely insofar as it is inherently formalist, and thereby relatively innocent of descriptions of material content), *or* deconstruction is indebted to a specifically European question regarding the position of the intellectual, essentially formulated as a contest between Sartre and Camus, Frenchman and Algerian. It would be a crude and cheap trick to effect a deconstruction between such poles of a simplistic binary opposition like this, although clearly such a deconstruction is invited. Perhaps more important is the observation that Derrida occupies—biographically, at least—precisely the terrain marked out by the contest of France and Algeria; and that much of his major influence has been felt outside of Europe (most obviously in the United States). The consequence, slight though it may appear at first sight, is simply that there is a relation between Europe and America in these matters, and that this relation is marked by an order of temporality or of *priority*. Deconstruction, we might say, is a form of jet lag or *Jetzt-lag*.

This *Jetzt-lag* is more than a joke.[13] The question at stake is that regarding instantaneity or the coincidence of my critical practices with my political practices. It has been a fundamental tenet of the leftist 'theoreticism' that I question in these pages that such a coincidence exists, such that my critical acts are always already and inevitably political acts at the same time. What I deny in this is simply the coincidence or cotemporality assumed between the two spheres of activity. The subscription to such a 'coincidentalist' position is one that has gained much ground in our contemporary era—the era of an often supposed precise and absolute contemporaneity itself. Vattimo has considered this in the midst of his meditation on politics in a supposedly 'transparent society'. The description of our contemporary society as 'transparent' is indebted to a credibility in the reality-forming powers of the mass media: 'The mass media, which in theory offer information in "real time" about everything happening in the world, could in effect be seen as a kind of concrete realization of Hegel's Absolute Spirit: the perfect self-consciousness of the whole of humanity, the coincidence between what happens, history and human knowledge'.[14] Vattimo, of course, questions this view, pronouncing it too monocultural and monolithic. For him, instead, the massification of our media of communication instead produces myriad realities, with the consequence that instead of witnessing a realisation of the Hegelian Absolute Spirit we find, rather, that, as foretold by Nietzsche, the 'true' world has become a 'fable', replete with myriad truths or points of view, none of which can claim any absolute foundational status. Yet despite the power of this (incipiently postmodern) contestation of a neo-Hegelianism, the marxisant left nonetheless held to the view of the increasingly absolute contemporaneity of all reality.

Vattimo can accept that the contemporary world is contemporary, yet it is so 'because it is a world in which the potential reduction of history to the level of simultaneity, via technology such as live television news bulletins, is becoming ever more real'.[15] Such a view not only reduces history to simultaneity, of course; it also, in this urgency, confounds the temporality of our thinking about a state of affairs with the temporality of our enacting of it. That is to say, it simply confuses the critical with the political. It is precisely such a confusion that cannot be permitted within a political criticism—such, perhaps, as deconstruction—that is worthy of the name, of course. As Vattimo indicates, we have here a 'radical revision of the very notion of history' such that 'the social ideals of modernity may in each case be described as guided by the utopia of absolute *self-transparency*'.[16]

In a word, the urgently political 'left' has grounded its criticism not only upon what is fundamentally precisely the erasure of the very history that it pretends to prioritise, but also upon the idea that its critical legitimacy stems from its self-evidencing (and therefore immediately transparent) status. That is to say, in institutional terms, truth lies (happy phrase) with the political left precisely to the extent that its enactment of critical practice reveals it to be of the left as such. This is of the essence of that criticism that has by now degenerated into the great absurdities of autobiographical criticism in which the fundamental task of critics is to reveal themselves, to advertise their identity (as working class, as antimasculinist, as Irish, as postcolonial—even as 'deconstructor'). Like bad readers of Rousseau, these critics can reduce truth to 'what is happening, now', but without any acknowledgement not only that 'now' is not the same moment for the totality of the world or that the 'now-time' might be genuinely internally fissured in ways that make it problematic to identify 'I' and 'now', or the formalities of a self-consciousness with the urgencies of a social force.

The simplest way of effecting the elision between form and force in order to establish such a principle of coincidence, or contemporaneity, is to highlight the power of 'reading' and to reduce things (in all their physical force) to signs of things (in all their aesthetic and formal regulatedness). Thus would the assumed legibility of political action make it supposedly immediately available; thus would real political states of affairs be confoundable with the signs of such states of affairs—and thus, also, can the critic schooled in the activity of reading the literary text supposedly transfer that skill into not only analysis of a political state of affairs but also into a political act itself. It is this move that, institutionally, has allowed criticism to be based on poor engagements with Derrida, in which deconstruction has often been simply a sophisticated hermeneutic, an 'approach', a way of reading. In this predicament, it is Agamben who indicates a possible project and allows us to see what might actually be at stake: 'To restore the thing itself to its place in language and, at the same time, to restore the difficulty of writing, the place of writing in the poetic task of composition: this is the task of the coming philosophy'.[17]

Hypocrite Lecteur! or, 'On Being Late'

In its reduction of history to simultaneity, then, 'leftist' criticism has effectively reduced criticism to autobiography. Further, it has evacuated politics of its political content, giving us instead a merely formal engagement with the political as such, in which engagements with generous abstractions take precedence over detailed political engagements, these latter being usually cast aside as 'micropolitical'. We have, in the institution of literary criticism, a politics without politics. Insofar, however, as the critical act is legitimised by its signature, by the identity of the critic who practises (and this is the situation, of course, tirelessly described and satirised by Fish in recent years[18]), then we can say that the critical act depends on a specific notion of authenticity. Criticism is authenticated by the signature that performs it, and thus it reveals the identity of the critic with the act of criticism and the act's objects (thus, I identify myself—however suddenly—as Irish, say, and identify thereby with 'the Irish'; and it is this very act of identification that now encompasses the total and self-evidencing substance of my politics). This, clearly, is another issue with which deconstruction would no doubt have difficulties, for the authentic is not and cannot be given as such.

In the face of this, I shall argue here that the only political criticism worthy of the name is one based on hypocrisy in the reader, a fraternal and even egalitarian reading as prefigured in Baudelaire's great address *au lecteur*.

If there is a 'project of modernity' (in any sense), then it is certainly tied up with the achievement of autonomy, with a project of 'giving oneself the law' or of oneself establishing the laws to which that self will have been answerable or responsible. The 'leftist' view has erroneously taken the establishment of autonomy to be identical with a politics whose aim is the achievement of subject identity, identification—sameness, *le propre*. Indeed, in Habermas, the very principles of 'communicative action' through which we will arrive at the establishment of a rational society are based on the idea of consensually available agreement; and it is within this agreement or accord that we can detect this fundamental drive for the establishment of an identity/identification of the self with its others. The belief that such an agreement is available is also a dream of the kind of transparency whose viability I have questioned above. Bennington questions the viability of such a position when he argues that 'there is communication only when there is a moment, however minimal, of non-understanding, of *stupidity* with respect to what is said. *Communication implies non-comprehension.* I am in a situation of communication with the other only when I do not understand what he, she or it says'.[19] A different way of putting this would be to suggest, following Lyotard, that even in its most 'reasonable' moments, there is always a violence inscribed in a claim to have comprehended the other, insofar as alterity is reduced to identity. Guillaume, in his discussions with Baudrillard in *Figures de l'altérité*, arrives at a similar position when he claims that 'dans tout autre il y a autrui' (in every Other there is an other-Self), that our communications with others refuses to acknowledge the absolute alterity that might be there, preferring instead to find points of assimilation (which we call comprehension) that are actually terroristic reductions of the other to versions of the same/self.[20] To get at the core of this, we might look at Agacinski, arguing for a singularity in the other that is irreducible to figures of the other—a force of the other irreducible to its form, so to speak.[21]

 A more fruitful way of approaching the question concerning politics is through an understanding of that politics within modernity as being grounded in a different inflection of the notion of autonomy, one in which the question of politics becomes, fundamentally, the question of freedom. To think the question of freedom is also, inevitably and intrinsically, to think the question of frontiers, extremes, boundaries, transgressions, limits; and that which limits freedom is, of course, death. To think freedom, thus, involves us also inevitably in a thinking of death; and, yet further, to think freedom, insofar as it involves us inevitably in a thinking of death, also involves us in a dying of thinking. To think freedom, paradoxically, involves the end of thinking as such; and the way in which this has usually been construed by the anglophone left is to establish a binary opposition between the realms of philosophy (thinking) on the one hand, and politics (practice, agency, urgent action) on the other. The way is then clear to seek a relation between the two, a conjunction or 'articulation' most readily given by the notion of reading. That this implies a political agency that is unreflective has been an abiding problem for this left, and one to which the name of Althusser used to be invoked in order to reestablish the identity between class struggle and philosophical critical theory.

For this political criticism, the achievement of autonomy is marked by the extent to which I can equate my freedom with my living and vital agency and with my subjectivity. Thus, 'I' enact something in such a way that the 'I' is contained by, accounted for, constrained within and identified as the action itself, regardless of any philosophical intention that might have lain behind that action. The left can disregard intention in this way precisely because of its subscription to the principle of coincidence in which the urgency of the political overrides the delays of the philosophical. Further, this gives such political criticism its construal of authenticity, in that the manifestation of the 'I' revealed in and through its action is authentic, not contaminated by any other subject who might have forced me to commit my action. Indeed, to this way of thinking, that 'I' which is not so contained in or accounted for by its action is precisely the subject who can be identified as—and criticised for being—inauthentic, living in and enacting an ideology to which it remains blind. In this mode of understanding, a philosophical criticism is always necessarily working ideologically for the simple reason that it is not immediate, not unmediated. Ideology would be avoided by the principle of absolute transparency or self-coincidence. Against this, of course, we might set de Man:

What we call ideology is precisely the confusion of linguistic with natural reality, of reference with phenomenalism. It follows that, more than any other mode of inquiry, including economics, the linguistics of literariness is a powerful and indispensable tool in the unmasking of ideological aberrations, as well as a determining factor in accounting for their occurrence. Those who reproach literary theory for being oblivious to social and historical (that is to say ideological) reality are merely stating their fear at having their own ideological mystifications exposed by the tool they are trying to discredit. They are, in short, very poor readers of Marx's *German Ideology*.[22]

De Man's object of criticism here, of course and among others, is precisely the *soi-disant* left who 'reproach literary theory' for its supposed philosophical hermeticism. In their privileging of the urgent (political) over the delayed or untimely (philosophical), or in their subsumption of the latter under the former, it is they who are confusing linguistic with natural reality. Not only are they poor readers of Marx's *German Ideology*, they are also fundamentally weak in their thinking through the questions concerning freedom and its relation to authenticity. That relation is one that involves, perhaps paradoxically, the establishment of a criticism that is necessarily inauthentic in that it is grounded in a specific kind of 'hypocrisy', 'seemingly' reading, reading from the point of view of the 'hypocrite lecteur,— mon semblable,—mon frère'. To understand my claim here, we must address the relations of freedom and autonomy to death: to 'being late'.

On Friday, 14 November 1975, Levinas opened his seminar by asking 'Que savons-nous de la mort?' (What do we know of death?), and in the first instance he considers the question of the death of another and not of oneself:

Que savons-nous de la mort, qu'est-ce que la mort? Selon l'expérience, c'est l'arrêt d'un comportement, l'arrêt de mouvements expressifs et de mouvements ou processus physiologiques qui sont enveloppés par les mouvements expressifs, dissimulés par eux—cela formant 'quelque chose' qui se montre, ou plutôt *quelqu'un* qui se montre, fait mieux que se montrer: s'exprime. Cette expression est plus que monstration, plus que manifestation.[23]

What do we know of death, what is death? If we think of it in relation to experience, it is the stopping of a behaviour, of expressive movements and of physiological movements or processes that are contained within expressive movements, hidden by them—this all forming 'some thing' that shows itself, or rather *some-one* who shows himself, does better than show himself: expresses himself. This expression is more than a revelation, more than a demonstration.

Death, according to this, is the disappearance of this super- or extraexpression: the moment when 'le visage . . . devient masque' (the face . . . becomes a mask).[24] In this early formulation of the question in his seminar, Levinas describes the relation to the death of the other as one given through the *visage*; and, as is well known, the face of the other, for Levinas, is what calls me to responsibility:

Quelqu'un qui s'exprime dans la nudité—le visage—est un au point d'en appeler à moi, de se placer sous ma responsabilité: d'ores et déjà, j'ai à répondre de lui. Tous les gestes d'autrui étaient des signes à moi adressés.[25]

Someone who expresses himself in nakedness—the face—is one to the extent that he calls to me, places himself within my responsibility: from now onwards, I have to respond to him. Every movement of this other was a sign addressed to me.

Responsibility is thus tied to the establishment of a relatedness whose primary condition is that of the availability of death: it is the fact that the other may die that calls me to response; and response is of the essence of an autonomy that is based not on the establishment of a selfsame identity for the subject but rather on the realisation that the subject is always already grounded in a fundamental alterity. Such alterity is not only given by the fact that the subject is freely existing only to the extent that she is in relation to her others, but also by the fact that, given the essential unavailability of these others as stable or fixed identities, the subject is internally different from herself. Contesting the view that 'l'identité du Même avec soi est la source de tout sens' (the identity of the Same with itself is the source of all meaning)—and it is this belief that underpins what I have described as the anglophone left's view—Levinas asks rhetorically:

Mais la relation avec autrui et avec sa mort ne remonte-t-elle pas à une autre source du sens? Le mourir, comme mourir de l'autre, affecte mon identité de Moi, il est sensé dans sa rupture du Même, sa rupture de mon Moi, sa rupture du Même dans mon Moi.[26]

But does not the relation with another human and with his death amount to another source of meaning? Dying, as the dying of the other, affects my identity as Myself, and is felt in its rupturing of the Same, its rupturing of Myself, its rupturing of the Same within Myself.

When Derrida considers the question of responsibility, appropriately enough for this argument in *The Gift of Death*, he sees it precisely as an engagement of sorts:

In order to be responsible it is necessary to respond or to answer to what being responsible means. For if it is true that the concept of responsibility has, in the most reliable continuity of its history, always implied involvement in action, doing, a *praxis*, a *decision* that exceeds simple conscience or simple theoretical understanding, it is also true that the same concept requires a decision or responsible action to answer for itself *consciously*, that is, with knowledge of a thematics of what is done, of what action signifies, its causes, ends, etc. In debates concerning responsibility one must always take into account this original and irreducible complexity that links theoretical consciousness . . . to 'practical' conscience (ethical, legal, political).[27]

Responsibility, according to this, is shaped by a linking of the theoretical (it is thematic, a matter of consciousness) and the practical (it is a matter of conscience, be it ethical, legal, or political). Responsibility is not 'at once' theoretical and practical; it is a linking of the theoretical and the practical. In this linkage of consciousness with conscience we can identify that which we usually call autonomy or agency (these being other terms that can substitute for 'responsibility'); yet the relation of consciousness with conscience is not simultaneous, not coincidental, but complex. The autonomous subject knows the laws that she answers to for her actions (for the simple reason that those laws are given to and given by herself—and in this these laws actually constitute her consciousness); and the authentic subject knows the sociocultural effects of her actions, the practical consequences deriving from them. Where political criticism has confused these two, making consciousness immediately a matter of conscience (and, in passing, we can note that this explains a certain 'political correctness', in that what I know is shaped not by knowledge but by conscience), Derrida allows for a more complex and mediated relation, one that allows for a separation of autonomy from authenticity.

Derrida pushes Levinasian thought a little further by shifting attention from the death of others to the death of oneself. Levinas, in the seminar from which I have already quoted, states that 'La mort est décomposition; elle est le sans-réponse' (death is decomposition; it is that which does not respond).[28] If death marks the end of the ability to respond in this way, then it becomes a liminal point of responsibility as such. For Derrida, ostensibly counterintuitively, death becomes precisely the moment at and through which one has the possibility of being responsible at all:

Now to have the experience of responsibility on the basis of the law that is given, that is, to have the experience of one's absolute singularity and apprehend one's own death amounts to the same thing. Death is very much that which nobody else can undergo or confront in my place. My irreplaceability is therefore conferred, delivered, 'given,' one can say, by death. . . . It is from the site of death as the place of my irreplaceability, that is, of my singularity, that I feel called to responsibility. In this sense only a mortal can be responsible.[29]

It would be an oversimplification here to see in this passage Derrida simply following Heidegger. For Heidegger, authenticity is given through the relation of *Dasein* to death, which *Dasein* acknowledges as the possibility of the end of all possibility. In this way, of course, it is *Dasein*'s being-towards-death that introduces the question of urgency (that is, of the political) in the first place. Yet the take on death here in Derrida is not as straightforward as this. Death is that which 'gives' singularity, which is not yet authenticity; indeed, such singularity, as marked by the feeling of being called to responsibility, is primarily a matter of consciousness rather than of conscience. Death, therefore, is not that which introduces urgency (the political), but rather that which introduces delay (in that I am not yet dead, not yet at the point of death itself).

Agamben offers a useful gloss on this in *Il linguaggio e la morte*. Agamben begins his seminar with the uncontroversial observations regarding Dasein: 'Il *Dasein* è, nella sua stessa struttura, un essere-per-la-finé, cioè per la morte e, come tale, è sempre già in relazione con questa' (*Dasein* is, in its very structure, a being-towards-the-end, indeed towards death and, as such, is always given in relation to that). He goes on, however, to introduce the question of *negativity* as the primary condition of *Dasein*'s selfmost possibility:

L'esperienza della morte, che è qui in questione, prende, invece, la forma di una 'anticipazione' della sua possibilità. Questa anticipazione non ha, però, alcun contenuto fattuale positivo. . . . Essa è, piuttosto, la possibilità dell'impossibilità dell'esistenza in generale. . . . Solo sul modo, puramente negativo, di questo essere-per-la-morte, in cui fa esperienza dell'impossibilità più radicale, il *Dasein* può accedere alla propria dimensione più autentica e comprendersi come un tutto.[30]

The experience of death, which is here in question, takes, from now on, the form of an 'anticipation' of its possibility. This anticipation, however, does not have any positive factual content. . . . It is, rather, the possibility of the impossibility of existence in general. . . . Only in the purely negative mode of this being-towards-death, in which it makes the experience of the most radical inpossibility, can *Dasein* arrive at its own most authentic dimension and understand itself as a whole.

Such negativity, of course, is a linguistic matter; from which it will follow, on the sixth day of Agamben's seminar, that 'Il pensiero della morte è, semplicemente, pensiero della Voce' (the thinking of death is, simply, the thinking of the Voice),[31] and that 'L'esperienza dell'essere è, cioè, esperienza di una Voce che chiama senza dire nulla, e il pensiero e la parola umana nascono soltanto come "eco" di questa Voce' (the experience of being is, therefore, the experience of a Voice that calls without saying anything, and thinking and human speech are born only as an 'echo' of this Voice).[32]

This brief excursus into Agamben has the purpose of reminding us that there are at least two ways of regarding the question of an authenticity given by a being-towards-death. For the left, the authenticity in question is that of being and is thus marked by an urgency that collapses consciousness into conscience. Yet there is also another possibility, in which authenticity is a question of voicing or, more generally, of language. It is this latter authenticity that is at stake in deconstruction; and here, responsibility is a matter of answering (be it vocally or in writing) to a law that is given according to the logic of negativity, or, in my preferred term here, 'hypocrisy'.

Blanchot has it that 'literature is its own negation',[33] that 'as soon as honesty comes into play in literature, imposture is already present'.[34] He adds that 'in the final analysis literature, by its very activity, denies the substance of what it represents',[35] and that 'what is striking is that in literature, deceit and mystification are not only inevitable but constitute the writer's honesty, whatever hope and truth are in him'.[36] This ostensible necessity of a drive towards negation in literature can be explored more fully. For Blanchot, writing is inherently paradoxical:

A person who wishes to write is stopped by a contradiction: in order to write, he must have the talent to write. But gifts, in themselves, are nothing. As long as he has not yet sat down at his table and written a work, the writer is not a writer and does not know if he has the capacity to become one. He has no talent until he has written, but he needs talent in order to write.[37]

This paradoxical situation is clearly one that is characterised by a specific tension and, yet more precisely, by a specific grammatical tense. The demand to write is urgent; the possibility of enactment of that desire marked by delay. The consequence of this is that writing becomes something of the order of the event. As Lyotard would much later put it, the writing is done in a future anterior tense:

A postmodern artist or writer is in the position of a philosopher: the text he writes, the work he produces are not in principle governed by preestablished rules, and they cannot be judged according to a determining judgment, by applying familiar categories to the text or to the work. Those rules and categories are what the work of art itself is looking for. The artist and the writer, then, are working without rules in order to formulate the rules of what *will have been done*. Hence the fact that work and text have the characters of an *event*.[38]

This eventual status of writing can now be described for what it is: writing as the quest for and the question of authenticity. In other words, writing/criticism cannot stem from authenticity, cannot be grounded in it: authenticity is what it is looking for in the first place. The paradoxical situation here arises if and only if we accept the 'event status' of the object of our criticism; and, further, it is only in accepting such an eventuality of the text that we can allow the act of criticism itself to be of the order of an event (that is, something whose outcome is not preestablished, something less than dogmatic or orthodox—in short, something historical). That is to say, authenticity is the outcome of a critical engagement and not its predetermining or legitimising basis. That basis must be one that is, literally (etymologically), hypocritical.[39]

This can be explained still further if we consider the centrality of the act of reading itself to our question. It will be recalled that my gambit here is that deconstruction cannot read politics, that the problem in the relation between deconstruction and politics is not overcome through a simple assertion regarding the availability, or, more precisely, the legibility, of the political for a deconstructive criticism. It is worth considering Blanchot again in relation to this. Blanchot argues that the opposition established between the realms of action on the one hand, and the realm of written literature as some kind of passive/passionate sphere on the other, is an 'abusive' opposition; and he writes that 'If we see work as the force of history, the force that transforms man while it transforms the world, then a writer's activity must be recognized as the highest form of work'.[40] He offers the example of the man who builds a stove, an action that is shaped of both positive and negative aspects. The building of the stove 'affirms the presence in the world of something which was not there before, and in so doing, denies something which was there before'. The making of the stove transforms the world; and, yet more importantly, it transforms the conditions and being of its maker as well. The resulting heat 'will also make me someone different'. In writing, claims Blanchot, this transformation is writ large, and the book that the writer makes 'is precisely myself become oth-er'.[41] Insofar as the self is 'altered' in and through writing, one can say here that the authentic self would be the consequence or product of the act of writing; and the way towards the establishment of such authenticity is of necessity the way of masking the self, or of an essential hypocrisy: *larvatus prodeo* is the slogan of the writer.[42]

This paradox also affects the issue of reading. When MacIntyre ex-plores the medieval conception of reading, he finds the roots of our para-dox in Augustinian culture:

In medieval Augustinian culture the relationship between the key texts of that cul-ture and their reader was twofold. The reader was assigned the task of interpret-ing the text, but also had to discover, in and through his or her reading of those texts, that they in turn interpret the reader. What the reader, as thus interpreted by the texts, has to learn about him or herself is that it is only the self as transformed through and by the reading of the texts which will be capable of reading the texts aright. So the reader, like any learner within a craft-tradition, encounters apparent paradox at the outset, a Christian version of the paradox of Plato's *Meno*: it seems that only by learning what the texts have to teach can he or she come to read those texts aright, but also that only by reading them aright can he or she learn what the texts have to teach.[43]

The idea that reading, like writing, is a transforming activity, or an event, is structured on exactly the temporal paradoxicality of the future anterior-ity that is required for the act of reading (now every bit as 'historical' or as 'active' as the making of a stove). The reader, like the writer, must also therefore 'step forward, masked', the *hypocrite lecteur*.

The alternative to such a state of hypocritical affairs is, simply, one of 'the Reign of Terror', as Blanchot puts it. In those decisive historical peri-ods to which we give the name 'revolution', freedom aspires to realise itself in the '*immediate* form of *everything* is possible'.[44] In this immediacy—pre-cisely the refusal of delay and thus the oversimplification of the relations between conscience and consciousness—or in this urgency, it becomes clear that 'the only choice left is between freedom and nothing', with the consequence that 'the only tolerable slogan is Freedom or Death':

Thus the Reign of Terror comes into being. People cease to be individuals work-ing at specific tasks, acting here and only now: each person is universal freedom.

. . . No one has a right to a private life any longer, everything is public. . . . And in the end no one has a right to his life any longer, to his actually separate and physical existence. This is the meaning of the Reign of Terror. Every citizen has a right to death, so to speak: death is not a sentence passed on him, it is his most essential right.[45]

Yet in this 'right to death', we lose the responsibility of the mortal, for we lose the singularity of the self's being-towards-death; and instead, we have a self that is a universal being-towards-death. Such universality is of the order of an abstraction. Paradoxically, therefore, that 'left' criticism that sees itself as based in authenticity and historical being ends up being based on a false notion of autonomy and on a philosophy that cannot account for singular or particular action at all—nor, in the end, can it account for the deaths that it claims so much to honour. Less grandly, it cannot account for the transformative nature of reading, in which readers strive to seek authenticity from their position of fundamental hypocrisy. As Blanchot has it, in a brief remark that should put paid to any theory of reading based on identity politics: 'it is dangerous to write for other people, in order to evoke the speech of others and reveal them to themselves: the fact is that other people do not want to hear their own voices; they want to hear someone else's voice, a voice that is real, profound, troubling like the truth'.[46] In the paradoxical situation in which the eventual hypocritical reader finds herself, as MacIntyre points out, the reader requires two things: first, a teacher; second, a trust that the transformed self towards which that teacher might lead her is, in fact, a necessity or that there are indeed good reasons for transforming herself in the fashion that the text appears to require.

In short, we need a reading friendly and hospitable to otherness.

Friendly Reading

Hospitality is culture itself, argues Derrida in his pamphlet *Cosmopolites de tous les pays, encore un effort!*[47] By this, he means to point out that hospitality is not some ethical position that is available within culture, such that we might choose or not to be hospitable. Rather, insofar as there is culture at all, there is also this ethics of hospitality. Many of Derrida's recent engagements with this question of hospitality have a clearly definable political source, in that he has been active in questions pertaining to immigration in Europe. In this brief concluding section, I shall examine the centrality of hospitality to the mode of hypocritical reading that I argue above to be inevitable for a criticism that would address the relations of deconstruction to reading and to reading politics.[48]

Intrinsic to the claims in the foregoing argument is the notion that reading is itself an act of 'altering/othering'. The hospitality in question for my purposes here is that which is marked by what Derrida calls *hospitalité absolue* (absolute hospitality), in his discussions with Anne Fourmantelle in their book *De l'hospitalité*. There, Derrida distinguishes this 'absolute hospitality' from our everyday understanding of the term, according to which we would offer shelter to a stranger, perhaps, but in so doing, we would effectively assimilate her or him to our home and our family. Absolute hospitality is much more radical than this:

l'hospitalité absolue exige que j'ouvre mon chez-moi et que je donne non seulement à l'étranger (pourvu d'un nom de famille, d'un statut social d'étranger, etc.) mais à l'autre absolu, inconnu, anonyme, et que je lui *donne lieu*, que je le laisse venir, que je le laisse arriver, et avoir lieu dans le lieu que je lui offre, sans lui demander ni réciprocité (l'entrée dans un pacte) ni même son nom.[49]

absolute hospitality demands that I open my home and that I give not only to the stranger (furnished with a family name, with a social status as foreigner, etc.) but to the absolute other, unknown, unnamed, and that I *give place* to him, that I allow him to come, to arrive, and to take his place within the place that I offer him, without asking either reciprocity (the entering into an agreement) or even his name.

It is precisely hospitality such as this, according to which I entertain an absolute other, that the logic of reading hypocritically requires. That is to say, the reader 'cultivates an ethics of hospitality' towards the other that the text will make her, precisely by opening herself to the other (the absolute other) that the text is and must be. To put this in perhaps polemical terms, we have no culture (no hospitality) when we read an other that bears a name and a social status (for example, when we read, say, James Kelman for the sake of his identifications with or identifiability as 'working-class Glaswegian'). In these readings, there is no hospitality, and as a consequence, no culture at all. I do not say, of course, that we do not read such writers. Rather, I argue that we seek a reading based in friendship or hospitality according to which I accept that I cannot know what it might mean to be an authentic 'working-class Glaswegian', or a 'black woman', or indeed any other category associated, in the end, with a politics of identity. A hospitable reading attends to singularity, on the grounds that anything else is both egocentric and inimical to culture, growth, *Bildung*. Agacinski makes this clear in her meditation on racism in *Critique de l'égocentrisme*, where she argues persuasively that 'racism' is that which fails to attend to the singularity of the other who comes to me as an event.[50]

To accept this, of course, is also to accept the requirement for a greater hospitality to be shown to those other writers (for random examples: Chaucer, Spenser, Milton, Dryden, Swift, Pope—partly for the sake of tendentiousness, my 'random' choice are all DWEMs) to whom we have become, institutionally, less than friendly in recent decades.

The erasure of these names from many university syllabi is carried out in the name of a project of identity politics. Behind the project is a drive that effectively allows a 'cultural' university education to be a seamless continuation of everyday life, where classes and criticism address 'interests' assumed to be central to the everyday lives of students. To dignify this theoretically, one would have to appeal to the thought of one such as Raymond Williams, who famously advocated that 'culture is ordinary', that 'culture' can be semantically reclaimed as that which describes not just a selected number of books or aesthetic productions, but rather modes of living. Although sympathetic to the aim behind this—to dignify the lives and work of those deprived of high culture—it nonetheless has been complicit with precisely the institutional history that has deprived many people of the cultural capital that comes from an engagement with high culture. Culture may indeed be ordinary, in a particular sense; but it is an error to equate, say, an activity of randomly shooting at people (ascribable to 'gun culture') as 'cultural' in the same sense as, say, reading Cormac McCarthy. Likewise, it is a theoretical error to assume that the 'popular' is 'cultural'; for if anything is urgent in the sense in which I have used that term here, it is the production of those artifacts that are the elements of popular quotidian cultural industries. Although it is desirable to dignify the culture of working-class people, it is not at all desirable (or politically defensible, in my view) to defend the value of the productions of the culture industry so avidly devoured by so many disenfranchised people.

The important question is not so much whether we read such writers as the DWEMs mentioned above, but whether we read them according to a logic or politics of identity. If we do so, then, I claim, we are failing to engage *either* critically (deconstructively) *or* politically. The relation of deconstruction to politics is not one to be resolved through a logic of identity or identification, but rather one whose complexity can only be addressed by attending to the temporal paradox of the future anterior, and to the logic of a hypocrisy that will result in a genuine—absolute—hospitality, a hospitality that is at once the mark of culture and of politics.

CHAPTER 3

. . . Declining the West . . .

Deconstruction—criticism—is not new; and it originates, I have argued above, in what is essentially akin to a postcolonial situation, in the 'absurd' or irreducible moment of the play of forces that constitutes our 'situatedness'.[1] In this, I mean to suggest a link between the formalities of a logic that drives the critical consciousness and a 'geography' or writing of location and of the structures of the earth. We know this most intimately in the sophistications of and arguments within postcolonial theory; but it has had a percussive effect through a general cultural history, as in the work of so-called radical geographers, for whom representations of geographical realities are imbued with the production of cultural meanings and memories.[2] It is by now almost a commonplace to assume that our situatedness determines—predetermines—our criticism or even that it limits the possibilities of our consciousness; yet, in that predetermination, it is clear that there is also not just a problem of 'prejudice', as discussed in Chapter 1, but also what we should call a 'prevention' of criticism,[3] which I hinted at in Chapter 2.

The term 'prevention' here has a particular sense, which I derive from George Herbert's great seventeenth-century 'poem of place', *The Temple* (1633). *The Temple* is an interrelating web of texts that constitute the building of a location for the poet and his reader, a mapping of a temple that is also the mapping of a relation to God. Throughout the collection, Herbert strives to be simple, to arrive at a simplicity that would be the resolution of the complexities of his theology. Central to this is the ostensibly self-contradictory relation between Herbert and God, a relation that is marked by the logic of what Herbert thinks of as a problem of temporality. His problem is that he feels his words to be, in some essential sense, predetermined. In the fact that his poems derive from the Bible and from a theological logos or fiat, Herbert is aware that his language is always derivative, a reiteration of something already said. It thus appears to lack originality, and also sincerity, for every time he strives to say something to God that is drawn essentially from the very source and origin of his own self, he discovers that yet again he is repeating what God said or what God might have said. In this, Herbert laments that his every attempt to be original, authentic, autonomous is doomed in advance. It is doomed for the straightforward reason that he can never surprise God: God has always got there first, or has literally 'pre-vented' Herbert. As he puts it at the opening of 'The Reprisall':

> I have consider'd it, and finde
> There is no dealing with thy mighty passion:
> For though I die for thee, I am behinde.[4]

It is useful to recall here the structure, discussed in my opening chapter, of *Jacques Derrida*, in which the demand that Derrida 'surprise' Bennington is itself always 'prevented'. We might now add to this a more general proposition regarding how we read. In his early work, Stanley Fish proposed a theory of reader-response criticism that was organised around the idea of reading as 'surprise'. This drove not only his study of Milton, *Surprised by Sin*, but also his more explicitly early theoretical texts, initially those organised around his studies in the seventeenth century, as in *Self-Consuming Artifacts*. For the early Fish, surprise was not only possible, but even a necessary fact of right reading: it was fundamentally a sign that the reader was actually *doing* something. However, later, the 'pragmatic' Fish declines ever to be surprised by anything, entirely accepting a logic of locatedness in which he suggests that he would always have been able to predict what any critic says, once given that critic's theoretical or conceptual principle, her or his 'critical location', as it were. How is this shift possible?

The problem—of a surprise that turns out always to have been predictable—is essentially the temporal equivalent of the politics of space surrounding postcoloniality. For what the later Fish is actually saying is something like, 'Had I known what you were going to say, I would have been able to predict it'. Another way of putting that is to imagine the possibility of being in two different temporal moments or instances; and another way of putting this is to imagine the possibility of teaching, in which the pupil is intrinsically situated 'behind' the teacher in time but ahead of the teacher in space, sitting at the desk while the teacher patrols and supervises.[5] The logic that brings together pedagogy and postcolonial space is one that ensures that the colonised can never surprise the coloniser (or Fish); and the reason for this is a tardiness that is ascribed to the colonised by the teacher/coloniser/reader.

A more genuine kind of surprise, we might say, is what we should now properly consider as an 'event', as that would have been understood by Lyotard, for instance. An event for Lyotard, as for those sympathetic to his construing of the postmodern, is something that happens but whose happening could never have been predicted from what had gone before. It is, as it were, the instantiation of a singularity, something whose taking place is not dependent on what was in place before it took place. In this seemingly linguistically clumsy formulation, I am trying to ensure that we can hear the issue of the postmodern as a 'taking place', and thus hear it as something intrinsically related to precisely that logic of place that, imbricated with a temporality, I argued above, structures the critical consciousness as such. The question before us now is simultaneously simple and difficult: is the event of reading possible? More precisely, is it possible to engage in a reading that allows the reading Self to engage with the presumed alterity of the Other as writer? Is it possible for a westerner, say, to read 'the east' and/or vice versa? Further, is it possible to do so without prejudice, without an already inscribed structure of power that predetermines the reading, and thus denies it the status of an event?

For Herbert in his temple, this brings together a poetics of place with a poetics of temporality. He wants to be in the truth, to find in his words an adequate relation to a transcendental truth, and yet he realises that whatever he says can only ever be a repetition or a rehearsal of a preordaining 'it is written that'. In short, he realises that whatever he might say is but a rehearsal of what is available within the possible repertoire that is already spoken in the voice and word of God. Truth predates—better, prefigures—Herbert; and thus it can never originate with him or in him. He can never tell the truth, even and most especially at those moments when he strives most resolutely to speak the truth. The consequence of this is that he realises that truth is not to be found in his words or in his speaking; and yet his every word is precisely such a seeking after truth. Thus it is that, proto-Shandy, the more he writes, the more he falls away from an originary truth; and thus the more he needs to write to try to regain such a truth.[6] *The Temple* marks the impossibility of identifying the voice or writing with the truth; yet this impossibility coincides with the incessant demand for precisely such an identification. The success of *The Temple*, as the building of a place for the poet to inhabit, is marked by the failure ever to construct an adequate place, the inadequacy in the case resulting from the temporal disjunction between the poet and the place. Inversely, however, such failure is precisely what makes the poems successful, in that the failure demands that more poems be written, that the attempt to get closer to the truth that Herbert finds in God be reiterated again and again. For Herbert, truth could be defined as a fundamental alterity: it is the other that demands a relation with the self, but that also escapes the self precisely as it makes such a demand. God calls to Herbert, but then moves on and evades the response. That structure is what we can call temporality itself, for it calls Herbert ever forward, such that his temple becomes the inhabiting of time (an essential restlessness, like the life of the fugitive) as well as an architectural construction of location.

The temporal structure here is also, of course, an ethical structure. *Tempus fugit*: and in that flight of time, we see also the fugitive and the refugee. In arguing that criticism has a foundation in a situatedness that is at once spatial and temporal, I am also claiming here that there is an ethics at the base of modern criticism. That ethics, however, is neither abstract nor formal; rather, it is an ethics that has its root in the complexities of a postcolonial logic whose effect is to translate the spatial or geographical relation into a temporal or historical one. It is probably Homi Bhabha who has come closest to articulating this complexity in his explorations of 'newness', broadly correlative with what Herbert would have thought of as spontaneity or authentic original speaking. For Bhabha,

The borderline work of culture demands an encounter with 'newness' that is not part of the continuum of past and present. It creates a sense of the new as an insurgent act of cultural translation. Such art does not merely recall the past as social cause or aesthetic precedent; it renews the past, refiguring it as a contingent 'in-between' space, that innovates and interrupts the performance of the present. The 'past-present' becomes part of the necessity, not the nostalgia, of living.[7]

What is at stake here is the question that we have now come to recognise as the problem of the postmodern, in which the 'new' is set to be the event of an interruption whose force is that it requires an 'act of cultural translation' if it is to be understood, or even properly experienced. In short, the postcolonial relation is always silently inscribed with a temporal relation; and whenever temporality manages to break its silence, we see the postcolonial relation as one that is marked not just by politics (for that would be purely—merely—geographical), but also by ethics. In this chapter, I shall explore what this might mean by calling the relation 'east/west' to account before the relation 'modern/postmodern'.

Having opened with Herbert, let me add another seventeenth-century writing, in which John Donne maps an erotic relation in geopolitical terms:

> My face in thine eye, thine in mine appears,
> And true plain hearts do in the faces rest,
> Where can we find two better hemispheres
> Without sharp north, without declining west?[8]

This poem, ostensibly about the intimate relation between two bodies in space, is, of course, a poem about time. 'The Good Morrow' wants to open the lovers to a future, to the day or morrow ahead; but a future without death[9]:

> What ever dies, was not mixed equally;
> If our two loves be one, or, thou and I
> Love so alike, that none do slacken, none can die.

The west here is aligned, fairly conventionally, with the setting of the sun, and thus with the passing of the day; and, by extension, therefore, with death itself. Donne wants a world without 'declining west'; or, to put it briefly, he declines the declining west. It is this that gives me the title of the present chapter.[10]

In claiming that criticism begins, effectively and for shorthand purposes, in the relation 'east/west', and that this occludes an equally significant relation of 'modern/postmodern', I am also suggesting that we must consider the nature of the partition between these two sets of oppositions. In what follows, I shall be considering the partition between east/west; the partition between modern/postmodern; and, finally, the partition between, on one hand, the partition of east/west and, on the other, the partition of modern/postmodern. The argument falls into three sections: in the first, I attend to the deictic nature of 'the west'; in the second, I consider the politics of such a deictic and meditate on the frontier that is 'Europe'; and finally, I consider the place of Egypt in such a configuration or constellation of east/west relations.

A brief word is required here to clarify my take on the postmodern. I follow Lyotard, not Jameson: I take the postmodern as mood or attitude, rather than as periodising concept. The mood is characterised by the differend: that impasse in thinking where, as Lyotard has it, we have 'a case of conflict between (at least) two parties, that cannot be equitably resolved for lack of a rule of judgement applicable to both arguments. One side's legitimacy does not imply the other's lack of legitimacy'.[11] The consequence of this is a radical pluralism, a multiplicity of points of view that cannot be resolved into a unity: an 'east/west', if you will, that cannot become one world (and thus, if we think about it carefully, an 'east' that cannot be to the east of the 'west'; and a 'west' that cannot be the east's west). To explain the predicament of criticism or judgement in this postmodern mood, according to which all judgements face a crisis of legitimation or grounding due to the lack of any universal foundational philosophy, Lyotard has recourse to Kant. In the *Critique of Judgement*, Kant makes a distinction between two forms of judgement. On one hand, Kant claimed, we have 'determining' judgement, in which our judgements are made in conformity with a rule and are predetermined by that rule (and, furthermore, the rule is acceptable to all parties to the judgement: a kind of 'Supreme Court of Appeal', the legitimacy of whose ruling will be universally acceptable); on the other hand, we also have 'reflective' judgement, in which there are no rules—as in aesthetics for example, where there are no rules governing what constitutes 'the beautiful', but where we still face the necessity or requirement of making judgements ('I like this'; 'I dislike that'; 'this makes me weep'), even though we lack the agreed criteria requisite for universal agreement. For Lyotard, the modern mood would be that which prioritises determining judgement (often to such an extent that reflective judgement disappears, or at least is relegated to a secondary position—'the arts' and not 'science/knowledge'); and the postmodern is that which reengages reflective judgement, with all the legitimation crises that follow from that. The importance of this will become more apparent when I discuss the case of an Egyptian text below.[12]

Deictic Wests

Let me begin from Said's view of 'the west'. In his later works, such as *Culture and Imperialism*, Said is fairly explicit about how we identify 'the west'. The west is identified as something that 'rises' to prominence during the nineteenth century, when it becomes increasingly identified as Britain and France:

> At the centre of these perceptions is a fact that few dispute, namely, that during the nineteenth century unprecedented power—compared with which the powers of Rome, Spain, Baghdad, or Constantinople in their day were far less formidable—was concentrated in Britain and France, and later in other Western countries (the United States, especially). This century climaxed 'the rise of the West', and Western power allowed the imperial metropolitan centres to acquire and accumulate territory and subjects on a truly astonishing scale. Consider that in 1800 Western powers claimed 55 per cent but actually held approximately 35 per cent of the earth's surface, and that by 1878 the proportion was 67 per cent, a rate of increase of 83,000 square miles per year. By 1914, the annual rate had risen to an astonishing 240,000 square miles, and Europe held a grand total of roughly 85 per cent of the earth as colonies, protectorates, dependencies, dominions, and commonwealths. No other associated set of colonies in history was as large, none so totally dominated, none so unequal in power to the Western metropolis.[13]

In this, we should note that the west characterised by Said and identified as 'Europe' has its own internal west (Britain, France), and that it also has another, external, west (the United States). Something happens in this passage that allows Said effectively to elide other great historical imperial powers (Spain, Portugal, the Netherlands) all of which had colonies to their west as well. The west in question is thus clearly rather uncertain; Said offers a *constructed* west, designed to identify the west with that specific instance of imperialism whose roots lie in the nineteenth century. This, I suggest, oversimplifies the case, however magisterially it serves the purpose of highlighting that instance of imperial power, and however well it serves what is, in the end, an ideological critique.

The point that I would make is made much more eloquently and forcefully by Aijaz Ahmad in *In Theory*. Said, argues Ahmad, is indebted to 'an idealist metaphysic' inherent in the humanist tradition against which Said ostensibly writes. That idealist metaphysic would claim that

a)there *is* an unified European/Western identity which is at the *origin* of history and has *shaped* this history through its *thought* and its *texts*; b)this seamless and unified history of European identity and thought runs from Ancient Greece up to the end of the nineteenth century and well into the twentieth, through a specific set of beliefs and values which remain essentially the same, only becoming more dense; and c)that this history is immanent in—and therefore available for reconstruction through—the canon of its *great books*. Said subscribes to the *structure* of this idealist metaphysic even though he obviously questions the greatness of some of those 'great books'.[14]

The fundamental problem that I am finding here with Said's influential (and, for many, uncontroversial) view of the west is that it homogenises the west and its histories. Such a move is precisely one of the moves made by those orientalists who were the object of Said's fundamental criticism in *Orientalism* and since. Orientalism had homogenised the east, the orient, Islam, as if these were all part of one great totality, graspable without attending to intrinsic tensions, contradictions, pluralities.

To state the obvious, then: there are many 'wests', and they all shift around, depending on the position from which one 'orients' oneself (West Beirut; West Belfast; West Jerusalem; West Berlin as was; the West End of London, Glasgow, and Cairo; West Britain; California, but before that on the great migrations, the Dakotas, Wyoming, Idaho; not to mention those mythic wests identifiable in Yeats or in Synge's *Playboy of the Western World*; in Wyndham Lewis; or the 'west Britons' who are the object of scandalised disgust among the nationalists in Joyce's 'The Dead'; Erich Maria Remarque's 'western front' on which all is said to be quiet; the west of *West Side Story*; the west implied when Milton writes of what happened 'east of Eden'; and so on). So much, so simplistic, you will rightly say; but let us now try to see what happens if we take the idea of a plurality of wests more seriously.

I turn to Spengler's once massively influential book, *The Decline of the West*. The first time that Spengler makes mention of the phrase 'West European', he calls up a lengthy footnote:

Here the historian is gravely influenced by preconceptions derived from geography, which assumes a *Continent* of Europe, and feels himself compelled to draw an ideal frontier corresponding to the physical frontier between 'Europe' and 'Asia'. The word 'Europe' ought to be struck out of history. There is historically no 'European' type, and it is sheer delusion to speak of the Hellenes as 'European Antiquity' (were Homer and Heraclitus and Pythagoras, then, Asiatics?) and to enlarge upon their 'mission' as such. These phrases express no realities but merely a sketchy interpretation of the map. . . . 'East' and 'West' are notions that contain real history, whereas 'Europe' is an empty sound. Everything great that the Classical world created, it created in pure denial of the existence of any continental barrier between Rome and Cyprus, Byzantium and Alexandria. Everything that we imply by the term European Culture came into existence between the Vistula and the Adriatic and the Guadalquivir and, even if we were to agree that Greece, the Greece of Pericles, lay in Europe, the Greece of to-day certainly does not.[15]

Spengler's irritation here derives from his anti-Kantian, proto-Lyotardian stance with respect to history and historiography. The neo-Kantian view, rejected by Spengler, would be that it is possible (at least in principle) to construct a universal history, a single unified story of the world in which 'the east' would be 'the west's east' and 'the west' would be 'the east's west'; and both would be unified in one world. Spengler sees this univocal version of history as a product essentially of two things: first, the triumph of the mathematical and abstract logic of a cause-and-effect structure as the method through which we should understand the flow of history, a structure that, of course, prioritises narrative as the explanatory mechanism of history; and second, what he calls the 'Ptolemaic' view of history that places the European who writes the resulting historical narrative at the centre of all meaning and value (a confusion, if you will, of narrator with 'author' or source: precisely the kind of 'confounding' that is precluded in Herbertian prevention).

Spengler's counterarguments to this derive from the (very contemporary) observation that all perspective is relative: that the world as seen from Konigsberg, Paris, Edinburgh is not identical with the world seen from Dublin, Alexandria, Cairo. Further, Spengler is of the view that we can-

not find 'the truth' of history simply by adjudicating between the competing narratives of its events. Our adjudications are themselves relative and
are the products of our own historical position. In this he is Nietzschean
('there is no truth; there are only interpretations. And this, too, is an interpretation'); but he is also proto-Lyotardian, in offering us the problem
that Lyotard identifies as that of the differend. Spengler's 'Copernican turn'
in historiography is his advancing of the protostructuralist 'morphological
method', which allows for an overview to be taken of events that ostensibly
differ significantly from each other, but in a fashion that sees those events
with a sufficient degree of abstraction required to enable the structure of
history (necessity/Destiny, in Spengler's terms) to become apparent; and
thus, although one is inevitably making these abstractions from a particular place and time, their meaning is neither construed in narrative terms
nor dependent on the position from which one views them.[16]

In an uncanny (and unlikely) prefiguring of Adorno, Spengler allows
for methods of historical explanation that are based on modes of reason
other than the mathematical/computational (so, perhaps, farewell to Said's
impressive statistics). Further—and this is my key point—Spengler ac-
cepts that there are multiple histories of ostensibly singular events.

The Kantian/Ptolemaic view, as Spengler points out, faces a legitimation problem. As merely relative, it has no legitimate validity; yet it must
try to advance itself as truth. Thus, this historiography must find a way of
privileging its own perspective as the truthful perspective; and the way that
it does this is by calling itself 'modern'. History is now (at the turn of the
twentieth century) 'partitioned', split into three parts: ancient, medieval,
and now (for the first time) 'modern'.

This modern epoch is added, Spengler points out, 'on Western soil,
and it is this that, for the first time, gives the picture of history the look of
a progression'.[17] This, he argues, is profoundly antihistorical. He is able to
make a simple link that allows him to equate Eurocentrism with an antihistorical view: 'The ground of Western Europe is treated as a steady pole,
a unique patch chosen on the surface of the sphere for no better reason, it
seems, than because we live on it'.[18] Uncannily, and uncomfortably, Spengler prefigures Lyotard and also many within the mainstream of postcolonial studies. More importantly for present purposes, Spengler, in alerting
us to the validity of the postmodern device of multiple and undecidable

narratives, is also able to identify Eurocentric thinking as intrinsically spatial, nonhistorical. It is in these primarily spatial terms that we tend often to think of the mapping of east/west: as a political division, a partition based on the differences of politics and of polities. It is to this political issue that I now want to turn more directly.

Frontiers

We often think of partition, such as that between east/west, between India/Pakistan, say, or within Ireland, as 'essentially' political, in that it often involves the establishment of a frontier that divides, demarcates, describes the realms of the proper and the alien. Recall Bennington's formulation that 'wherever there is a frontier, be it between two countries, be it between literature and philosophy . . . there is something of the order of politics'. What this means is that wherever there is undecidability such as we see it in deconstruction, there is politics. For Bennington, such thinking originates in the old *quis custodiet* paradox, 'stated by Kant before Marx', as he puts it, 'of knowing who will educate the educators'.[19]

Such thinking, however, constitutes an example of what Spengler called 'Eurocentric' thinking: its notion of the frontier is essentially spatial. From it, however, we can see that partition is an inevitable condition of European thought; and that it situates the political always and necessarily as an act of containment by frontiers or transgression of frontiers—or, indeed, both at once, in the form of imperialist expansion in which Britain (say) transgresses its own borders to 'contain' or 'protect' other territories.

Why is partition essentially and inevitably the structure and condition of European thought? Because if Europe thinks itself as 'modern', then it faces a temporal version of Bennington's *quis custodiet* question: 'who, if not the modern, will modernise those who would be modern?'— or, more succinctly, 'whose perspective is *so modern* (perhaps *postmodern* enough) that it is able to allow the identification of other perspectives— including those of the east, say—as less modern, underdeveloped, tardy?' Europe, therefore, *must* work through the partition of itself from itself, and through the partition of itself from its external other—which it will call the east—in order to legitimise itself at all.

We need a textual example. Let me turn to Beckett. Towards the end—if there is an end, if there is anything other than ending—in *The Unnamable*, the Unnamable says:

perhaps that's what I feel, an outside and an inside and me in the middle, perhaps that's what I am, the thing that divides the world in two, on the one side the outside, on the other the inside, that can be thin as foil, I'm neither one side nor the other, I'm in the middle, I'm the partition, I've two surfaces and no thickness, perhaps that's what I feel, myself vibrating, I'm the tympanum, on the one hand the mind, on the other the world, I don't belong to either.[20]

Beckett's great question here is eventually identified as a temporal one: 'you must go on, I can't go on, I'll go on'. I shall argue here that we must understand this unnameable partition, this 'thing that divides the world in two' this structure of 'east/west' thought as part of the problem of history and of time, and not simply as that of space.

Spengler, we recall, shows that the idea of historical progression in a single narrative is fundamentally a product of a thought in which 'the west' or 'Europe' must identify itself as modern: it is this modernity that legitimises Europe's otherwise dangerously relativistic point of view. We might add to this Rorty's take on Hegel, for whom the progress of Spirit towards self-actualisation was identified geopolitically as a 'westering' motion that, for Rorty, leads to America being the locus of a pragmatic version of truth today. In these, 'the west', identified as constant modernisation or self-modernisation, is identified firmly with futurity. Now, let me return to Beckett. Beckett's unnameable 'partition' is clearly a frontier, a place or nonplace 'between'; and it owes its very being, such as it is, to the division of the world between the alien and the proper. In situating the identity of the Unnamable thus, Beckett is constructing the subject-as-such in the form of 'partition'; and because partition is that characteristic which we have identified as the fundamental ethos or character of 'Europe', then it follows that we can now name the unnameable: Europe.

So much for a spatial identity, we may say; but what of the temporal? Europe, I suggest, must not only be 'here' in this form of thinking; it must also be 'now'. Like Eliot in *Four Quartets*, 'History is now and England'. This prioritisation of a present moment as a 'modern' moment has its analogue in earlier philosophy: Descartes, for example, famously allows the meaning of the world—the world as epistemology—to fall on his own subjectivity. His 'I' is that which mediates between the world as being and the world as meaning; or, in a word, Descartes is the 'partition' that divides the world in two, but that also returns the world to us, making it available once more after its radical disappearance in the moment of doubt. Augustine offers a similar kind of example when he considers whether it is possible to be alive and dead at the same time (that is, whether Christian resurrection is possible, or, more crudely, whether he can believe in ghosts). In *Civitas Dei*, Augustine divides being into three parts: before death, in death, and after death; and he proves that it is impossible for the moment 'in death' ever to have any substantive existence, on the grounds that, at any given instant, we are *either* alive (before death) *or* dead (after death). In this, the moment in death, like the moment of the present, sandwiched between a past and a future, effectively disappears or loses its substance. In this, Augustine prefigures Derrida; but, perhaps more importantly for our present purposes, he effectively equates 'experience' (being in the present moment) with dying. If we experience at all, it paradoxically follows from this that we must be passing through that otherwise insubstantial moment 'in death'. It is almost as if experience depends on our being simultaneously alive and dead, on our being ghostly, like the figure of the mummy. It is to this that I can now turn, in an effort to politicise this ghostly figure in relation to our presiding issue of the relations between east/west and between modern/postmodern.

Irish Egypt

Imagine the moment of 1922 for the London intellectual or cultural critic. *The Waste Land* appears; *Ulysses* appears, and your friend in Paris smuggles you a copy. Modernism, we can safely say, is with us. Both these great texts come, in a sense, from 'the west': one is written by an American who, most interestingly in this context, models the text on a pilgrimage by recalling Chaucer in its opening lines, before taking the pilgrimage eastwards to a Sanskrit culture. The other is written by a Dubliner who brings Greece westwards to Dublin, and who makes the text while moving around modern metropolitan cities, such as Paris, Zurich, and that great frontier city between Europe and whatever lies to its east, Trieste. The appearance of this 'Irish' text causes something of a stir, especially among intellectuals who might be interested in Irish politics, for Ireland is just beginning its proper (if incomplete) secession from Britain.

But the intellectual I have in mind has other pursuits. Imagine him interested in history and in the great works of art that are to be found in London's museums. He might have been reading Spengler (in the German, for the work won't be translated until 1926); and perhaps he has been reading how, today, 'Pathetic symbols of the will to endure, the bodies of the great Pharaohs lie in our museums, their faces still recognizable'.[21] Perhaps this critic is asking the kinds of troublesome, curmudgeonly question2 that are now routine: how did these pharaohs get here, into these museums of the west? Perhaps, on 26 November 1922, this intellectual has taken his copy of Spengler on an archaeological dig. For he is Howard Carter, and on 26 November 1922, he has just broken through the partition wall into a tomb: Tutankhamun's tomb.

This mummy, however, is one that will not be taken westwards unproblematically, because Egypt, like Ireland, is asserting its autonomy, and it has established itself as independent again on 21 February 1922. Michael North is very good on this incident in his *Reading 1922*. Carter, North points out, tries to justify his theft of remains by saying that Egyptians are untrustworthy (it is thus, incidentally, that we know Carter has not been reading Spengler, whose views on Egypt are uniformly extremely positive). As North glosses this:

British science [through its museums] . . . must represent Egypt against itself, serving for a time as a sort of stand-in for the mature political entity that has yet to develop. . . . In this very familiar way, Great Britain interposes itself between modern Egypt and its own ancient history, offering itself as rightful heir and inheritor of all the glory of the past, no matter where it might have occurred.[22]

This gloss is useful precisely because it characterises Britain *as* the partition, as that unnameable *between* Egypt's *proper* and *alienated* histories. 'The west' here is that which severs Egypt from itself, acting *as* partition and partitioning Egypt; but this time, the partition is *historical*, for Britain is inserting itself as a mediating present instant between Egypt's past and its future.

It is, of course, not just Britain that does this: it is Europe itself. Said comes close to getting at what I mean here in his analysis of Verdi's great opera, *Aida*, mounted for the first performance in Cairo as the inaugural opera for the new Cairo Opera House in 1872. Said's case is that, when

Khedive Ismail built this opera house, he was fascinated by 'the west'; and the opera house effectively partitioned Cairo into two cities, a West Cairo that was European, a 'Paris-on-the-Nile', and an East Cairo that was left underdeveloped, with its poor 'teeming quarters of Muski, Sayida Zeinab, 'Ataba al-Khadra'.[23] We can add to Said's analysis in the following terms: West Cairo was to be led into modernity, effectively through the operatic death/mummification of Aida and Radamès; East Cairo to be left in the past, in the figure of Amneris, wailing at her lost opportunity, unable to move forward in time.

It is worth noting here that what is true of Cairo is also true of Egypt itself in that Egypt was seen as, in Said's terms, 'the focal point of the relationships between Africa and Asia, between Europe and the East, between memory and actuality'.[24]

What is at stake in this splitting of Cairo, and behind that, of Egypt itself, is a temporal and historical issue. Egypt is proposed as a frontier between past and future: at the threshold of modernity, it is always thus in an 'unnamable' or unknowable, unidentifiable situation. If I characterised Beckett's unnameable as Europe, then, it would follow, Egypt, in this characterisation as a point or frontier between memory and futurity, as this liminal point called modernity, is also 'Europe'. In short, here in Cairo we are also 'in the west'. Further, insofar as Cairo/Egypt in these terms occupies this liminal point, it is a place without rules, without criteria: it requires a postmodern mood for its inhabiting.

What, we might say, has happened to the east? Where has it gone?

Another date and place: it is Ireland, 1972. Seamus Heaney, having just moved south from Derry to the countryside outside Dublin (across a 'border') is contemplating the writing of *North*. Yet let us recall the major trope shaping his writing at this moment: archaeology. He carries forward the notion of 'digging' for the past in his native Irish soil into a series of poems that have him, like Yeats before him, looking eastwards. Whereas Yeats looked to Byzantium, Heaney looks to Denmark, where he finds the mummified bodies of the bog people, the Tollund Man, the Grauballe Man, the Bog Queen. In this move, Heaney effectively identifies the west, his west, with the present moment, a vantage point from which he can mine an archaeological past; and it is this west that these bog people must pass through in order to allow Heaney to come to a full articulation of his—and Ireland's—identity (or future). Structurally, this repeats the imperialist consciousness of Carter. It simply displaces the location of the west. In this structure of consciousness, the east is always the site of an archaeological memory. It can be allowed to come to futurity—to modernity—only by passing through the prism of its controlling west. It follows, in this, that the east, by definition, can only ever be the west's version of the east.

Can we contest this structure of consciousness? One easy way, of course, would be to retreat to precolonialist theory, to Kipling, say, and to proclaim that we will ignore the locatedness of cultures. That, however, does not solve the problem. It simply evades it.

Let us therefore return to the stakes of this original question, and to the division of modern/postmodern. I, a Scottish intellectual (from the west of Scotland: Glasgow; but from the east of Glasgow), read, let us say, *Bayn al-Qasrayn* (*Palace Walk*), the first volume of the great Cairo trilogy of Mafouz. Let us say that I am a modern; and so I would critique Mafouz from within the terms of a 'determining judgement'. That is to say, I would take the rules of the novel as I know them and would compare Mafouz's ability to compose plot, character, and so on with, say, the skills of Dickens or Thackeray, both of whom are able to represent a great city in their texts. (It is this, incidentally, that Said does when he characterises Mafouz as an Egyptian Dickens or Zola.) Mafouz, though, published this text in 1956; and so I might apply the rules of the midcentury novel, especially of those novels marked by a religious interest, such as those of Greene; and here, I would set and judge al-Sayyid Ahmad alongside, say, Greene's 'whisky priest' or Catholic gangsters, looking for an analysis of guilt and morality. In all such cases, I am judging Mafouz by criteria that are not his own— indeed, criteria that are frankly alien. The response, though, is not to hypothesise that I can be Egyptian, for that is as impossible as me becoming a contemporary of John Donne. Rather, a more appropriate response might be to think of myself not as modern, but as postmodern; and I would then read *Palace Walk* 'without criteria'. Hence, I might not immediately rush to judgement when Ahmad throws Amina out of the house; or if I do judge (which I must), I would not judge according to the criteria either of (western) feminism or of (eastern) Islam. I thus accept the necessity of judging that great scene; but I also accept the impossibility of finding a ground of judgement that would be equally acceptable to the Islamist and to the European feminist. As Beckett might have put it: 'you must judge, I can't judge, I'll judge'. In doing this, of course, I actually come to inhabit precisely the position of both Ahmad and Amina at once; and it is in reading thus that the scene achieves its great power.

This situation—'you must judge, I can't judge, I'll judge'—is what Lyotard calls a differend. I prefer to call it 'the east'. By 'declining the west' or 'declining modernity', we can strive to find the east as it occasionally affords glimpses of itself precisely as the condition of the postmodern. The east is thus not a repository of world history, the site of an archaeological memory; rather, the east is a frame of mind that allows us to enter a futurity, or, as Marx might have said, to get history started at last, before it is too late. Another way of putting this is to say that we need to learn the ethical friendship that is a hospitality that we can show towards futurity, or towards the possibility that the future will—must—differ from the 'here, now'. The ethics in this, therefore, is a temporal ethics, a hospitality towards the possibilities of the culture to come.

The Potential of Aestheticism

CHAPTER 4

Aesthetic Education and the
Demise of Experience

The philistine is intolerant.

—BENJAMIN, 'EXPERIENCE'

Love naturally hates old age and keeps his distance from it.

—AGATHON, IN PLATO, *Symposium*

In 1913, Benjamin was a central figure alongside his teacher, Gustav Wyneken, in the German Youth Movement, agitating for substantial reforms in the German educational system and, beyond that, in German society. He placed one of his first serious publications, an essay entitled 'Experience', in *Der Anfang*, the magazine of the movement, as a contribution to the debates. In this essay, he points out that a society's elders have a bad habit of legitimising their views through recourse to their 'experience' (*Erfahrung*), their amassing of 'felt life', as we might call it, which is axiomatically greater than that amassed by youth. Youth—like a contemporary emergent 'modernism'—claims to offer something new, something requiring *synthetic* and not merely *analytic* judgement, in Kantian terms; but the old and established refuse to legitimise such novelty, and resist it, in a pragmatic world-weary analysis whose purpose is to assimilate the shocking to the normative and to contend that 'experience' will show youth the error of their ways and the validity of the elders' ways of thinking.[1]

For this young Benjamin, a mode of thinking or of criticism is required that will go beyond what we have already described as 'criticism as analysis'; and it will go beyond such 'mere' analysis in order to engage the possibility of *difference* that can be brought about through experience or what we might call actual and sensual life. For Kant, 'Judgments of experience, as such, are always synthetical',[2] and synthetical judgements are what he calls 'augmentative' in that they 'add to our conceptions of the subject a predicate which was not contained in it, and which no analysis could ever have discovered therein'.[3] Such augmentation we might call education or even culture itself, in its primary senses of edifying growth and development.

Benjamin writes that 'In our struggle for responsibility' (by which he means something like youth's struggle for autonomy, for self-determination, or for the independence needed to determine a new and different future), 'we fight against someone who is masked. The mask of the adult is called "experience"'. He goes on:

> But let us attempt to raise the mask. What has this adult experienced? What does he wish to prove to us? This above all: he, too, was once young; he, too, wanted what we wanted; he, too, refused to believe his parents, but life has taught him that they were right. Saying this, he smiles in a superior fashion: this will also happen to us—in advance he devalues the years we will live, making them into a time of sweet youthful pranks, of childish rapture, before the long sobriety of serious life. Thus the well-meaning, the enlightened.[4]

The present living of the youth—*Erlebnis*—is effectively evacuated of content. Youthful *Erlebnis* is denied substantive reality by this rhetorical manoeuvre practised by the elders; for reality, being the amassing of experiences (*Erfahrung*) is what, by definition, the youth has not yet attained.

Benjamin's point, arising from this, is that such thinking is precisely what substantiates and validates the philistinism of a culture whose terms are defined by the elders: 'herein lies his secret: because he has never raised his eyes to the great and the meaningful, the philistine has taken experience as his gospel'. Benjamin thus wants here to stake a claim for something 'other-than-experience', something characterised in terms of values or spirit, and, more precisely still, in terms of values or spirit that are in a profound sense 'modern', youthful, up to date: 'Why is life without meaning or solace for the philistine? Because he knows experience and nothing else. Because he himself is desolate and without spirit. And because he has no inner relationship to anything other than the common and the always-already-out-of-date'.[5] Benjamin's essay allows us to see that the fundamental effect of this is to deny one kind of experience (*Erlebnis*: the content of the moment as it is lived in its intensity, the content of Baudelaire's 'transient, evanescent' moment; 'felt life') precisely as it validates another (*Erfahrung*: the accrued mass of such moments, no longer in their lived actuality, but rather in their general, abstract, total form: Baudelaire's 'eternal' or 'immutable'). As he puts it in 'The Return of the Flâneur', in terms indebted to Baudelaire, 'There is a kind of experience that craves the unique, the sensational, and another kind that seeks out eternal sameness'.[6] The elders legitimise the triumph of the latter, yielding a triumph of the sensible form of life over its sensual content; and the sense they give to such form is, paradoxically, senselessness itself, philistine 'meaninglessness'.[7]

Here is the kernel of Benjamin's 'modern' thinking. He notes the contest between, on one hand, the material *content* of a lived experience, transient if intense, and, on the other hand, the abstract and unreal ideality of the *form* that such an experience assumes when it is construed in terms of a 'monument of unaging intellect'. The absolute prioritisation of the latter is to be contested. In the present case, the aim is not simply to rehabilitate the lived actuality of material existence as such, but rather to claim that there is something valuable in the 'other than experience' constituted by the German Youth Movement's trajectory towards and into modernity, into a spirited occasionalism, or a being 'always already up to date'.

This opposition, between the materiality of content and the abstract ideality of its form, is utterly fundamental to Benjamin. It lies, for instance, behind the argumentation of his most celebrated essay, 'The Work of Art in the Age of Mechanical Reproduction'. That essay sets up an opposition between, on one hand, the work of art in its singularity, shaped by its very specific history, and, on the other hand, the work of art reproduced and thus effectively divorced from that specificity. In viewing the former, we are profoundly aware of the work of art as a work located in its material place and time and we see it as filled with ontological content; in viewing the work abstractly reproduced, we see the form of the work—and this effectively means that we see the work emptied of its ontological fullness of being and filled instead with 'merely' aesthetic and epistemological interest. We see the beauty of a picture, say, and not the struggles that gave the picture its essence. The analogy with the political sphere then becomes clear. Benjamin is aware of how undemocratic societies survive by giving their peoples the form of a democracy (its mere appearance or manifestation through a ballot box and institutionalised political parties, say) while denying them the actual and material content of democracy (the right to change property relations, as Benjamin sees it). As he succinctly and elegantly puts it, 'The growing proletarianization of modern man and the increasing formation of masses are two aspects of the same process. Fascism attempts to organize the newly created proletarian masses without affecting the property structure which the masses strive to eliminate. Fascism sees its salvation in giving these masses not their right, but instead a chance to express themselves'.[8] In our terms, what is at stake here is the fact that we have, in our times, the forms of democracy without any of the content.

It is important to recall that for Benjamin, the elders against whom he ranged himself were also 'teachers'. Benjamin saw education as being properly concerned with 'the nurturing of the natural development of humanity: culture'.[9] It would follow that if actual experience—the *Jetztzeit*—is denied, then culture is being denied; for culture is the activity of becoming, the educational development (*Bildung*) of the human into her or his being, and being requires that there be a content to the 'now-time', that there be substance and legitimacy in *Erlebnis*.

It did not trouble Benjamin that his movement was rather an elite and not at all a mass educational movement. In a letter to Wyneken, he writes, 'we are always very few, but we don't really care about that'.[10] My occasional references above to experience cast in terms of a 'felt life' have been intended to hint at an ostensibly unlikely collocation of Benjamin with the later Leavis. Leavis famously celebrated the elite (although not in the same terms as Benjamin) and resisted the idea of culture's availability to the masses. Both men share a conviction that a serious aesthetic education is necessary for resisting the advance of 'philistinism'. Leavis, however, explicitly excluded the mass from culture, arguing that the elite was itself under threat from a populist media (Northcliffe's newspapers) whose very vulgarity was damaging the existence of the public sphere necessary for the maintenance of a literary civilisation. Against this, more recently, leftist theory has followed rather a later Benjamin, and has advanced the cause precisely of those 'excluded' from a supposedly 'normative' (if 'elderly') history of civilisation.[11] The question now concerns the place of aesthetic experience in education: the legitimacy of *Erlebnis* in the face of the authority of *Erfahrung*. Another way of putting this: how youthful is culture? My contention is that, in our time, aesthetic experience (like youth) is denied legitimacy by the elders (the dominant ideology of education) in a society (ours) that celebrates and legitimises a philistinism and vulgarity that deny human potential.

This chapter, in taking its stance against such a predicament, effectively revisits the terrain mapped during the first half of the twentieth century by John Dewey in his attempts to forge the intimacy of a linkage between democracy and a specific kind of education or culture. We may take as a guide to our argument here two passages from 'The Basic Values and Loyalties of Democracy', first published in *American Teacher* in 1941. The first passage affirms that 'The freedom which is the essence of democracy is above all the freedom to develop intelligence; intelligence consisting of judgment as to what facts are relevant to action and how they are relevant to things to be done, and a corresponding alertness in the quest for such facts'. For Dewey, another word for this developing intelligence was 'culture' itself, and education was the primary vehicle for the enhancing of culture, democracy and thus freedom. Against this, Dewey sets a version of democracy that seems to have triumphed in our times, but a version that, for him at least, was anathema to actually experienced democracy: 'The attempt to identify democracy with economic individualism as the essence of free action has done harm to the reality of democracy, and is capable of doing even greater injury than it has already done'.[12]

Experience into Event

Aesthetic experience—that feeling that provokes me to say 'I like this' in my encounter with art—has been rather disreputable in sophisticated or in institutional modes of critical reading. On one hand, it has been seen as the trivia of subjectivity, a local irrelevance in the face of the abstract general truths about art that can be derived from a reasoned response. In the eighteenth century, of course, aesthetics begins precisely from this contest between sense and sensibility; reason is proposed as that which will effectively regulate the senses, enabling thereby a mode of criticism that is geared towards truth. On the other hand, however, experience is making a return, exemplified by the recent autobiographical turn in criticism. Such a turn is, of course, the logical development of partisan or committed criticism, in which the critic is seen not as a specific individual, but as an individual whose specificity derives, paradoxically, from her representativeness (as representative, exemplar, of a generalised class, gender, race, sexual orientation, and so on). My position here differs from both these tendencies and derives from the fundamental question: 'why are we so wary of the particularity of a specific aesthetic experience?' Such wariness is odd if we see culture precisely as something experienced, lived, by specific individuals and their societies, rather than as something detached from human being and from 'human becoming' as such.[13]

Another available instructive originary moment exists for this examination of our question, one that long predates Benjamin. When Montesquieu died on 10 February 1755, he was blind—indeed, he had suffered from near-total blindness during the last years of his life. Shortly after his death, when his fragmentary and still incomplete *Essay on Taste* was published, it became immediately apparent what such an affliction might have meant to him. In that essay (probably begun around 1726, and so contemporaneous with the birth of aesthetics in the texts of Hutcheson[14]), Montesquieu highlights the primacy of vision in matters of aesthetic taste. In the section entitled 'Of Curiosity', he points out that 'As we like to see a great number of objects, we'd also like to extend our vision, to be in several places at once, to cover more space . . . thus it's a great pleasure for the soul to extend its view into the distance'.[15] How to do this? What technology exists in 1726 to allow for such a prosthetic extension of vision? Montesquieu's answer is that art (and here, he means primarily visual art) will enable such an advance. Art not only extends the possibilities we have for vision, for imaging, but, in doing so, it offers us, as its primary content, the beautiful. The blind Montesquieu, then, is denied beauty, denied 'imaging otherwise', or, simply, imagination and 'youth'.

Montesquieu's thesis in his *Essay* starts from the proposition that we are always hungry for experience: as we grow and develop, we want to see as much as possible, to extend our view as far as possible (or even as far as impossible; into what we would now—post-Romanticism—term the imagination). We are never at rest, always seeking more experience, more engagements with objects whose difference and distance from us grant us our self-awareness or enable our autonomy. These objects, constituted through distance and difference, lead us always and inexorably further onwards and outwards in a restless desire for more and more experience.

As will be the case with Benjamin some two centuries later, experience (and particularly aesthetic experience) becomes *constitutive* of culture and of its acquisition. It is through the experience—intense moments of being or of becoming—offered by our engagement with art that we can imagine things undreamt of in our philosophies—or, to put this more simply, that we can *learn*. For Montesquieu, then, education depends on such aesthetic experience; as for Benjamin, the lived experience of youth ought not to be discounted if we are to have an educational system that will contribute to culture rather than to the endorsement of philistinism.

However, our present elders are also suspicious of the validity of such 'mere' experience, preferring the instrumentalism of a reason that has been abstracted from our personal being or development.[16] This, of course, is the poverty of that view of 'education' prevailing among European and American governments (however 'young' or 'modern' they may purport to be). Education is seen simply as the acquisition of a transferable skill, preparation of the individual for the taking of her or his place in an uncritical workforce. In such a state of affairs, the idea that an aesthetic education might have a value that is 'spiritual' or 'occasional', in Benjamin's terms, is simply anathema: aesthetics have value for our 'elders' only to the extent that art contributes directly to the economy. This is the most extreme form of instrumentally rationalist abstraction: art and sensibility purely as commodity. Sadly, however, this conservative position is shared by that tendency in leftist theory or criticism that resolutely refuses to engage with the primacy of our aesthetic experience (spirited occasionalism) or with a nonquantifiable, noncomputable (untheorised) 'sensibility'.

What might it mean for youth to engage with art in these circumstances? What might it mean to have an experience evacuated in advance of its content, to accept Jameson's contention that 'texts come before us as the always-already-read'?[17] Agamben explicitly follows Benjamin in some recent work on *Infancy and History*, where he claims that 'modern man's average day contains virtually nothing that can still be translated into experience. . . . Modern man makes his way home in the evening wearied by a jumble of events, but however entertaining or tedious, unusual or commonplace, harrowing or pleasurable they are, none of them will have become experience'.[18] Things may happen, but they no longer acquire the authority of experience, as attested to by our elders, teachers, governors. This is akin to that situation in which we suspect that 'modern man' may spend the day reading books, hearing music, seeing pictures; but that it is all vacuous, productive either of ignorance or of trite rehearsals of orthodox 'criticism'. This is one direct consequence of the age of 'information': the information/aesthetic overload allows no time to engage properly with any of it. We are thereby radically blinded, like Montesquieu; or, as Baudrillard has it, we prefer simulacra or simulation.

Vattimo addressed such a state of affairs in *The Transparent Society*. There, a key part of his argument is that the society of generalised communication and of mass media—and for him this is constitutive of the postmodern society—is one where we have, ostensibly, the promise of a pure transparency of experience. He comes at this through a consideration of the *Jetztzeit*, here called 'contemporaneity'. The contemporary world is contemporary, he writes, 'because it is a world in which a potential reduction of history to the level of simultaneity, via technology such as live television news bulletins, is becoming ever more real'.[19] The consequence of this is a 'radical revision of the very notion of history', such that 'the social ideals of modernity may in each case be described as guided by the utopia of absolute *self-transparency*. The further result of this, however, is that, in the society of generalised communication, there is an eruption of myriad 'dialects' that question the assumed normative self-transparency of a previously central 'language'. This is a way of describing decolonisation, for instance, argues Vattimo; and it is also, of course, a way of explaining the tendency to assume that all dialects are equally sites of culture (thus 'youth culture', 'football culture', 'business culture', 'rap culture', 'working-class culture'—and so on in various reifications of culture as commodity). Instead of returning us to the fullness of the *Jetztzeit*, this state of affairs leads us back to Nietzsche's famous proposition that, perhaps, finally, the true world ends in a fable, that truth dissolves into a multiplicity of fablings. Thus, we might have experience, but there is no truth to such experience. Once more, *Erlebnis* becomes vacuous, despite our seeming validation of all kinds of experience; and, 'truthless', it has little relation to education.

Against this, we might set Paul Zweig, who argues that our knowledge of adventure tends to be literary nowadays, rather than being drawn from our everyday life: 'adventures are precisely what few of us know from experience'. Yet, he suggests, our familiarity with adventure might be more common than we routinely think: 'Haven't all of us, now and then, experienced moments of abrupt intensity, when our lives seemed paralysed by risk: a ball clicking round a roulette wheel; a car sliding across an icy road; the excruciating uncertainty of a lover's response; perhaps merely a walk through the streets of a strange city? The cat's paw of chance hovers tantalizingly, and suddenly the simplest outcome seems unpredictable'.[20] Another way of putting this would be to say that with the unpredictability of the simplest outcome, we enter the realm of the event.

This entry into the event is precisely the entry into youthful experience; and more precisely still, it is the entry into play. Our critical task is to rehabilitate such experience, to refill it with content; and to regard such content as not only 'meaningful' but also 'eventful', as thereby serving education and culture materially. Zweig's case is that the entry into the event can be as banal as a walk in the streets of a strange city: that is, the event arises through the defamiliarising contact with the unknown. Another word for this is *reading* or any such related aesthetic activity. The text always already read by elders/teachers such as Jameson is the text paralysed; and it is also the reader/student blinded, the cultural event or history arrested.

Experience, Life, and Death

Football isn't a matter of life and death; it's much more important than that.

—BILL SHANKLEY, APOCRYPHAL

In his famous theses on the philosophy of history, Benjamin proposed what has become a major insight for contemporary criticism, when he indicates the double-sided nature of 'cultural treasures' that embody what we call 'civilisation'. Famously, 'There is no document of civilisation which is not at the same time a document of barbarism'.[21] This insight drives that major recent critical tendency—fundamentally semiotic-deconstructive, and operating as a 'corrective' to the norms of a bourgeois high culture—indicating that values (especially aesthetic evaluations) are themselves shaped and conditioned by the political values of the victors in the triumphal procession that we call a history of civilisation. That is by now a commonplace.

Lurking within the observation is a yet more telling and a rather different question. If culture is genuinely double-sided, might it not also follow that 'there is no document of barbarism that is not also and at the same time a document of civilisation'? This would be the shocking possible corollary of Benjamin's famous thesis. The status of the document would thus become genuinely problematic: aesthetic documents—the artefacts of culture—are neither intrinsically civilised nor intrinsically barbaric. Rather, the document manifests itself as the merest potentiality for either civilisation or barbarism. 'Culture' would now be the name that we give to the inhabiting of this potentiality. Intrinsic to such culture would be a fundamental aesthetic education that we can now say, following Dewey, is an education tied to the possibilities of actually-living democracy. Those who decide the status of the document see culture instead as the determination of the potentiality and thereby make the document (and culture itself) a commodity, an object, or a sum of objects (*Erfahrung*), rather than a process of eventful living (*Erlebnis*), living as itself the processing of contestations or of indeterminacy.

Putting the question of experience in terms of a contest is also to understand experience in terms of Aristotelian *energeia*, energy. To explore this properly, we might relate Benjamin's concern for the (youthful) *Jetztzeit* to Agamben's understanding, derived from Aristotle, of potentiality. The simplest way to do this is to reconsider the metaphysics of presence. Augustine long predates Derrida—and Benjamin—in being troubled over this. In both *Civitas Dei* and *Confessions*, Augustine famously pondered the issue of temporal being. Crucial to his thinking is that there is a distinction to be made between a present that is filled with substantial content and a present that has a merely formal existence, as a structural bridge enabling us to think the relation between past and future (or to think narrative, as it were).

Augustine begins from a consideration of the great transgressive moment of death. Meditating on the question whose theological basis is doubt about resurrection, Augustine asks whether it is possible to believe in ghosts: 'can one be living and dead at the same time?' In response, he proposes a sophisticated argument in which he establishes an absolute opposition between being alive and being dead. That strict opposition then allows him to elide the very moment of dying itself, for at any given instance, he claims, one is either still alive or one is already dead, and therefore, one is 'never detected in the situation of dying, or "in death"'. Yet more importantly for our purposes here, 'the same thing happens in the passage of time; we try to find the present moment, but without success, because the future changes into the past without interval'.[22]

The consequence of this is not only that the moment of death is emptied of content, but so also is the moment of the present. The present is now marked always by the traces of past and future that crowd in on it and shape it, thereby stifling any self-presence therein. In other words, the present moment is merely a moment of potential. We might say that experience (in terms of the *Jetztzeit* or 'felt life') is thus only at best potential energy. By analogy, therefore, any 'present' engagement with an aesthetic object can be an engagement with either barbarism or civilisation; and it is the sustained inhabiting of that potential *energeia* that is 'culture'. By extension, barbaric philistinism, manifested in the determination of an aesthetic object as a commodity whose essence can be 'analysed', is anathema to culture and also, simultaneously, to democracy.

The realisation of the text is an act of realising potential, converting potential energy to kinetic energy (most usually, in the form of an avowed political energy). My contention here is that the premature politicisation—'realisation'—of the text or of the aesthetic encounter is always barbaric and anathema to culture, for it actively denies the experience of the present moment, refuses the encounter with death that is at the centre of all art, an encounter that is actually a moment of transgression, a moment of engagement, an event or an adventure whose outcome cannot be given in advance.

What I am resisting is the partisan position whereby the preference for one reading kills the other (14 May 1948 marks the celebratory and emancipatory establishment of Israel, say, thereby disposing entirely of the

Palestinian view of that date as characterised by catastrophe, *nakba*; or vice versa). Rather, I am stressing that the preference for one reading must always maintain the other reading as an unrealised potential or possibility; and that it must maintain it as ghostly, as a potential guest in a spirit or occasion of hospitality. That hospitality is what I will now identify firmly with and as culture; or, as Derrida has it in a different context, 'Hospitality is culture itself and not simply one ethic amongst others'.[23]

This, then, is a counter to partisan reading or to a reading that is a priori determined by political choice, or by the premature decisionism that would lead a critic to place the commitment to a reading before the experience of reading. That partisanship—when it precludes the possibility of 'hospitality', as in cultural critique—is what I'll call, in our normal, everyday sense of the term, *philistine*. Although such determinism may be appropriate in the political sphere, it is out of place in the cultural; and although an analogy may be available between what happens in aesthetics and what happens in politics, it is a philistine error to elide the difference between these two realms. Instead, the only commitment required is a commitment simply to the aesthetic encounter. But that commitment itself has some important consequences. The first is that 'culture' is not an abiding condition, but rather an episodic event: the spirited occasion in which it becomes possible to inhabit a potentiality.[24]

Criticism, Play, Dance

Montaigne opened his great essay on the force of imagination with a citation: 'fortis imaginatio generat casum' (the strong imagination creates the event). We might compare here the great poet so beloved of aestheticists, Keats, in whose famous letter of 22 November 1817 to Benjamin Bailey we find that 'The Imagination may be compared to Adam's dream—he awoke and found it truth'.[25] Adam dreamt of companionship, and I shall return to the centrality of such companionship to our 'new aestheticism' in what follows. Montaigne's essay is about the strength of an imagination that can realise things in material actuality. For example, Montaigne writes, when he is in the presence of one who persistently coughs, he himself begins to experience pulmonary irritation: 'Someone insistently coughing irritates my own lungs and throat. I visit less willingly those ill people towards whom I have duties than I do those in whom I have less interest and who mean less to me. I seize upon the illness that I witness, and embed it in myself'.[26] Montaigne advances in the essay a materialist view of imagination, indicating that imagination realises itself through the body (as especially in sexual desire), and thus gives an actuality of experience to that which is ostensibly 'merely' imagination.

The usual way in which we have configured this question is, broadly, post-Romantic. It comes in the form of the question whether art makes any material difference to life. As a self-proclaimed 'last romantic', Yeats, 'old and ill', put it thus, in what is possibly the most celebrated question of Irish literary history: 'Did that play of mine send out/Certain men the English shot?'; to which Auden would, equally famously, reply that 'poetry makes nothing happen . . . it survives,/A way of happening, a mouth'.[27] At issue between Yeats and Auden, however, is rather the centrality of play and more especially of the play of imagination; for it is this kind of play that is, really, another word for the potentiality of which I write here.

The idea of play as central to aesthetics is not new, of course. Schiller had been at pains to stress the importance of play, *Spielen*, and of the 'play-drive', *der Spieltrieb*, in his *Letters on Aesthetic Education* (specifically in Letter 24). For Schiller, this (deliberately ambiguous) term, hovering between notions of theatricality and of childhood self-entertainment, effectively regulates the opposition in our consciousness between the two competing drives of 'sense' and of 'form' (or between sensibility and reason; between particulars and universals; or, more pertinently here, between event and the dead weight of elderly authority, between *Jetztzeit* and philistine 'maturity'): 'The sense-drive demands that there shall be change and that time shall have a content; the form-drive demands that time shall be annulled and that there shall be no change. That drive, therefore, in which both the others work in concert . . . the play-drive, therefore, would be directed towards annulling time within time, reconciling becoming with absolute being and change with identity'.[28] Such 'play' gives a content to time while also giving it a formal sense; it reconciles the particular experience with the more general sociocultural general authority.

Recently, using entirely different sources, Isobel Armstrong argues something similar: 'Play, that fundamental activity, is cognate with aesthetic production . . . I understand play . . . as a form of knowledge itself.

Interactive, sensuous, epistemologically charged, play has to do with both the cognitive and the cultural'.[29] Here, inter alia, Armstrong is writing against the crude philistinism of a British educational system that has become increasingly Gradgrindian in its concentration on education as pure instrumentality. Play is now seen as a waste of time for politicians who see children simply as fodder for political statistics or the achievement of pedagogical 'targets'. Just like

> Thomas Gradgrind, sir. A man of realities. A man of facts and calculations. A man who proceeds upon the principle that two and two are four, and nothing over, and who is not to be talked into allowing for anything over. . . . With a rule and a pair of scales, and the multiplication table always in his pocket, sir, ready to weigh and measure any parcel of human nature, and tell you exactly what it comes to.[30]

Or, as the much later Adorno and Horkheimer have it in their devastating critique of a crude Enlightenment, 'whatever does not conform to the rule of computation and utility is suspect'.[31] Oh, that we had some of Dickens's anger now.

Thankfully, Armstrong does. Armstrong rightly wants to rehabilitate youthful play as a central pedagogical activity. She considers childhood play, in which 'things lose their determining force', or, in my preferred terms here, where things become pure potentiality. Play, she argues, transforms perception, as when a stick becomes a horse, say, where the stick 'becomes a "pivot" for severing the idea of a horse from the concrete existence of the horse, and the rule-bound game is determined by ideas, not by objects. Play liberates the child into ideas'.[32] 'Quadruped. Graminivorous. Forty teeth . . . ' and so on, if taken as definitive of a horse, does not. The former is culture; the latter, barbaric government 'not to be talked into allowing for anything over', and barbarous criticism by the 'man of realities'.[33]

The poem is such a pivotal object, releasing its reader into the experiencing of ideas, into thinking as such. That 'eventful' thinking, eventful precisely to the extent that its outcome cannot be predetermined, is what we might properly call culture, but culture as activity, culture as potentiality, or, more simply, education: the forming and informing of a self in the spirit of growth, development, and imagining the possibility that the world and its objects might be otherwise than they are. Another word for this is metaphor (or even, in fact, democracy); but metaphor as a practice of thought, or, in the words of Ricoeur, as a process of 'cognition, imagination, and feeling'[34]: in my own terms, a thinking that is always hospitable to otherness and is thus 'companionable'.

A useful way of characterising the play at issue here is to see it as dance. Valéry, in particular, made great play with dance as a key figure in philosophy; but it is more recently Badiou who has argued for dance 'as a metaphor of thought'. For Badiou, following Nietzsche, dance is 'all that the child designates', an always new beginning prompted by the 'altering' event. Dance is a 'wheel that moves itself', a 'circle that draws itself and is not drawn from outside', a pure and simple act of affirmation.[35] This, however, is not the dance that is imposed from without, regulated by external forces (be it that of choreography, rock music, or the rhythms of mechanical/industrial production); it is dance that does not submit to an external regulation. By analogy, we need a criticism that is self-determining, autonomous: playful, between sense and form. For Nietzsche, the opposite of dance is 'the German', marching to the military beat with strong legs. Dance, by contrast, resists what Nietzsche called such 'vulgarity', marked by the spontaneous reaction of the body to external forces.

Badiou appropriates Nietzsche in these terms: 'Dance would be the metaphor of all real thinking linked to an event. For an event is precisely that which remains undecided between taking place and no-place, an emergence that is indistinguishable from its disappearing'.[36] This kind of dance is what allows experience to occur as event: 'Thus we see that dance has to play time into space. For an event founds a singular time from its nominal location. Traced, named, inscribed, the event designs, in the "it happens that" (*le "il y a"*), a before and an after. A time brings itself into existing. . . . Dance is that which suspends time in space'.[37] We should here recall Montesquieu, for whom play is pleasurable because it satisfies our avarice for experience. Within such play, dance in particular pleases us by its lightness, grace, beauty, 'by its link to music, the person who dances being like an accompanying instrument; but above all it pleases thanks to a disposition of our brain, which is such that dance secretly encompasses the idea of all movements under certain movements, of most attitudes under certain attitudes'.[38] Lurking more explicitly behind Badiou, however, is Valéry. In *L'âme et la danse*, Valéry offers a Socratic dialogue, in which Phèdre tells Socrates to look at a young dancer: 'Look at her fluttering!

You'd say that the dance comes out of her like a flame', to which Socrates replies,

What is a flame, my friends, if it is not the *moment itself*?. . . . Flame is the act of that moment between earth and sky. My friends, all that passes from a heavy to a subtle state passes through the moment of fire and light. . . . Certainly the unique and perpetual object of the soul is that which does not exist; that which was, and which is no more;—that which will be and which is not yet;—that which is possible, that which is impossible,—there indeed is the business of the soul, but not ever, *never*, that which is![39]

Valéry argues that the body of the dancer, in refusing to be localised in one place as a simple object, thus becomes multiple: playful. Such play, in its multiple release of possibility, is itself also thought, but thought in the form of event, or thought realised as potentiality. This is the materiality of imagination, and by extension, it is the materiality also of reading.

Reading thus becomes a matter of companionship. By this, I do not mean to suggest that (as in Booth, say) there is an implied relation between reader and writer,[40] nor (as in Leavis) that an elite 'common pursuit' is established between teacher and student.[41] Rather, I mean that reading-as-culture produces an attitude of readiness for companionship, and in this, it is like dance, where movement is autonomous yet also ready for relation with—hospitable to—the movement of other partners. What else is this but a founding condition of the possibility of democracy? Cultural reading such as this is what happens between determinacy and indeterminacy: culture, we might say, is the *potentiality* for culture.

In this regard, Socrates learns a deal from Diotima, in Plato's *Symposium*. Discussing the nature of love, Diotima first of all rejects the simple oppositions between good and bad, wisdom and ignorance, beauty and ugliness, reinstating the middle terms whose occlusion proves so useful to Augustinian sophistry. Love, she then argues, is itself such indeterminacy: 'Love is between mortal and immortal. . . . He is a great spirit, Socrates. Everything classed as a spirit falls between god and human'.[42] If culture is also such indeterminacy, then we might say, modifying Derrida, 'love is culture itself and not simply one ethic among others'. The aesthetic attitude I propose, then, is one that aligns love, companionship, hospitality; and it is the inhabiting of these, not as stable conditions but as episodic events, potentiality, that is culture.

The dancer may then be like the *flâneur*. 'As he walks, his steps create an astounding resonance on the asphalt. The gaslight shining down on the pavement casts an ambiguous light on this double floor. The city as a mnemonic for the lonely walker: it conjures up more than his childhood and youth, more than its own history'.[43] And it is this *flâneur* that the aesthetic must accompany, rehabilitating memory, youthful *Erlebnis*, ambiguity and the exponential potential for *more*: more dance, more love, more hospitality, more experience.

CHAPTER 5

The Passion of the Possible

In the previous chapter, I have established the link between democracy and what we might term 'possibility'. In crude terms, we might say simply that democracy, although never a constant state of affairs, provides the episodic opportunity for the maintaining of one's human possibilities. As Dewey has it, 'democracy has always professed belief in the potentialities of every human being'.[1] However, when Dewey wrote this, he had explicitly in mind that it would be education that enabled the actualisation or realisation of those potentialities. My own contention, modifying this, is that democracy in a certain sense refuses such realisation, preferring instead what I called the 'possibility of democracy' or the maintaining of possibilities for human change at all times. In the present chapter, I shall explore more fully the precise nature of such possibility; and I shall begin from an examination of what has been a major trope in modern literary criticism: possibility in the form of ambiguity.

The Romance of Ambiguity

The concept of ambiguity has been an especially enriching one for modern literary criticism. It was in 1930 that William Empson (then aged twenty-four) wrote his first major critical work, *Seven Types of Ambiguity*, in which he systematised the workings of ambiguity in English poetry, argued that our awareness of its centrality in literature allowed us to have an improved sense of the beauty of that literature, and required the urgent further theorisation of ambiguity.

The kind of thinking that shaped Empson's study was, of course, very much of its early twentieth-century moment. It would be a useful exercise to place Empson's *ambiguity* alongside several other key tropes that were determined as central to the subsequent hugely influential work of the American New Criticism, for instance. Where Empson privileges ambiguity, Cleanth Brooks was to discuss *paradox*, Allen Tate *tension*, Wayne Booth a little later *irony*. Paradox, tension, irony, ambiguity: four figures in search of an author or founding moment. These tropes are all centrally concerned with a form of 'double coding' or double thinking; and the foundation of this, I suggest, lies in the work of I. A. Richards (Empson's teacher in Cambridge).

The influence of this on the American New Criticism, I note in passing, is important for the larger-scale argument of this book, thanks to the complex relation between that New Criticism and a specific inflection of an American national identity that was characterised by democracy. This school of criticism, developed in the smaller liberal arts colleges and not in the richer Ivy League institutions, rests on the assumption of a certain equality before the text. In establishing the twin fallacies of authorial intention and of readerly response, critics such as Wimsatt and Beardsley effectively bracketed the text off from its wider institutional contexts and knowledges. The effect of this is to place students from different cultural backgrounds (the rich, well acquainted with books and from a 'cultured' parentage alongside the poor, from rather less literate backgrounds) on an equal footing before the text in terms of what might be said about the text. Both have to respond to 'the words on the page', to that which is directly experienced in the reading. The argument, which cannot be explored at length here, is that this establishes an ostensibly democratic relation among rival readers of the same text, in which divergent readings can be accommodated under the sign of the positive evaluation of texts as richly 'ambiguous, ironic, paradoxical, held in tension'.[2] Such a position regulates the possibility of any action that could be taken as a result of one's reading and moderates any desire for such action through the tolerant ability always to see the other person's point of view and to sympathise with it. For some, this might be construed as a form of democracy; yet it obviously has substantial and significant problems. Those problems derive from the fact that the ambiguity in question requires further examination.

In 1924, when Empson was just arriving in his rooms as a new and brilliant student, I. A. Richards proposed his *Principles of Literary Criticism*. Richards's formation, it will be recalled, was partly in what we would now call psychoanalysis; but it is his literary genealogy that more immediately interests me here. In his *Principles*, he famously distinguishes the poet as one who is able to entertain the full experience of her or his entire mental apparatus, or 'impulses', and whose work is the manifestation of the imposition of order on those impulses. Thus, for the greatest example, Richards argues for what we might think as the ambiguous response most applicable to tragedy. In 'the full tragic experience', he writes, 'there is no suppression. . . . The mind does not shy away from anything, it does not protect itself with any illusion, it stands uncomforted, unintimidated, alone and self-reliant'. Further, tragedy is a site in which we can see the resolution of the most ambiguous response, drawing us towards both pity and terror at once:

What clearer instance of 'the balance or reconciliation of opposite and discordant qualities' can be found than Tragedy. Pity, the impulse to approach, and Terror, the impulse to retreat, are brought in Tragedy to a reconciliation which they find nowhere else. . . . Their union in an ordered single response is the *catharsis* by which Tragedy is recognized, whether Aristotle meant anything of this kind or not. This is the explanation of that sense of release, of repose in the midst of stress, of balance and composure, given by Tragedy, for there is no other way in which such impulses, once awakened, can be set at rest without suppression.[3]

In the midst of this, Richards quotes from Coleridge (on whose work he would specialise). That 'balance or reconciliation of opposite and discordant qualities' of which Richards speaks is taken from Coleridge's *Biographia Literaria*, chapter 14, where Coleridge describes the condition of being a poet:

The poet, described in ideal perfection, brings the whole soul of man into activity, with the subordination of its faculties to each other, according to their relative worth and dignity. He diffuses a tone and spirit of unity that blends and fuses . . . each into each, by that synthetic and magical power to which we have exclusively appropriated the name of imagination. This power . . . reveals itself in the balance or reconciliation of opposite or discordant qualities: of sameness, with difference;

of the general, with the concrete; the idea, with the image; the individual, with the representative; the sense of novelty and freshness, with old and familiar objects.[4]

In this, we see that specifically Romantic predicament from which Richards takes his extremely influential idea. That predicament is one shaped by a specific ambiguity; and the ambiguity in question arises from the contest, within the eighteenth century, between the primacy of reason and the primacy of sensibility, between what Coleridge depicts as the general and representative on one hand, and the concrete particular or individual on the other. This is the ambiguity that is thematised for us in the nineteenth-century *Bildungsroman*, where we see it typically dramatised in the central character, to whom we typically respond ambiguously because she or he is of necessity living ambiguously. The protagonist of the *Bildungsroman* hovers between, on the one hand, the psychological demand that she answer to herself or that she be autonomous, while also acknowledging the social requirement that she behave in terms acceptable as a representative member of the general society.[5]

This, in fact, is the ambiguity that is central to modern criticism: should we respond to a poem 'reasonably' or should we respond 'feelingly'; yet more importantly, what happens when these two responses are in conflict with each other, as they must be? They must be so simply because in the reasoned response, we respond from the position of the general, whereas in the feeling or sensible response, we respond from that of the individual: and the individual is, by definition, opposed to or distinct from the general. That is to say, our response *must* be ambiguous.

I can offer some useful examples here to demonstrate the kind of ambiguity I have in mind. Consider, for example, Archibald MacLeish, in a text that is used by W. K. Wimsatt to demonstrate the validity of an 'intentional fallacy': 'A poem should not mean / But be'. Wimsatt provocatively uses this to justify a nonepistemological response to poetry, yet it occurs within a poem. Logically, therefore, the phrase itself *cannot mean* that a poem should not mean; it therefore precisely fails to prove what it proposes in the mode of proof. That paradoxical response to the text is the kind of ambiguity with which we are familiar. A similar example might be found in Empson's own test case of the newspaper headline: ITALIAN AS-SASSIN BOMB PLOT DISASTER. In this, says Empson, 'we have the English language used as a Chinese system of key-words', and our response to it semantically is compromised by our response to it semiotically. More recently Terry Eagleton tried something similar. In his *Literary Theory*, Eagleton attempted to dispose of the claim that literature is marked as a 'special' use of language, that it is characterised against ordinary language by its ambiguity. If that is so, he mischievously suggests, then the signs that we see on the London underground—'Dogs must be carried on the escalator'—are poetry. Behind this lies what I think will turn out to be a significant example, in Kierkegaard's *Either/Or*, a text that thematises ambiguity and dramatises it: 'Pressing done here'.[6] Perhaps, however, the best single example of this kind of ambiguity is an ancient one, much favoured in postmodern considerations of paralogy: the Cretan liar paradox, most concisely stated in the sentence, 'I am lying'. If that sentence is true, it is false; and if false, it is true. Our response to this is at one level rational, but given the impossibility of final semantic resolution, it also becomes visceral, a matter of feeling.

To this last example, Keats would have offered the modern response. In his famous letter of 21 December 1817, to George and Thomas Keats, Keats praises Shakespeare for his 'negative capability', that state 'when man is capable of being in uncertainties, mysteries, doubts, without any irritable reaching after fact and reason'.[7] This negative capability is required in modern criticism as the condition of our literary response, and is systematised in those key tropes of irony, paradox, and, above all, ambiguity. It may sit uneasily with the modern pretensions of the scientific cast of mind; but it is precisely the characteristic of poetry or literature that enables us to distinguish poetry from science at all. Negative capability, we might say, as an equivalent of the *ambiguous consciousness*, is that which marks off a presiding characteristic of modern literature: that characteristic is the problematisation of linguistic reference.

Modern literature is *modern* and is *literature* precisely to the extent that it eschews validation in terms of reference: that is to say, the texts of modernity cannot be *legitimised* or grounded in something called a nonlinguistic reality that is thought to precede them. We cannot find the truth about Dublin from reading *Ulysses*; we cannot find the unadulterated truths about colonialism or imperialism by reading Conrad; we cannot find the truth of woman by reading Woolf; and so on. Rather, in our readings here, we are engaging precisely with ambiguity as such: on the one hand, these texts may be giving us something truthful about Dublin, or Africa, or woman; but equally, and simultaneously, they are giving us the opposing view. They give us truth as ambiguous. As Wilde famously has it, 'truth in literature is that whose contradictory is also true'.

Ambiguity literally (and unambiguously) means 'driving both ways'. There is a political aspect to this, of course; and again, we can see it in its literary form in the critical stance adopted by Edward Said:

The history of thought, to say nothing of political movements, is extravagantly illustrative of how the dictum 'solidarity before criticism' means the end of criticism. I take criticism so seriously as to believe that, even in the very midst of a battle in which one is unmistakably on one side against another, there should be criticism, because there must be critical consciousness if there are to be issues, values, even lives to be fought for.[8]

The phrase 'critical consciousness' here is, precisely, ambiguity; and it is also, of course, as I argued right from the start of this book, 'deconstruction'. I shall return to this Said passage at the end of this chapter.

Clearly, of course, I am not saying that ambiguity is invented with the Romantics; but I am claiming that in Romanticism ambiguity is raised to a privileged position within poetry and within the critical consciousness itself. Modernity, after Romanticism, foregrounds and thematises ambiguity as its very condition. More recently, we see the persistence of this ambiguity in its deconstructive figuring as 'undecidability'.

Nietzsche laid the ground for these kinds of ambivalences and paralogies in his famous claim that 'There are no truths, only interpretations; and this, too, is an interpretation'. By analogy, we might say something similar: 'In modern literature, there is no possibility of truthful proposition; there are only ambiguities; and our response to this lies therefore not in truth but rather in our authenticities'. Ambiguity, in these terms, would reflect authentic being.

Ethics as Ambiguity: The Possibility of Hypocrisy

It is by now a commonplace that modern literature has been concerned to hand a certain authority over to its readers. The abandonment of an omniscient point of view—the abandonment of epic, basically—led inexorably to the abandonment of univocal sense and meaning, and to its replacement by multiplicity, multiple readings. This is the meaning of the shift I have just traced, from truth to authenticity. We might find the source for this in Denmark—more precisely, in Elsinore, where one of the great and defining modern ambiguities is posed for us, when Hamlet asks 'To be, or not to be'.

Sartre had a useful response to this kind of question. In his celebrated attack on Mauriac, he asks: 'Voulez-vous que vos personages vivent? Faites qu'ils soient libres' (Do you want your characters to live? Make them free, then). Characters will 'live' precisely to the extent that they are seen to be open to possibility, to potentiality: the text portrays them in one way, but the reader has the sense, from the text, that they might be otherwise. Now here, we see an important turn in the location of ambiguity. For Empson, ambiguity was a condition of the consciousness of an author; for us, now, ambiguity is a condition of reading and is therefore to be located primarily within the consciousness of the reader.

A classic anglophone example of this is the ambiguous ending of John Fowles's *The French Lieutenant's Woman*. Here, we are presented explicitly with two (in fact three) different endings for the narrative, and we are invited to choose between or among them. We might paraphrase Sartre to describe this situation: 'Voulez-vous que votre récit vive? Faites que votre lecteur soit libre, et qu'il révèle sa liberté en choisissant' (Do you want your story to live? Make it that your reader is free, and that he shows his freedom through making choices). The choice that the reader makes, at the end of this text, is basically a moral decision in the face of an ambiguity. In making this moral choice, the reader bases her choice on what she feels to be authentic: 'this is how *I* would close this text'. In this, the reading subject resolves the ambiguity, closes the *récit*, and thus enacts a moral freedom.

I insist, however, on the extremely limited nature of this involvement of the reader; and I shall seek to replace it with what I shall call a properly ethical involvement. In this latter state of affairs, it will be axiomatic that the reader does not resolve the ambiguity in question. In a particular sense, the ethical and political freedom of the reader will depend not on the ostensible action of making the choice that resolves the ambiguity, but will depend rather on the reader maintaining what I call, after Kierkegaard, 'the passion of the possible'. I will now try to explain this.

I have already adverted to Shakespeare's Hamlet; and I now add Desdemona. Recall the great ambiguity that she faces when she stands before Brabantio and Othello; and there, she tells her father that 'I do perceive here a divided duty' (1.3). The rather shocking thing about this brief interlude is that it resolves the fractious situation extremely quickly. Desdemona acknowledges a duty to her father, but also, now, to her husband—and Brabantio's reponse is brutally short: 'God be with you! I have done. Please it your Grace, on to the state affairs'. If there ever was the possibility here of what Eco would eventually call an *opera aperta*, the 'open work', then it is rapidly closed off as *un'opera chiusa*. Whenever this happens—whenever the possibility of openness is closed off by the making of a choice—I claim that we are in the realm of morality, but not yet of ethics. Further, I contend that we may well experience a sense of freedom in which freedom is made manifest by the availability of a choice as such; but we are not yet in the realm of democracy.

Freedom reduced to the articulation of choices is precisely the basis of that fallacious version of democracy that Dewey saw as inadequate because it was identified simply with 'economic individualism', not with human potential. Choice, especially consumer choice, does not equate with freedom and is not a constituent of democracy at all. The reason for this is that we have not yet properly entertained the possibility of ambiguity. Rather, we have replaced one possible truth ('I am Brabantio's daughter') with another ('I am Othello's wife'). Ambiguity disappears, and with it, the question of authenticity that it was supposed to raise and open. In other words, the existentialist version of authentic being that grounds authenticity in the enactment of choice is itself anathema to democracy, being instead complicit with economic individualism.

For authenticity to appear, as the proper counterpart of an achieved ambiguity, we need to maintain and preserve the condition of ambiguity as such. We need to see the maintenance of a negative capability or, quite simply, of possibility/potentiality. The consequence of this, I shall argue, is that we also find a link not between 'free' choice and authenticity, but rather between ambiguity and hypocrisy: paradoxically, ethics is to be marked by the possibility of hypocrisy.

When Kierkegaard writes his great text of ambiguity, *Either/Or*, he considers a protoexistentialist question. The writer of the 'Diapsalmata' section (usually referred to as the aesthete) writes: 'Were I to wish for anything I would not wish for wealth and power, but for the passion of the possible, that eye which everywhere, ever young, ever burning, sees possibility. Pleasure disappoints, not possibility'.[9] In this 1843 text, we should hear an echo of the Keats of the great odes, writing of the 'still unravish'd bride', the heard melodies that are sweet, while 'those unheard/Are sweeter' (in the 'Ode on a Grecian Urn'). Kierkegaard's aesthete character sees the possible—the ambiguous—not as something that is to be resolved by an action that will resolve the possible into an achieved pleasure; rather, action is to be replaced by passion, that passionate commitment to ambiguity as such, that he identifies as 'the passion of the possible'. It would be a little like reaching the end of *The French Lieutenant's Woman* and refusing to choose. Yet more than this, it would be like reaching the end of that text and refusing to choose between, on one hand, the option to choose, and on the other, the option to refuse to choose.

To consider this complication further, I turn to Giorgio Agamben, whose work foregrounds the concept of *potentiality*. In Aristotle, Agamben points out, there are two kinds of potentiality: the former is essentially trivial, for it is the potential that we have to grow up, say, or to become a head of state—this generic potentiality, I shall suggest, is that which is to be aligned with 'morality', or with the enactment of a choice. Against this, Aristotle sets a more interesting potentiality, exemplified by Agamben in the figure of the architect, who 'has the *potential* to build', or the poet who 'has the *potential* to write poems'.[10] The difference between this existing potentiality and the generic potentiality is that poets or architects have the potential to write or to build whether they actually do so or not. They do not lose or use up their potential in or through its enactment; the poet does not lose the potential to write whenever she writes a poem, and thus also has the potential to 'not-write' as a constituent part of her potential as a poet.

By analogy, of course, readers do not lose the potential to read when they complete *The French Lieutenant's Woman*. If freedom is marked by potential, then we can now say that the maintenance of freedom is marked also by the maintenance of potential—that is to say, freedom depends on negative capability or on the ambiguous consciousness. However, we now have two ways of understanding this. The former is that of existentialist thinking, in which our freedom is realised through the using up of our potential, through its realisation, as we say, in a committed action (so, for example, I choose ending 'A' over ending 'B'). The latter would be what I am now calling the ethical mode, in which we accept that the reality proposed by our reading of the text is one shaped by ambiguity. Reading the text will not effect our freedom (nor, indeed, will it affect it).

I promised to return to Said. The passage I quoted earlier is problematic. How might I read it? To agree with it is, effectively, to express my solidarity with it; and yet this very solidarity is what the passage is warning me against. If I disagree with it, then I am, effectively, criticising it and thus demonstrating in my practice precisely what the passage is calling for. Therefore, the only way that I can show my agreement with it is by disagreeing with it: the response must be ambiguous. That response is not a matter of committed action or engagement; rather, it is a 'passion', a feeling—and an uncomfortable one at that. In forcing this kind of response, the passage demonstrates that freedom is always about to be, not yet effected, and certainly not effected through the simple reading of a text. Freedom is still to be fought for, perhaps most especially the freedom to say that 'freedom is still—always still—to be fought for'. It is like the unheard melody adverted to by Keats: an 'always still' to counter our contemporary trend that privileges the 'always already'.

Finally, what has this to do with the ethics of hypocrisy? Ethics I take in a Levinasian sense as being shaped through the encounter with alterity. Such an encounter requires that the Other be fundamentally unknown, that the Other be a site of the possible or the ambiguous. Our response, in our face-to-face encounter with such alterity, must be passionate, a 'passion of the possible'. It would be an error to assume a knowledge of this Other, for any such knowledge would be a resolution of the ambiguity that she presents into a closed and univocal meaning; and that meaning would be 'always already' given by the shape of my own consciousness. This error allows for the possibility of moral judgement; but it is a judgement that, in denying freedom—and indeed otherness—to the Other, fails to rise to the level of the ethical. The ethical requires 'negative capability'.

The encounter is dramatised for us in literature and in our critical engagement with it. We might respond to it 'authentically'. To do so, however, would be to fall into the error of assuming a knowledge of its otherness, thereby collapsing its otherness and difference into an encounter with the reader's self, her authentic identity that was always already given prior to the act of reading. The ethical response requires a different attitude.

The attitude required might be thought of as hypocritical in that it refuses the possibility of authenticity. It is that 'criticism under criticism', that *hypo*critical attitude hinted at in our appropriate response to Said: the 'always still'.

CHAPTER 6

Potential European Democracy

Blacked out fallen open true refuge issueless towards which so many
false time out of mind. Head through calm eye all light white calm all
gone from mind. Old love new love as in the blessed days unhappiness
will reign again. Ash grey all sides earth sky as one all sides endlessness.
Scattered ruins ash grey all sides true refuge long last issueless. Never but
in dream the happy dream only one time to serve. Little body grey face
features crack and little holes two pale blue.

—SAMUEL BECKETT, 'LESSNESS' (1978)

In modernity, death has usually been seen as an ultimate and determining horizon of experience. Put simply, death—as the point beyond
which ostensibly we have no further material living to do—is the point
therefore at which we can sum up the content of all our lived experiences,
and at which we can cast retrospective shape and even a determinate—un-
ambiguous—totality of meaning on our lives. It thus becomes the moment at which, finally, we identify or define ourselves, the moment at
which becoming stops and being starts (but a being whose start is precisely the end of becoming and thus also its own end). A better, although less
simple, way of putting this would be to say that death is determining in
these senses precisely because, paradoxically, it is itself rather indeterminate. As Wittgenstein famously put it, 'Death is not an event in life. Death
is not lived through'.[1] It is the very indeterminacy of death—its openness,
infiniteness, indefinition, or lack of a determinate intrinsic ending for it-

self—that allows us to give a determinate shape to a life, and therefore to the experiences—the various 'becomings'—that shape that life's history or temporal being.

This is most current for us in the wake of Heidegger, of course. *Dasein*, knowing that it will die, is always oriented towards death as the horizon of its being, and the being-towards-death informs every present moment of *Dasein*'s engagements. For Heidegger, death is thus ever-present; or rather, death is present in every instance in which a subject might try to identify itself. Such thinking, as I indicated earlier, can be traced back at least as far as Augustine. Famously, Augustine considered death as a kind of 'transitional' moment, determining what is on both sides of it (a time 'before death' and a time 'after death'), while yet itself always escaping self-determination (given its 'threshold' status, as an always-in-between condition). He then makes the analogy between this indeterminate moment of death and the moment of the present itself, always hovering indeterminately between a past and a future, always (as Derrida will much later think it) carrying the traces of that which it is not. The present, and death: both are 'always-in-between' conditions, and therefore unamenable to definition or appropriation.[2]

This kind of thinking is, on the face of it, paradoxical (even if, after deconstruction, the paradox in question is one with which we are very familiar). Perhaps because it is paradoxical, it has often been poetry that has accommodated such preoccupations, from Donne's Divine Meditation 10: 'Death be not proud . . . /One short sleep past, we wake eternally,/And death shall be no more, Death thou shalt die', to T. S. Eliot's 'In my beginning is my end' (from 'East Coker') or, much more insistently all the way through 'Little Gidding': 'In the uncertain hour before the morning/Near the ending of interminable night', or

There are three conditions which often look alike
Yet differ completely, flourish in the same hedgerow:
Attachment to self and to things and to persons, detachment
From self and from things and from persons; and, growing between them, indifference
Which resembles the others as death resembles life,
Being between two lives—unflowering, between
The live and the dead nettle.[3]

The present moment, we say—the moment in and through which we are living, experiencing a specific set of becomings that constitute the present moment in its full material and sentient reality—is informed by death, by the moment that is described as the end of becoming as such, the moment at such a limit of experience that it cannot itself be experienced. Death defines by being indefinite, or even infinite. In philosophy, it is perhaps Blanchot who has given this its paradoxical sense:

> And there is no question that we are preoccupied by dying. But why? It is because when we die, we leave behind not only the world but also death. That is the paradox of the last hour . . . to die is to shatter the world; it is the loss of the person, the annihilation of the being; and so it is also the loss of death, the loss of what in it and for me made it death. As long as I live, I am a mortal man, but when I die, by ceasing to be a man I also cease to be mortal. I am no longer capable of dying, and my impending death horrifies me because I see it as it is: no longer death but the impossibility of dying.[4]

It follows from such thinking that experience itself—the inhabiting of a present moment in all its fullness—is always already in the condition of death, and dying haunts our every transient moment, because the present is, like death, an 'always in between' condition, like death. Further, given that death is 'the impossibility of dying', then experience becomes a confrontation precisely and paradoxically with impossibility itself.

This collocation of death and of the present conditions the possibility of experience itself now. To consider the present as such a 'mortal' transitional threshold is, inevitably, to raise the question of its substantiality. For experience to have a substance—for the 'now-time' (Benjamin's *Jetztzeit*) to have a material content or for us to be 'living', 'here, now'—the present moment has to be thought of as something conditioned by an interiority of being whose substance is partly given by that which is exterior to it (past/future; before death/after death): experience is what is 'within' the present moment, or what is 'specific' and 'pertinent' to it, what is 'appropriated' in it and by it. Agamben reveals that the consequence of this is the aestheticisation of the political. He writes, 'All living beings are in the open, reveal themselves and revel in their appearance. But only man wants to appropriate this opening to himself, to seize upon his own appearance, his own manifest being. Language is this appropriation that transforms nature into *face*. Thus appearance becomes for man a problem, the site of a struggle for truth'.[5] This, in fact, is the condition in which we might claim that modern life is purely—in the sense of merely—aesthetic. Experience within modernity is always in this 'always in between' condition, and, as such, it is always mediate and mediated; and, further, experience, we can say, is always in between possibility and impossibility—or, in a term that Agamben will make his own, experience is always potential. When Agacinski considers the question of contemporary democracy, she notes that there are at least three forms of representation in question: party-political representation (effected through the ballot); public representation (effected through opinion polls); and 'a form of "representation" of the people, not concerning the people's public self-expression or its political representation, but rather its aesthetic visibility: the people want to see themselves. . . . The people today require images with which to identify themselves'.[6] Modern life sees experience not in terms of an actual felt life, but rather in terms of a mediated—between—condition. It is such thinking that conditions all experience as aestheticised, or as a matter of a problematic relation between appearance and some other supposed condition called reality. It is also such thinking that allows for an aestheticisation of politics, such as was most famously attacked by Benjamin.[7]

The thinking in question here, in fact, is precisely akin to Baudelaire's great definition of beauty in modernity, for in it the transient and the eternal are united: 'the beautiful is made of an eternal, invariable element, whose quantity is extremely difficult to determine, and of a relative, circumstantial element, which can be, as you please, turn by turn or altogether, the epoch, fashion, morality, passion'.[8] This second element is itself the stuff of modernity as such: 'Modernity is the transitory, the fleeting, the contingent, the half of art whose other half is the eternal and the immutable'.[9] In this formulation, we can think experience as *Erlebnis* or as the content of the *Jetztzeit*, both transient (and thus a site of possibility); but shaped and determined by death as eternal and immutable (and thus a site of impossibility). The thought is not far removed from the Socialist Christianity of John Macmurray, who argued in *Creative Society* that 'The eternal is the reality of the temporal *in the temporal'*,[10] keen to see the present of the eternal in the present (as against Marxism which, argues Macmurray, refers the eternal to an 'outside' or 'beyond' or 'afterwards' of the present). In this sense, for us, death has also shaped our consideration of aesthetics, or of the beautiful. Is it therefore possible to go beyond aesthetics?

Death shapes experience and aesthetics; and, as we know, it also shapes politics in Europe after the twentieth century. How, indeed, is politics possible in the wake of the death camps of the twentieth century in Europe?

Much of Agamben's thinking—itself heavily influenced by Benjamin and profoundly engaged with him—might be seen as a counter to such an eschatological tendency or problem. In this chapter, I shall bring together the strands of this second section of my argument: experience, democracy, and potentiality; and I shall establish their relation to my opening section on what we might call the 'absurd postcoloniality' of critical consciousness. I shall organise the argument around three tendencies in Agamben's thinking. The first we might call a transition between the 'being-towards-death' and a new condition of experience which I'll call a 'being-towards-love'. In this, it is the concept of the *amiable singularity* that is novel and productive. Second, I explore sovereignty in relation to autonomy; and sovereignty here means not just political sovereignty, but also the power to assert a control over one's living as such, over one's bare life. Finally, I'll explore the condition of democracy that might be available in the wake of Agamben's current thinking; and here, a key issue is the notion of substitutability and of the refugee.

Being-Towards-Love

All meaningful knowledge is for the sake of action, and all meaningful action for the sake of friendship.

—JOHN MACMURRAY, *The Self as Agent* (1957)

Agamben follows Benjamin in seeing that experience has become rather problematic for the contemporary world; and indeed, he goes so far as to claim that 'experience can be approached nowadays only with an acknowledgement that it is no longer accessible to us'.[11] Benjamin traced what Agamben calls the destruction of experience back to the fact of mass death in war, and to the image of soldiers returning from the battlefields where technological processes had effectively alienated them from direct experience (with bodily experience 'contradicted' by 'mechanical warfare', as Benjamin put it), after which, of course, all other experiences might become trivial. For Agamben, we do not need anything as cataclysmic as war: everyday life demonstrates amply the 'destruction of experience': 'Modern man's average day contains virtually nothing that can still be translated into experience. . . . Modern man makes his way home in the evening wearied by a jumble of events, but however entertaining or tedious, unusual or commonplace, harrowing or pleasurable they are, none of them will have become experience'.[12] The reason for this is that, in our time, 'no one . . . seems to wield sufficient authority to guarantee the truth of an experience'.[13] What this means, in effect, is that no particular individual carries sufficient authority to allow that his particular experience can legislate for others or for a general state of affairs: no one particular can represent the general. This—fundamentally and essentially a crisis of representation—is also a crisis of authority, of experience, and indeed of foundational philosophy itself. It is also, clearly, a crisis in that form of thinking—which we can call 'modernity'—that sees its goal or task as the regulation of the relations between the relative claims of the particular and the general, the individual and the universal, the idiosyncratic or idiomatic and the law.

Agamben traces this decisive shift in modernity back to the transition from Montaigne to Descartes. Montaigne, as Agamben points out, was able to take his own experience as, in some ways, unproblematically representative of a more generalised humanity, in ways that the later Descartes was not.[14] Indeed, it is Descartes who ushers in the age of suspicion, the age in which we need to abstract knowledge from experience and displace it onto reason itself, or, more precisely, onto the language—logos— in which reason speaks itself.

The substance of Montaigne's *Essais* is, of course, nothing more or less than Montaigne's own shifting experiences and reflections upon experience. The experience in question here is of a kind that Agamben calls 'traditional'; and this kind of experience

remains faithful to [the] . . . separation of experience and science, human knowledge and divine knowledge [or, in my terms above, modern/transient and eternal]. It is in fact the experience of the boundary between these two spheres. This boundary is death. Hence Montaigne can formulate the ultimate goal of experi-

ence as a nearing to death—that is, man's advance to maturity through an anticipation of death as the extreme limit of experience.[15]

Once more, we see experience here oriented towards death. Descartes effects a shift in this, ushering in the moment when we will no longer trust
experience as the ground of knowledge at all, and thereby effecting a strict
separation and distance between science and experience. To some extent,
the delegitimation of traditional experience founded in Descartes remains
with us, for as Agamben points out, 'it is the character of the present time
that all authority is founded on what cannot be experienced, and nobody
would be inclined to accept the validity of an authority whose sole claim
to legitimation was experience'.[16]

When Descartes makes this move, what he does effectively is to reconfigure the very notion of the human subject as such. It has long been a
commonplace that Descartes refounds knowledge upon human consciousness, upon the instance of the *Cogito*; but in fact, the ground or foundation on which Descartes rests is much shakier than this. We have become
'used to representing the subject as a substantial psychic reality' when, in
fact, 'In its original pure state, the Cartesian subject is nothing more than
the subject of the verb, a purely linguistic-functional entity, very similar to
the "scintilla synderesis" and the "apex of mind" of medieval mysticism,
whose existence and duration coincide with the moment of its enunciation'.[17] The Cartesian subject is one grounded not on experience but rather in language, in the *loquor* that speaks it into being. The consequence of
this is a significant modification of our relation to experience. 'Traditional'
experience, oriented in the last analysis towards death, yields 'the anticipation of death as the idea of an achieved totality of experience— . . . something complete in itself'; but now, displaced onto language, experience
is referred instead to the subject of what we recognise as science and, as
such, it becomes radically incomplete, 'something it is possible only to *undergo*, never to *have*: nothing other, therefore, than the infinite process of
knowledge'.[18] In short, ontology is now radically split from epistemology;
knowledge is separated from action—or, in a word, theory becomes possible. We might push this a little further and venture the claim that theory
becomes potential.

Despite this radical shift, however, it remains the case that experience can still be characterised as an 'always in between' condition: either it

occupies that terrain marked by the indefiniteness of death, or it occupies the terrain marked by the infinite and interminable process of knowledge, equally indeterminate. The shift to the prioritisation of the speaking of experience simply reinforces the fact of its indeterminacy, its mediate condition, for language is itself a privileged site precisely of indeterminacy.

We now therefore have a problem regarding this new 'split' subject. The way in which most contemporary philosophy has attempted to deal with this has been by finding ways of regulating the status of the claims of individuals against the general. At the basis of this lies the aesthetic philosophy of Francis Hutcheson, whose great and abiding formulation is that beauty is found wherever there is 'uniformity amidst variety', or where we find the applicability of a general rule (uniformity) while at the same time acknowledging the specificity of a particular (various) case.[19] That formulation, as its roots in aesthetic philosophy should suggest, yields only the kind of aestheticisation of the political whose limitations we have already outlined above: the inherent orientation towards death fails to address experience as the site of an indeterminacy.

Agamben offers a route beyond this impasse with his concept of the 'whatever singularity', *una singolarità qualunque*. The relation of particular to general yields a notion of individuality as determined by predicates, qualities, or properties. An individual, in these terms, might be identified as a member of a specific class; but her individuality is given by the combination of 'properties' that she shares with all members of that class and some properties that are ostensibly not thus shared (they might be unique, but more likely they pertain to another class). Thus, for instance, I might identity myself as 'British'; but when asked to characterise this 'Britishness', I offer a list of predicates ('speaking English', 'born in the British Isles', 'dogged, phlegmatic, solidly empirical', for random examples) that, taken together, constitute 'Britishness'. This uniformity shared with others from this same classification is not enough to identify me in my particularity, however, so I add some other qualifications or further 'properties' ('speaking English but with a Glaswegian accent', 'born in Scotland', 'stubborn, ironic, impractical', and so on). The assumption is that this will eventually yield the essence of my subjectivity or identity. To each, thus, a specific set of identifiable qualities or specific properties is shared, even if marked by distinctions. As Ophelia has it in *Hamlet*, 'There's fennel for you, and columbines. There's rue for you, and here's some for me. We may call it herb of grace o' Sundays. Oh, you must wear your rue with a difference' (4.5). I am I (or Ruth is Ruth, and rueful) precisely to the extent that I 'wear my rue with a difference'; but even this difference is itself to be characterised as a sum of identifiable qualities or properties. It is this difference within similarity, this particularity within generality, this uniformity within variety, that yields 'my' identity, an identity to be appropriated precisely because it comprises properties. In this, the sum of my identity is made up of the sum of 'my' experiences; but this is precisely what we have seen above as the aestheticisation of politics and the being towards death.

Agamben argues against this—that, for instance, when I love someone, I do not love her for her properties or qualities. Love is not directed towards qualities or properties but rather to its object such as it is: I love her being 'such that it is' (*il suo essere tale qual è*) and not because of any 'properties'.[20] From this (essentially derived from Scholastic philosophy), Agamben is able to make the argument that 'the coming being' entails a specific kind of singularity. The singularity in question, he writes, 'takes its singularity not from its indifference with respect to a shared property (from a concept, for example: being red, French, Muslim), but only from its being "such that it is". Thus, this singularity renounces the false dilemma that requires that knowledge choose between the ineffability of the individual and the intelligibility of the universal'.[21] In its place, Agamben offers a singularity not to be grounded in any predicates at all, but rather simply in its being 'such that it is': a 'somewhat' inasmuch as it is 'such'. That singularity can now be defined in relation to its 'amiability': 'the singularity revealed as such is whatever-it-is, or in other words lovable'.[22]

With the emergence of this singularity, a singularity that has nothing to do with the regulation of particular with respect to universal, we can thus make a move not only beyond the impasse in thought that is representation, but also, as a corollary, a move 'beyond aesthetics' and beyond the aestheticisation of the political, so to speak. We can propose a condition of the subject in which identity is not given by 'properties', the corollary of which is that we can envisage a subject whose being is not 'towards-death', but rather a singular amiability, a being 'towards-love' in all its uncertainty.

Infant Sovereign

The 'being-towards-love' brought about by the realisation of this singularity stems from a belief in the possibility of 'loving without cause', or of 'being without content' (to adapt Agamben's own adaptation of the title of Musil's *Der Mann ohne Eigenshaften*). In *King Lear*, we can see the stakes of this mentality. Lear's daughters, depriving him of his retinue, draw him in the figure of a 'bare life'. They ask what need he has for twenty-five, ten, five, or even one man to assist in his retinue, to which Lear replies,

> O reason not the need! Our basest beggars
> Are in the poorest thing superfluous.
> Allow not nature more than nature needs,
> Man's life is cheap as beast's. (2.4)

Lear's great problem, of course, is that for him, love is quantifiable; and its quantity can be precisely measured, classified, turned into property (the land as dowry that is being left aside in this great opening scene for what Lear hopes will be Cordelia's betrothal to Burgundy). The singularity of which Agamben writes is one devoid of property and is tied to a 'bare life' in ways that I shall explore later. Here, however, the implications of such a singularity need to be examined further. Most importantly, we have an important question to answer: if there is no cause that initiates or inaugurates this love, then whence does it arise? I began the present study with the question of how we might locate and identify the source and origin of the critical impulse as such. But now we might widen this, to ask the yet more political question, 'What is the source or origin—the ground—of a groundless singularity?'

Recently, Derrida has argued that 'Death is very much that which nobody else can undergo or confront in my place. . . . It is from the site of death as the place of my irreplaceability, that is, of my singularity, that I feel called to responsibility. In this sense only a mortal can be responsible'.[23] For Agamben, a different argumentation is available—indeed, necessary. Agamben considers Montaigne's essay 'De l'exercitation', in which Montaigne points out that, unlike almost everything else, we get only one shot at dying: 'with respect to death, we can only try it out once; we are all apprentices when we arrive there'.[24] The proto-Wittgensteinian point here is that we don't 'experience' death like other things. Montaigne describes a near-death experience following a fall, which prompts him to consider those 'in-between' moments, like that between sleeping and waking. In a meditation whose content prefigures the start of Proust's *A la recherche du temps perdu*, Montaigne considers the status of ostensibly involuntary actions. He then writes that

> Each of us knows from experience that there are parts [of our bodies and our muscles] that stir themselves, stand up or lie down often without our willing it. Now those passions that only touch us superficially cannot call themselves 'ours'. To make them ours, it is necessary that a man is engaged entirely in them; and the pains that our foot or our hand feel when we are asleep do not belong to us.[25]

Agamben discovers a similar critical moment in Rousseau's *Rêveries du promeneur solitaire*, but in this instance, the fall provokes a meditation not on death, but on birth as itself just equally such a 'transitional' moment of 'experience'. From Montaigne, Agamben derives the observation that there are experiences that we have that are, in a particular sense, 'not ours'.[26] From Rousseau, whose meditation is further witness to the 'surging emergence of the concept of the unconscious',[27] Agamben derives something of further significance. Unconscious experience is not in any simple sense 'subjective'; yet psychoanalysis has shown that it is this unconscious experience that might be even more important than 'subjective' experience. It follows, Agamben suggests, that 'the limit of experience has been turned around: it is no longer deathwards, but backwards towards infancy'.[28] The being-towards-love is thus also a being-towards-infancy, in a very peculiar sense of that term. The infancy in question is not that typically adumbrated and explored in British Romanticism, by Blake or Wordsworth (although the latter comes close in the "Ode: Intimations of Immortality"); rather, it is the condition of being in a position that Agamben describes as 'between the human and the linguistic', or in that space prior to a speech that would, in being spoken, reduce experience to something known and abstracted from the *Jetztzeit*. As he puts it, 'In terms of human infancy, experience is the single difference between the human and the linguistic. The individual as not already speaking, as having been and still being an infant—this is experience'.[29]

To have bodily experience that is not mine is, in a sense, to call into question my sovereignty over my body. Further, it calls into question the

link between private and public, between experiences that can be identified as 'mine' and those that are shared, those that pertain to a community
('yours', 'ours'). It also raises the question of when—at what moment—the
speaking subject, in and by becoming a speaker, enters into the community at all. In short, this raises the issue not only of sovereignty but also of
democracy, or sovereignty in the public sphere.

In this present section, I ground these political questions by more
fully exploring the question of the inauguration of the causeless act. This
involves a consideration of aesthetics and of taste. We have long since become used to the idea that questions about 'origins' are, in a particular
sense, nonquestions, this despite the persistence of a vulgar psychoanalysis that refers neurosis back to chronological beginnings in childhood. The
postmodern has accustomed us to the view that philosophy has no foundations, that judgements can have no stable and secure grounds or bases
shared by all. Deconstruction has likewise accustomed us to the permanent undecidability of origins, in that every origin will itself be seen to be
derivative of prior origins, themselves interminably recurring. This endless
recursivity has led either to an ostensible abandonment of critique (Baudrillard, some readings of Lyotard) or to a certain pragmatism (Rorty, later
Fish).[30] Agamben offers a different way of considering the question, and,
indeed, of escaping the false dilemma we always find ourselves in when we
ask whence an action derives.

We should begin by acknowledging the central problem of modernity as the problem of autonomy. As Todorov has it, 'Autonomy is, incon-
testably, a conquest of modernity; its first political value'.[31] The formulation of the question has, until now, been cast in terms of the regulatory
mechanisms governing the relative weight to be given to the individual
and the social or, in terms from the present argument, the logic of representation. Most famously, of course, Marx raises the issue at the start of
the *Eighteenth Brumaire*, when he points out that 'Men make their own
history, but they do not make it just as they please; they do not make it
under circumstances chosen by themselves, but under given conditions
directly encountered and inherited from the past. The tradition of all the
generations of the dead weighs like a nightmare on the brain of the living'.[32] Putting it in this way—in terms of a representation now discredited
by Agamben—allows (as Marx makes clear) for only one way of address-

ing the issue: how can we escape determination by our immediate precursors? The name for that question, in aesthetics, was modernism; and paradoxically, it yields a politics that is grounded in a purely linear chronology, whose telos—death (or the dictatorship of the proletariat, or the 'end of history')—predetermines the value of all events.

Agamben rethinks the question of autonomy in terms of what he calls (following Carl Schmitt) the logic of the 'sovereign exception'. This logic puts an end to recursivity, for, as Agamben has it, 'The paradox of sovereignty consists in the fact that the sovereign is, at the same time, inside and outside the juridical order': 'The sovereign, having the legal power to suspend the validity of the law, legally places himself outside the law. This means that the paradox can also be formulated this way: "the law is outside itself," or: "I, the sovereign, who am outside the law, declare that there is nothing outside the law"'.[33] This enables us to consider the sovereign as an 'exception', whose very exceptionality allows the grounding of a system of law as such. That is to say, we can break the vicious circle whereby the sovereign is dependent on the law for his position, and the law is dependent on the sovereign for its existence. Instead of endless recursiveness, we now finally have a ground—the sovereign exception—on which to base a law. The sovereign as 'he who decides on the state of exception' therefore becomes the locus of the inauguration of action: the sovereign is autonomous, in short; and such sovereignty is tied not to death but to infancy.

The consequence is that autonomy is not to be found in the enactment of experiences that can be identified as 'mine' or 'yours', but rather in this logic of 'exceptionality'. Until now, we have been accustomed to consider autonomy in modernity as being somehow related to, or even grounded in, the intimacy of an experience; and the experience in question has most often been aesthetic. 'Sensibility'—the ostensibly immediate or unmediated sensible response to a work of art—has been seen as undoubtedly 'mine'; and the problem has always been one of how we might generalise this particular condition, in order to establish regulatory laws for a community of subjects who are characterised by reason and by sensibility at once. In this state of affairs, reason and abstraction have been the mechanism whereby we have resolved the potential conflict between differing sensibilities, while at the same time permitting those sensibilities full play with no overt repression. The consequence, of course, has been the degradation of humanistic study and the triumph of 'opinion'. This is lamented explicitly by Alain Badiou, in *Petit manuel d'inesthétique*, where he asks: 'y a-t-il autre chose que de l'opinion, c'est-à-dire . . . y a-t-il autre chose que nos "démocraties" . . . Notre temps vaut mieux que la "démocratie" dont il se targue' (is there anything else more than opinion, that's to say . . . is there anything other than our 'democracies' . . . Our time is worth more than the 'democracy' on which it prides itself).[34] Such a triumph of 'opinion', such a triumph of 'choice', not only circumscribes the very freedom that it is supposed to celebrate, but also is anathema to any actually experienced or living democracy.

However, we can approach the issue differently. The question of autonomy is, as my citation of Marx makes clear, a question concerning how we can get a genuine history started; or (the better formulation here), what is the infancy of the present? How can a human subject or subjects initiate an event that is not always already given by the pure linearity of happenings that prefigure and determine it, thereby foreclosing its possibilities and limiting its intrinsic freedom? Agamben offers an answer: 'for everyone there is an immediate and available experience on which a new concept of time could be founded. This is an experience so essential to human beings that an ancient Western myth makes it humankind's original home: it is pleasure'.[35] Pleasure—what I call 'play', Schiller's *Spielen*—here can be related to taste. Both offer humanity the liberation from the constraints of a linear temporality that has predetermined outcomes, limited the freedom of human subjectivity, and foreclosed human potentialities. It is in this sense that taste can be positively historical, in ways that the institutionalisation of tastes cannot. Tastes have been institutionalised within modernity—within criticism—as forms of knowledge; moreover, they have been concretised in the collection, in the museum or university (which Agamben describes as both 'playland' and a 'museum for ghosts' all at once[36]). What is at issue here is the intimacy or otherwise between pleasure and taste. In the same way that we can 'have' experiences that are 'not ours', so likewise we can have tastes that are 'not ours'. What might that mean?

There is a simple sense in which we know what this means already: taste is something learned, appropriated, and not at all something 'pleasurable' or spontaneously occurring.[37] In a more theoretical, less sociological, sense, it might also be related to the condition of 'exceptionality' as a grasping of foundations or of autonomy in the form of sovereignty. Agamben traces two significant moments in the foundations of modern aesthetics. In the first of these, he indicates (following Valéry) that 'good taste is essentially made of bad taste'; and in the second, he points to that major shift in which the artist's consciousness, paradoxically, is distanced from the artwork.

The former of these is, broadly, sociological. Taste becomes identified, paradoxically, with the loss of sensibility and the loss of experience, in that it becomes rather a social matter. As the 'man of taste' emerges in the late seventeenth and early eighteenth centuries, he discovers that 'the man of taste cannot, in fact, follow his tastes, but only likes what he ought to like'.[38] This taste, then, is always already 'not ours', but rather the taste of a subject that we hypothesise as a 'man of taste'; and that 'man of taste' is, of course and further, no specific individual, but rather an imagined community of taste. If autonomy is to be grounded in such an aesthetic sensibility, and especially on one based in such a logic of representation, then it is inevitably the case that autonomy is always hypocritical, and thus self-destructive.

Let us consider the second condition, in which aesthetics exists partly to effect a distancing between the artist and the work that she or he makes. The emergence of the category of taste also serves to distance the audience from the artist, in that taste becomes purely a matter of perception, of looking at the completed artwork. The previous supposed intimacy between artist and spectator, or artist and audience—that very intimacy on which a critic such as Wayne Booth will try to found an ethics—is broken in the very originary moment of modernity. Agamben alludes to Paulhan's distinction between 'rhetoricians' and 'terrorists': 'There are the Rhetoricians, who dissolve all meaning into form and make form into the sole law of literature, and the Terrorists, who refuse to bend to this law and instead pursue the opposite dream of a language that will be nothing but meaning, of a thought in whose flame the sign would be fully consumed, putting the writer face to face with the Absolute'.[39] The Terrorist seeks to make art into a fullness of experience, consuming itself as it is undergone; the Rhetorician acknowledges that experience exists only in the form of the speaking-of-experience, and that it is therefore always to be located in the site of indeterminate play or pleasure. The growth of taste, in this situation, serves to ensure that the work of art becomes a 'thing', ostensibly complete in itself (full, thus, of 'terror'); but the consequence is that this taste effectively drives the artist away from a primary engagement with the social and into aesthetics. Such a movement duplicates the drive from meaning into form; and this drive ostensibly gives an autonomy to the work of art itself. Taste supposes that it is possible to guarantee the autonomy of the spectator—the historical subject—from its relation to another autonomous form, that of the artwork itself. The result is that 'The artist, faced with a spectator who becomes more similar to an evanescent ghost the more refined his taste becomes, moves in an increasingly free and rarefied atmosphere and begins the voyage that will take him from the tissue of society to the hyperborean no-man's-land of aesthetics'.[40] The artist thus eventually becomes 'the man without content'; but the artist is without content in the sense that he is rather like the 'sovereign exception'. It is this being without content, analogous to the loving without cause, this 'singularity' that becomes the ground for a more genuine autonomy. Exceptionality thus gives a content as the initiating ground of the ethical engagement that art requires.

Loving without cause is also the condition of pleasure. It is related to the pleasure associated not only with childhood play—the infancy of the present—but also with the achievement of autonomy. The autonomy in question here is rather like that towards which Hegel struggles in his introductory lectures on aesthetics, where he asserts that 'artistic beauty stands *higher* than nature'.[41] This 'higher' standing results from the fact that artistic beauty is, in a particular sense, not necessary. It stems from an inaugurating act of the human mind; and in that inauguration, we find freedom, according to Hegel. This 'gratuitous' beauty is what I can now relate to something I can call grace. For Agamben, the grace of which I write here derives from sovereignty; it is akin to the act whereby I make myself a singularity through the logic of exception—but that logic is applied not only to myself but also to the other. The consequence is the emergence of a freedom based on sovereign singularity, and the experience of such freedom is one that is linked to the limit case of infancy. Experience, as that space of 'difference between the human and the linguistic', is intimately related to infancy; but now, so also is sovereignty. The infant and the sovereign, as inaugurating instances of the potential for history, are yoked together. Any initiatory act must also be related to freedom or to grace; and the name that we usually have for such gratuitous giving is hospitality or, more basically, love. Can there be a democracy based on such metaphysics?

Refuge and Democracy

One of Europe's greatest scandals in our time is the way in which its member states have tried to outdo each other in terms of the harshness with which they treat refugees. In this, of course, contemporary Europe mirrors in reverse a certain mythology of 'America', famed for its welcoming of the refugee. How, we might ask, can a democracy vaunt its lack of hospitality so fiercely? This final section considers European 'democracy' as a paradigmatic case of the problem concerning contemporary democracy. That problem can be briefly stated: is democracy available or possible?

The question concerning sovereignty above is also, clearly, also a question concerning democracy, inasmuch as it fundamentally relates to the free autonomy in and through which peoples forge their future potentialities. Agamben finds in the establishment of the legal writ of habeas corpus in 1679 a particular politicisation of the body in the roots of modern democracy. Habeas corpus determines that 'democracy is born precisely as the assertion and presentation of this "body"'.[42] Crucial here is that it is a body, and not a person, at stake; for in this, Agamben sees the origins of a politicisation of 'bare life' (our simple, unadorned, biological—or, better, zoological—existence) that is at the source of modernity. 'Bare life' is what we are when we are stripped of all rights and reduced to biological being; but modernity is that which has politicised this bare life as such.[43] In its most extreme form, bare life is the VP, the *Versuchspersonen*, or human guinea pigs in the concentration camps of Nazism. Such people are, in Agamben's terms, *homines sacri*, by which he means to indicate that they can be killed without a (legally defined) murder being committed. In crude terms, their life is not that of a singularity, and thus not sovereign. It has been determined politically that they cannot be loved.

Such was the case with the concentration camps. Horrifically, however, Agamben's argument is that the camp is still with us. The camp, he claims, is 'the very paradigm of political space at the moment when politics becomes biopolitics and when the *homo sacer* can be virtually counfounded with the citizen'. Thus the real question facing us is not the hypocritical one ('how was it possible to commit such crimes against human beings?') but rather 'what juridical processes and political conditions permitted that people could be so stripped of rights and prerogatives that the acts committed against them no longer seemed criminal?'[44] As the paradigmatic political space, the camp is still with us in its moderated forms. Agamben considers detention centres at international airports as such a camp: 'In all such cases, a place that is in appearance anodyne . . . really delimits a space where the normal system is effectively suspended and where the carrying out of more or less atrocities depends no longer on law, but only upon the civility or the ethical sense of the police who are acting provisionally as sovereign'.[45] As with the detention hall, so also with suburban areas in big postindustrial cities or in the gated communities of wealthy American enclaves. In such circumstances, the refugee assumes a paradigmatic political importance.

The refugee, for Agamben, is a 'limit concept', in that she calls into question the link between nativity and nation[46]; or, to modify the terms slightly, between infancy and political identity in which the identity is given by a being-towards-death that denies the possibility of singularity for the subject. Given, however, that in a certain sense the camps are still with us, it follows that we are all refugees now. In this condition, the shape of a possible democracy is radically different from anything we have hitherto contemplated. Hitherto, democracy has been tied to a national arrangement, in which the *polis* grants an identity to subjects whose participation in and identification with the national public sphere gives them their identity in the first place. That circular condition is, as we have seen above, precisely the aestheticisation of politics that was so well understood by fascism and Nazism. We still find ourselves in this condition in Europe. For the moment, a genuine democracy is thus impossible in Europe, because such a democracy would require hospitality, the amiability towards the other that characterises the *singolarità qualunque*; and it would also require a conception of autonomy based on sovereignty (not understood in the usual political sense of the sovereign nation-state, but rather in terms of a new ground for action in a postfoundational 'infantile' philosophical condition). Finally, it requires an acknowledgement that we are all, as refugees, in a parlous predicament. The name that Agamben gives to this predicament is potentiality; and, crucially, potentiality means not just the possibility of something coming about, but also, and simultaneously, the possibility of that same something not coming about. Potential, in this sense, is that understood precisely by Hamlet when he asks 'To be or not to be'; for a potentiality is potentiality precisely to the extent that it can bring something about and also not bring it about.[47] Democracy, in Europe today, is just such a potentiality

Sovereign Democracy

CHAPTER 7

The Ethics of Hypocrisy

Philosophy and Lies; or, How
Fiction Loses the World

In his essay 'On Lying', Leszek Kolakowski begins from a fairly simple observation: 'The deliberate transmission of false information is, so to speak, part of the natural order of things. The butterfly says to the bird, "But I'm not really a butterfly at all, I'm just a dead leaf"; the wasp says to the bee guarding its hive, "But I'm not really a wasp at all, I'm a bee".'[1] We do not regard both these examples of lying in the same way. We praise the butterfly, but we condemn the wasp. Such a judgement is one based on what appears to be ethical grounds; and although we might easily ethically praise the attempt in extremis to preserve oneself and to continue in life, we can ethically condemn precisely the same action—lying—when it is used for maliciously self-serving ends. The first important point to note, however, in these examples, is the intimacy between, on one hand, the ethical judgements called for and, on the other hand, acts that are essentially acts of fiction or of fictionalising. Both butterfly and wasp engage in fictional pretences; and it is the fiction itself, seen as purposive (that is, with pretentions), that elicits—indeed demands—the ethical response. We might, of course, make the case more pressing and less trivial by adverting directly (following the logic of Agamben in my previous chapter) to the case of the prisoner in the concentration camps, such as Roman Frister. Frister recounts how he was raped by another prisoner, who then stole his cap. The theft of the cap is significant for the simple but deadly reason that any prisoner who appears at morning assembly without a cap is taken away and shot; and the theft is thus intended to protect the rapist by ensuring that the victim is silenced, killed. In this predicament, Frister then steals a cap from another prisoner and pretends that it is his own; and the prisoner without a cap is, surely enough, taken and executed the next morning.[2]

As Kolakowski points out, both Kant and Augustine have taken rather extreme positions in which lying is unjustified in any circumstances; but as Rousseau was aware, and as Molière had already shown in the example of the great theatrical precursor of Rousseau, the misanthropic Alceste, the social—the realm in which we live and communicate—is simply impossible without some forms of dissembling. In Molière's satire, we are presented with a fairly stark choice between two positions; and the fact of being placed in this dilemma is, as Rousseau later demonstrated, the very foundation of the ethical itself. On one hand, suggests Molière, one may be 'authentic' or 'sincere', certainly; but the price for such authenticity or truthtelling, for such absolute sincerity, will be exile or isolation, and hence the end of the social. We recognise this condition as that of tragedy, in that it describes the condition in which an individual becomes purely singular or individuated. That condition is one in which I am faced with my singular 'being-towards-death', the only act that 'nobody else can undergo or confront in my place'.[3] On the other hand, one may retain the possibility of the social, and with it that whole set of ethical demands without which sociability would be impossible—and, paradoxically, the price you pay for this is indeed that very sincerity or authenticity that is the ostensible basis for the ethical relation at all, for the fact of our social being requires that we 'represent' ourselves in the public domain, thus always establishing a discrepancy between the self who acts in the public domain and the self who is conscious of such acting—a fundamental (and even perhaps already hypocritical—certainly at least a moral) refusal of our singularity. In this dilemma, we have the basis of an ethical demand: as Lyotard might have put it, we must 'link' (*enchaîner*) with the 'phrase' or predicament that has been given us; or, more simply, we must choose between comedy (in the form of a sociable hypocrisy) or tragedy (in the form of an absolute sincerity that will inevitably lead to total isolation of the individual—or death).[4]

The great Scottish philosopher of Common Sense, James Beattie, took the view that lying is possible only and precisely because we are all inclined to truth-telling most of the time.[5] Liars must usually tell the truth; otherwise, their lies would be neither notable nor tactically, practically effective—they would not work. For the lie to work, we need a kind of commonality of sense (the real meaning of Common Sense: a shared reason grounded in aesthetic sensation); or, rather, we need a community bound in an ethical relation of 'faith', trust (or friendship) to each other. The social or public sphere, thus, is established as a kind of fiction, in that it exists precisely as a means of legitimation or validation of the private. In another context, Hannah Arendt has explained this seemingly paradoxical condition:

For us, appearance—something that is being seen and heard by others as well as by ourselves—constitutes reality. Compared with the reality which comes from being seen and heard, even the greatest forces of intimate life—the passions of the heart, the thoughts of the mind, the delights of the senses—lead an uncertain, shadowy kind of existence unless and until they are transformed, deprivatized and deindividualized, as it were, into a shape to fit them for public appearance. The most current of such transformations occurs in storytelling and generally in artistic transposition of individual experiences.[6]

We might say, thus, that fiction—storytelling—(and by extension aesthetic activity in general) offers the means by which the truth of the private realm is made possible, or realised. It is through fictions that we can establish that very commonality of sense—that 'faith' or friendship among a community—that allows us to validate or to identify as 'true' those specific attitudes (and even those 'facts') that will give the community its guiding identity or principles. In these circumstances, lying (the pretension to deceive)—as opposed to fictionalising—poses a threat to the very (ethical) substance of community itself; yet, at the same time, the community cannot be based on some preestablished 'truth', for it is through fictions that the truths governing a specific community can be elaborated in the first place.

In the Kolakowski examples that I cited above, the lying is carried out for strategic purposes; and it is arguable that it is the use to which lying is put that engages the ethical sensibility of the viewer/reader of the situation. This, I suggest, is precisely how we might describe the operations of fiction itself. Fiction is strategic lying—but, importantly, the strategic goal is not deception but rather the establishment of the faiths, trusts, and friendships that we call 'community', a commonality of sense or (if we are Marxists) ideology; which is, of course, simply a way of saying that fiction is one aspect of a 'possible worlds' philosophy.[7] Yet there is a still more appropriate kind of philosophy for us to consider here, one that will stress the importance of a commonality of sense, and with it, a set of ethical demands.

Fiction can neither make a claim to be truth (for that would be history), nor can it make a claim to be simply lies (for then it would be strategically unsuccessful); but rather, it operates as a way of thinking the world, or of representing the world, or of describing it, without making any simple 'truth claims'. In terms that I borrow from Todorov, we can make a distinction between *vérité-adéquation*, in which the truth being sought is one in which a description perfectly matches a preexisting reality, and *vérité-dévoilement*, in which we have a much looser attitude to truth. The first has an 'all or nothing' attitude to truth, the second a 'more or less' attitude:

Que X ait commis un crime est vrai ou faux, quelles que soient par ailleurs les circonstances atténuantes; et de même pour savoir si les juifs sont, oui ou non, partis en fumée par les cheminées d'Auschwitz. Si la question porte cependant sur les causes du nazisme ou sur l'identité du Français moyen en 1991, aucune réponse de ce genre n'est concevable: les réponses ne peuvent contenir que plus ou moins de vérité, puisqu'elles aspirent à dévoiler la nature d'un phénomène, non à établir des faits. Le romancier n'aspire qu'à ce deuxieme type de vérité.[8]

That X has committed a crime is true or false, whatever may be any attenuating circumstances; and it's the same if we want to know whether the Jews disappeared, Yes or No, in the smoke of the chimneys at Auschwitz. If, however, the question bears on the causes of Nazism or on the identity of the average Frenchman in 1991, no reply of this kind is conceivable: the replies here can only contain more or less of the truth, since they are trying to uncover the nature of a phenomenon, not to establish facts. The novelist aspires only to this second type of truth.

This loose attitude to truth, *vérité-dévoilement*, is clearly approximate to Rortean pragmatism, the ethics of which now start to reveal themselves.

Rorty has little difficulty in disengaging philosophy from something called absolute knowing or absolute truth. Although he would still make ethical claims for his philosophy, the ethics in question are not to be measured by how accurately his descriptions of the world match some prelinguistic ontologically present reality. In other words, 'truth' here is neither confused with, nor validated by, some preexisting 'reality'. For Rorty, there is no such reality independent of our descriptions; and it follows from this that it would be a mistake to think that we can somehow judge ethics by some absolute standard that preexists our judgements, actions, sayings, thinkings. Rorty's world is a useful place to start our investigation, or on which to ground it; for, in a special sense, that world is itself precisely fiction.

Rorty follows the distinction made by Russell between 'knowledge by acquaintance' and 'knowledge by description'; and argues that it is only the latter—knowledge by description—that we can have. In a neat near deconstruction, he argues that knowledge by acquaintance, indeed, would be simply one way of describing knowledge by description; and philosophy is that which—like fiction—offers us not the acquaintance with a world but rather a description of it, in these terms.[9] It would follow from this that it is not the case that Dickens, say, gives a more 'true', more mimetically adequate picture of London than does Thackeray; nor is it the case that both are somehow less 'true' than Marx or Engels or Gissing or Martineau or Carlyle or Mayhew; rather, we simply have various descriptions of London, serving different purposes, making different audiences, establishing different ethical relations or communities.

It is very important to note here that I am not rehearsing the trivial point often made regarding the supposedly total relativism of truth, and according to which truth has all but vanished as a meaningful term for the reason that it is entirely localised and relative to its speaker or listener.[10] More important is the observation that fiction is a description on which we agree to work: that is, it is a nexus around which we agree to constitute or identify ourselves as the autonomous agents of the fiction. By this, I mean simply that we deploy fictions in order to allow us to read fictions,[11] to master them, and thus to use them as guiding narratives or descriptions that allow us to constitute ourselves and our world, dialectically. One meaning of 'autonomous agent' in my phrase above, then, is simply 'reader'; but another meaning is 'free citizen', 'political agent', 'freely subscribing member of a community'. Fiction strategically collapses these two classes of meaning together.

According to this, what passes as truth, therefore, is itself subject to change, and most especially to that change that we call history—a change across and in time. As I shall argue, the real issue here relates not to the question of relativism in regard to truth, but rather to the question of the relation between truth (as something now firmly temporal, even secular) and experience, the ways in which truth is felt or subscribed to, which is the primary site of ethics as such. Before turning to this in detail, however, I need first to advert to the question concerning our 'autonomous agency', our capacity to be readers and citizens at once. In particular, I shall address here the troubling issue of the ostensible loss of 'authenticity' in the autonomous agent of our fictions. If, as seems to be the case, the agent (reader) is herself or himself constructed in and through the act of reading a fiction, or in and through the acts of fictionalising, then how can we have an ethics that is authentic, in the sense of being an ethics based on a true self-knowledge of a true or 'real' preexisting self? Fiction, we have said, is that which gives us both the identity of a self as well as our knowledge about it; and so it would appear to negate the possibility of authenticity, and with that, of truth in the public sphere.[12]

This question of authenticity (or of its unavailability) can be addressed through the philosophy of Gianni Vattimo, a thinker indebted to (and in some ways quite close to) Rorty. Vattimo has advocated a form of philosophy that he describes as 'weak', *il pensiero debole*. This 'weak thinking' derives from Vattimo's specific engagements with the history of hermeneutics, and, in particular, from his taking seriously both Nietzsche and Heidegger. From Nietzsche, Vattimo prioritises the claim that 'There is no truth; there are only interpretations. And this too is an interpretation'. The consequence of this has been to call into question how we ground or legitimise our linguistic propositions with regard to their truth content. No longer can we legitimise our claims by suggesting that our statements correspond to a nonlinguistic reality that precedes them; instead, we are caught up in what Ricoeur, from within the same hermeneutic tradition, called the 'conflict of interpretations'.[13] For Vattimo, the consequence of taking Nietzsche seriously is that a certain epistemological project is necessarily 'weakened'. One of the clear consequences of such a nihilism in hermeneutics, in which the erstwhile 'certainty' of philosophy or history with regard to truth is diminished, is precisely the validation of fiction as the ground for our knowledges. Fiction is a form of weakened epistemology; but, paradoxically, it is all the more important for that. Additionally, Vattimo takes from Heidegger a similar kind of problem, only this time relating to ontology, in terms of Heidegger's distinction between Being-as-such (which is elusive) and beings (which, although adverting to Being-as-such, cannot possibly embody or 'be' it); and from this, in parallel with the weakening of epistemology, ontology is also weakened for Vattimo. Through Nietzsche and Heidegger (and through Gehlen), Vattimo understands history as a process of secularisation, which he characterises as *kenosis*.[14] The consequence of such *kenosis* is that truth falls into the weaker 'interpretation', point of view, or stance (and as such, it becomes a disposition or ethos); and, correspondingly, Being falls into the weaker 'beings' (and as such, becomes fully secularised, positioned, located in a specific historical locatedness). Fiction, thus, is profitably described as a mode of *pensiero debole*, a nihilistic hermeneutic that offers only to advert to Being-as-such through its beings (we call them characters) and that offers to advert to truth as such through descriptions of what happens from the stance of characters (and we call this plot). It offers neither truth nor Being, but requires that we be content with the weaker 'as if'; and, consequently, it is both temporal and hypothetical.

Now, authenticity would be that which is marked by the subject who has full and direct access to truth as such and to Being-as-such; for it is only under such conditions of intimacy with both being and truth that a subject could claim simultaneously to know the truth and to be in the truth; and in that simultaneity, the subject would have circumvented the temporal predicament in which truth seems to be open to modification precisely because of its temporal or historical locatedness. Yet authenticity, as Augustine knew, is threatened precisely by the temporality of beings and the necessary locatedness of truth—our 'as if' condition. His many meditations on time are driven by the exigency of trying to know the substance of the present moment precisely at or in the present moment in which one undergoes an experience that is the ostensible object of knowledge.[15] By extension, one might say that authenticity in the sphere of fiction is that which happens if and only if the reading of the fiction entirely maps onto the living of a life in total and precise congruity (a situation satirised by Borges); and this is possible if and only if we lose the world of exteriority, for the position of such total congruity is available only to the writer who reads herself precisely as she writes, locked into a solipsistic—singular—

identity at the cost of a public sphere. Once again, then, it appears that we can have the social sphere only at the cost of authenticity; and that if we want to have access to an ethics based on truth, then we will of necessity lose the world of exteriority—the social—within which such an ethics could be lived or experienced.

We are left now with a complex predicament. Let us begin from the view that fiction is a kind of philosophy and that it has an intimate relation to the ethical in that, as a form of 'lying', whose strategic end is the establishment of friendship or of community, it evokes necessarily an ethical response. In simple terms, when we read a fiction, we ask ourselves whether this is the kind of lie to which we can subscribe (or, as we more usually put it, is this text 'good'; is it 'literature'; is it 'canonical'; does it suit our identity-forming principles or our nation-building principles; and so on). Alternatively, we might wonder whether the textual fiction in question is the kind of lie that we will despise (or, as we might put it, is it 'fantasy'; is it 'kitsch'; is it 'popular'; controversially, is it 'foreign'; and so on).

This much allows us to see that the relation of fiction to ethics can indeed be intimate. However, we have also drawn attention to the fact that the ethical demand here is shaped temporally or historically, in that this ethical relation requires that we establish some relation between truth and experience; and this experience is necessarily historical and thus the site of mutability. In short, what do we do with the ethical issue when we realise that truth can change, and that this change is related to experience? Further, what is it that is the object of experience in this way? The argument depends upon us seeing that the world is not there for us as an object of experience, awaiting the arrival of ourselves as subjects who will experience it in specific ways. Rather, the world is nothing but the communities that formulate themselves as autonomous—and ethical—agents. In short, what is there to this experience when fiction has effectively ensured that the world is lost; and what might be the ethical content of any such experience? I now turn to these two issues.

Secular Ethics; or, Ethics Without Foundations

I have already adverted to the intrinsic theatricality of fiction, its presentation of a figure of the world, its status as representation of a possible world, its status as a 'performing' of the world, just as the butterfly performs the leaf, or the wasp performs the bee. The success of its specific strategic lying often depends, of course, on the efficacy of the performance—on whether, that is, we will subscribe to its lies or not.

Something similar to this has been seen before. Rousseau, famously, concerned himself with the issue of our theatricality. In Rousseau's hypothetical 'state of nature', from which our present culture is a negative deviation, human relations were supposedly 'transparent', devoid of practice:

> Avant que l'art n'eût façonné nos manières et appris à nos passions à parler une langage apprêté, nos moeurs étaient rustiques, mais naturelles; et la différence des procédés annonçait au premier coup d'oeil celle des caractères. La nature humaine, au fond, n'était pas meilleure; mais les hommes trouvaient leur sécurité dans la facilité de se pénétrer récriproquement, et cet avantage, dont nous ne sentons plus le prix, leur épargnait bien des vices.[16]

> Before art had fashioned our manners and taught our passions to speak a borrowed language, our customs were rustic, but natural; and the change in conduct announced, at first glance, the difference in characters. Human nature, at bottom, wasn't better; but men found their security in the ease with which they could see into each other, and this advantage, of which we no longer feel the value, spared them many vices.

The nature of this transparency is such that relations between humans in this fictional state of nature are immediate, unmediated, the antithesis of theatrical performance or disguise; that is to say, they occur in a continuous present tense, and require (indeed, permit) no reflection. Another way of putting this would be to say that, in the state of nature, representation is unnecessary, even impossible. Here, there is no 'dissociation of sensibility' such as was to be lamented by Schiller and T. S. Eliot. As Rousseau is well aware, in the state in which we actually live (as opposed to the fiction that is the state of nature), we do not have such transparency. Instead, and in order to facilitate the very possibility of human relatedness, we have the formalities of decorum and politeness—the theatrical gestures or self-representations that make society possible. Politeness, for Rousseau, is marked by insincerity and by an essential drive towards hypocrisy, in that, for politeness to operate, the self has to be radically split internally. There is the self that is presented to the world, and there is the self that is occluded under such representations. This dissociation of the human subject from itself is not, however, just to be considered under the metaphors of a spatial 'veiling' of reality behind a simultaneous appearance; rather, insofar as it is opposed to the state of nature, it is opposed also to the condition of immediacy, simultaneity, that describes our being in the state of nature. For Rousseau, the social self is one marked by temporality, or simply by time itself. The consequence of this is that the subject in the world is marked by a temporal discontinuity with respect to itself, such that the being of the subject is marked by temporality rather than by the essentially timeless condition of that continuous present tense of existence in the state of nature.

We might explain this by reference to Rousseau's influential theories concerning the condition of language and its relation to democracy and politics in general. In the second *Discours*, Rousseau argued that language begins in some *cri de la nature* (cry of nature); and from this, he is able to develop what looks like an imitative, mimetic theory of language in which the speaker tries to accommodate the world outside the self (exteriority) by means of a language emanating from within the self (interiority) that will somehow match or adequately replicate that exteriority.[17] The consequence of this is a radical form of nominalism, and one that, interestingly for our present purposes, has a specific attitude to singularity:

Chaque objet reçût d'abord un nom particulier, sans égard aux genres, et aux espèces, que ces premiers instituteurs n'étaient pas en état de distinguer; et tous les individus se présentèrent isolés à leur esprit, comme ils le sont dans le tableau de la nature. Si un chêne s'appelait A, un autre chêne s'appelait B.[18]

Each object received first of all a particular name, without regard to genres or species, which these first teachers were in no condition to distinguish; and every individual presented itself in isolated form to their spirit, as they are in the tableau of nature. If one oak was called A, an other oak was called B.

The speaker in this state of nature has a skewed attitude to the world of exteriority. Living in what is essentially a timeless condition of the continuous present tense, the speaker is able to experience everything intensely, transparently, immediately. For this speaker, speech is action, epistemology is ontology (fiction is lived as it is written). The language in question would be extremely odd, for it would have to be coined entirely of neologisms: every new experience would require (or would be indeed dependent on) the invention of more vocabulary: *Finnegans Wake* as transparent referential realism. Furthermore, this speaker is unable to reflect on any experience that she undergoes, unable to know it as an experience; for she is unable to codify any experience through an act of memoration that would be precisely a comparison allowing the temporal distance between two experiences to be eliminated. Memory—denied in this hypothesis—is an act that serves to homogenise the ostensibly heterogeneous, to find what Hutcheson saw as the root of the beautiful (uniformity amidst variety).[19] If, following Ricardou, we define metaphor as 'the shortest distance between two points',[20] then, in the state of nature, there can be no metaphor. Representation here—and with it not only a fiction such as that of Proust, but indeed any fiction—is entirely impossible; and this is the case for the simple reason that, insofar as something is 'natural' at all, it is purely present in its entirety, and thus purely singular.[21]

Rousseau saw our 'problem' as being attributable to our temporal condition; and the deceptions on which the social are based are deceptions that depend on our temporal being. The subject-in-time—this *sujet-en-procès*—for him is problematic in that it cannot sensibly experience anything: its very interior temporality effects a rupture in the 'now' such that the subject can never be found in a present moment, but is always either anticipating it (and preparing the necessary mask to negotiate it) or is remembering it (and deluding herself about the efficacy of the performance). Politeness, it follows, might be necessary for the social, but paradoxically, it precludes the possibility of the subject's actually experiencing that social in the first place. The social thus becomes an empty space, surrounded by what are now vacuous or, at best, spectral subjects whose condition is that they are continuously 'becoming', in search of being. They are *personaggi in cerca d'essere*, as it were; or crowds flowing over London Bridge as in Eliot; or 'posthumous people'.[22]

In other words, we find ourselves in a predicament regarding authenticity. Authentic being requires that there be a world 'there' in relation to which 'I' can be authentic; but with the world now lost, in the sense that the social sphere has become entirely vacuous, such authenticity also disappears. It is important to note, however, that it is not just the social as a space that is lost, but also the social as a temporal moment. Not only have we lost the capacity to subscribe to the view that the social in relation to which we would be authentic cannot preexist our relations with each other; but also, and worse, the subjects who would form such an ethical relation are precluded from authentically doing so precisely because they are not there at the same time, they do not share the same moment, and they are temporally disjunctive with regard to each other. The consequence of this is that authentic ethical relatedness is impossible, in that the subject against whom I define myself as 'I' is always elusive, always disappearing, and therefore 'I' too must also elude myself. The 'I' here behaves like a ghost, like the dead, for it is always dying to itself, in a fashion reminiscent of Augustine's meditations on time.

We know now, from my preceding chapters, that, following a certain Augustine, the present moment, by analogy with the moment of dying, likewise cannot be an event in life. The present, having a formal existence only, can have no content, other than that of death. In simpler terms, 'experience', insofar as it is something felt in the present, can have no substantive existence, unless the experience in question be that of dying. More straightforwardly, nothing can be experienced at all; and this condition is precisely what makes knowledge (for whose truthful validation—or authentication—we must abstract ourselves from present experience) possible: epistemology is possible only through the evaporation of ontology, so to speak; or authentic knowledge depends upon inauthenticity in experience (authenticity depends upon an aesthetic fiction, as it were). Authentic knowledge depends upon our not being 'present' to the articulation of such knowledge; or, in short, it depends upon hypocrisy.

In this, our temporal being is what allows us to either imagine a past (and thus write a historical novel) or to hypothesise a future (and write a utopian or science fiction novel). Temporality is the condition of fiction, and fiction is the condition of a particular inauthenticity. This inauthenticity is conditioned by the fact that we cannot attend either to experience or to singularity. Imagine what this might mean in fact: we cannot experience exteriority (or, in other words, we can have no experience of another self, of another person); and further, we cannot attend to singularity (or even if we could attend to the other, we would be attending not to any specific other, but to the Other as such, in abstract terms). The consequence, thus, is that love, friendship, faith, trust, a commonality of interests that we call the social, becomes impossible—unless we live it as a series of lies—

or as fiction. This might be what we could call a condition of hypocrisy; indeed, if we think that the question of how we live together is the condition of ethics, then we already begin to see the shape of an ethics of hypocrisy here. In a final part of the argument, I shall explore some of the ramifications that derive from this seeming predicament.

The Goodness of Hypocrisy; or, Fiction and Friendship

One of the key aspects of Rousseau's philosophy regarding the state of nature is that he is perfectly willing to accept that it is simply a working hypothesis, that it is 'un état qui n'existe plus, qui n'a peut-être point existé, qui probablement n'existera jamais' (a state that no longer exists, that maybe didn't exist at all, that probably will never exist).[23] There is nonetheless a remarkable coincidence between this attitude to a lost state of nature and the attitudes of both Vattimo and Rorty. In both these thinkers, we see similar losses. For Vattimo, secularisation is determined by *kenosis*; for Rorty, the world as an entity capable of grounding our truth is simply not there. We might describe this attitude variously as 'romantic', 'nihilistic', 'pragmatic', certainly; but one thing shared here among such thinkers is a specific kind of 'modernity'. Hannah Arendt has traced an early response to a similar predicament, and in her response, we find one root of our modern human condition. She considers what happens when a community can no longer be gathered together in identity through a common or grounding belief in a shared public realm:

Historically, we know of only one principle that was ever devised to keep a community of people together who had lost their interest in the common world and felt themselves no longer related and separated by it. To find a bond between people strong enough to replace the world was the main political task of early Christian philosophy, and it was Augustine who proposed to found not only the Christian 'brotherhood' but all human relationships on charity.[24]

It is this 'charity' that founds the principle of the ethical relation based on fiction. This would be another way of describing modernity, most specifically literary modernity, in which we witness the development and triumph of fiction in the specifically ethical form of the novel. The charity in question here is better described for us moderns simply as that binding faith, friendship, commonality of purpose that constitutes the ethical relation among autonomous agents brought together into communities, groups, nations by the reading of fiction. It is in modern, 'mass' society that Arendt sees (like Rousseau, Vattimo, Rorty), that the world 'has lost its power to gather [the people] together, to relate and to separate them'; and it is in such society that we have had recourse precisely to function to establish the ethical—or indeed ideological—shaping of ourselves into community or society.[25]

The question of friendship has returned in some contemporary theory, perhaps most obviously in the recent work of Booth on *The Company We Keep: An Ethics of Fiction*; but it is important to note that, for a thinker such as Booth (as for liberal humanists such as Bayley in his *Characters of Love* before him), the friendship in question is a friendship between implied readers and implied authors. The fiction becomes something that establishes an interpersonal but finally individual mood between reader and author.[26] Against this, I see the text as an occasion for the establishing of friendships that are not, in the first instance, textual. In short, I see a link between the ethical demand and political issues—or, as Derrida could have already put it, there might be a 'politics of friendship', *une politique de l'amitié*, at stake in all this.

Derrida begins his study of friendship from a meditation on a phrase from Aristotle, as cited in Montaigne's *Essais*, and specifically in the essay 'De l'amitié': 'O mes amis, il n'y a nul amy' (O my friends, there is no friend). Let us begin instead from the first reference to Aristotle in Montaigne's essay, in which Aristotle makes explicit the link between friendship (and love) to politics: 'Et dit Aristote que les bons legislateurs ont eu plus de soing de l'amitié que de la justice' (And according to Aristotle, good legislators cared more about friendship than about justice). As Aristotle has it, 'Friendship also seems to be the bond that holds communities together, and lawgivers seem to attach more importance to it than to justice'.[27] As Aristotle glosses his statement, he goes on to make the more fundamental claim that 'Between friends there is no need for justice'[28]; and, in the terms of my own case here, we might claim that the reason for this is quite simply that friendship as such is justice, in that the friendship that constitutes community is also the ethical base—and, by extension, the juridical base—of that community in the first place.

Aristotle is taken as an authority for Montaigne's view that our human nature leads inexorably to the formation of societies, towards our being sociable or to a human essence of sociability and relatedness—the ethical base for society. Love—friendship—is the arena in which we assert our autonomy most vigorously, for Montaigne, because love is precisely a matter of singularity. As he puts it, if we ask him why he loves someone, 'je sens que cela ne se peut exprimer, qu'en respondant: "Par ce que c'estoit luy; par ce que c'estoit moy"' (I feel that that can only be expressed by replying: 'because it was him; because it was me').[29] Love here—the ethical relation—is of the nature of an 'event'; and it is the event that gives identity to the two subjects who are entered into relatedness through it.[30] For this, the subject is herself the product of ethics, and not the agent of ethical acts; or, in terms closer to the centre of the present argument, the subject is the product of fictions, but an already ethical product of such fictions.

We can now return to Derrida to take this slightly further. Derrida observes a kind of inequality between the lover and the loved, in that one can be loved without knowing that fact, but by contrast one cannot love and remain unaware of one's *amitié*. As Derrida has it, *l'amitié* is, above all and in the first place, a matter for the lover and not for the loved:

On peut *penser et vivre* l'amitié, le propre ou l'essentiel de l'amitié, sans la moindre référence à l'être-*aimé*, plus généralement à l'*aimable*. En tout cas sans avoir à en partir, comme d'un principe. Si nous nous fiions ici aux catégories de sujet et d'objet, nous dirions dans cette logique que l'amitié (*philia*) est d'abord accessible du côté de son sujet, qui la pense et la vit, non du côté de son objet, qui peut être aimé ou aimable sans se rapporter d'aucune façon au sentiment dont il reste précisement l'objet.[31]

One can *think and live* friendship, the proper or essentials of friendship, without the least reference to the *loved-being*, or more generally to the *lovable*. In any case without having to start from it, as from a principle. If we limit ourselves here to the categories of subject and object, we would say in this logic that friendship (*philia*) is first of all accessible from the side of its subject, who thinks and lives it, and not from the point of view of its object, who can be loved or lovable without reference in any way to the feeling for which he remains precisely the object.

Derrida here indicates an instability in the love relation, such that the very equality between participants on which it is ostensibly based reveals itself instead as a hierarchy—and, more importantly, as a hierarchy that depends upon a temporal priority: the lover is in advance of the loved, and friendship is an affair of the lover before it is an affair of the loved. The two subjects, insofar as they are effected by the ethical relation at all (friendship, love), or, as we might say, insofar as they have established a sociability or a society, a commonality of interest, are marked by an incommensurability: they must necessarily and axiomatically occupy different times, different moments, even as they pretend to occupy the same space. As Derrida has it, one cannot love and be loved *à la fois* (at the same time).

We might further gloss this, of course, to say that ethics is a matter of precisely this temporal predicament; and we should recall that this is also where we began the present study, where colonial consciousness presupposes that its victim colony is tardy, belated, 'underdeveloped', behind the times. The temporal predicament in question is that given to us as the condition of love and friendship; and because of the temporal condition of love, friendship, or the ethical relation as such, the possibility of authenticity or even of truth-telling is precluded, rendered impossible. Love, friendship, the ethical—all these are names for varying degrees of hypocrisy; and our way of salvaging ethics in this condition is to turn to fiction where the demand for authenticity is muted. Further, if it is the case that one of the functions of fiction is precisely to establish the possibility of the social itself, as we establish our communities around the fictions that sustain and identify them, it follows also that fictions must necessarily produce precisely this ethics of hypocrisy.

For the *Hypocrite Lecteur*

In all of the foregoing, it is silently assumed that there is some educative purpose in fiction: fictions are where communities try out or assay ethical relations, learning in this process which fictions to legitimise (or to pronounce 'good', 'canonical', and so on) and which to despise. Here, I wish finally to address more closely this pedagogical issue.

In his *Petit manuel d'inesthétique*, Alain Badiou indicates that the link between art and philosophy has traditionally been thought in one of three ways: didactic, romantic, and classical.[32] In the didactic mode, it is claimed that art is itself incapable of truth while yet offering a semblance of truth; and, accordingly, the task of philosophy in this case is to correct art, to banish or censor it, to treat it in a purely instrumental fashion. Philosophy here judges art (for shorthand purposes, we might name this Plato, or Kant). In the romantic mode, it is claimed that only art is capable of the truths that philosophy can merely suggest or imply. Art here is an incarnation or realisation of truth, and it is thus helps philosophy (let us name this Longinus, or Hegel, or Wordsworth). In the third mode, the classical, it is accepted that art does not propose the truth at all, but also that this is not a problem: for the classical view follows Aristotle in saying that the purpose of art is not to speak the truth but to make people feel better, to be therapeutic. Its domain, therefore, is not that of truth but rather of probability or fiction (name this Rorty, or Vattimo). Badiou's claim is that all three of these models are insufficient to our predicament.

Instead, argues Badiou, take it that art is itself a thought or a thinking (as I have argued this here, fiction is an event around which society and its subjects are constituted as an ethical relatedness or friendship). It would follow from this that art is the domain of a specifically educative or pedagogical set of purposes, in that it enacts truths unavailable anywhere else. Now, Badiou claims that art educates solely for the purposes of its own existence: the purpose of art is to make it possible to encounter art or—given that art is itself a thought or a thinking—to 'think a thought'. Art is that which forces us to think a thought, but to experience this thinking as an event; and further, I add, fiction is that which forces us to be ethical, but to experience this ethics as event, and hence as something entirely different from the kinds of action that we might associate with or judge according to a mere morality.[33]

The paradox, according to which art exists for the purpose of allowing us to encounter it in the first place, is not entirely new, as I hinted earlier. According to Alasdair MacIntyre, we have seen something very similar in the medieval conception of reading, as shaped by Augustine. As MacIntyre has it,

The reader was assigned the task of interpreting the text, but also had to discover, in and through his or her reading of those texts, that they in turn interpret the reader. What the reader, as thus interpreted by the texts, has to learn about him or herself is that it is only the self as transformed through and by the reading of the texts which will be capable of reading the texts aright. So the reader . . . encounters apparent paradox at the outset. . . . It seems that only by learning what the texts have to teach can he or she come to read those texts aright, but also that only by reading them aright can he or she learn what the texts have to teach.[34]

In this predicament, one thing that the reader requires is, simply, a good teacher (as MacIntyre himself points out); but what distinguishes the 'good' teacher is that—ethically at least—she does not know what it is that she has to teach. If the teaching is to be an 'event', then its outcome cannot be given in advance. Another way of saying this is that if teaching is itself to be ethical—if one of the communities in which we make ourselves is the university—then reading must be properly communal; and the participants must think against each other. In practice, what this means is that each reader must read as if from another subject position. Alternatively, and loosely following Wittgenstein, if thought is to happen (that is, if we are to experience thinking as event), the thinker must be radically split internally: the thinker must at least think to herself—but to herself as if she herself were an other.

Let us now call this thinker the reader of fiction. Such a reader must be 'other than herself' in the act of reading, if it is the case that the reading produces thinking at all; and consequently, the very idea that she can be authentic as a reader is now called into doubt. Authenticity would be what happens whenever the reader recognises herself or something that was already known or given in advance of the reading: that is, authenticity is what happens when the text fails to produce thinking but simply reveals or endorses previous judgements, determinant judgements, opinions. This would be that form of reading, for example, that is tied to an 'identity politics'; and my claim is a simple one: in that it fails to produce the event that is the establishment of the social—in that it fails to produce the ethical—such a critical attitude may be 'authentic', but it cannot be 'thinking'. To read in a fashion that would circumvent this kind of authenticity is to become a *hypocrite lecteur* (hypocritical reader), for it is only hypocrisy that makes thinking possible at all. Here is the ethics of hypocrisy, and the goodness of that ethic.

CHAPTER 8

Machiavelli and Modernity

To think the concept of hypocrisy in modernity is to confront the name of Machiavelli. Machiavelli's place within our understanding of the European Renaissance, that cradle of European self-modernisation, is well understood and relatively fixed. If we are critics of an explicitly sociopolitical disposition, his name is forever associated with modern statespersonship. In the major texts, *The Prince*, the *Art of War*, and, to a lesser extent, the *Discourses on Livy*, he outlines the conditions, it is said, of a rather harsh politics of the modern state, offering a foundational revision of Ciceronian republicanism based on what we have now learned to identify, after Isaiah Berlin, as a model of 'negative freedom'—that freedom that is established and enjoyed to the extent that I can engage my activities in an unimpeded and uncoerced fashion, and a freedom that Berlin associated with, among others, those philosophers of the French Enlightenment such as Montesquieu, Constant, or de Tocqueville, now coopted as 'liberals'.[1] Although it is no longer accepted that Machiavelli advocated in any crude and simple fashion that 'the end justifies the means' in all cases, no matter how intrinsically evil those means may appear to be, and no matter the social, political, or personal context, nonetheless, he is still taken as one who recommends that there be no illusions concerning altruism, hospitality, generosity, selflessness in matters of sociopolitical life, or military strategy in the state. At this level, we should assume that people—those in positions of control and therefore threatening to coerce us or impede our freedoms—are not intrinsically good, not intrinsically disposed to ensure our happiness, culture, or development; and we should then proceed to deal with this state of affairs as the matter of fact that it is. In this view, Machiavelli is taken as a strategic thinker who will advocate that we do or that we support the doing of whatever is required to protect our negative freedom.

For the critic who is more concerned with matters of art and aesthetics, with how Machiavelli might have influenced or shaped a culture (understanding culture here as a sum of aesthetic manifestations or productions), Machiavelli occupies a place that is, once more, more or less consensually agreed. He gives us the model for a number of characters who come new and fresh to the stages of European Renaissance drama. Richard or Iago or Aaron, to mention only the most celebrated Shakespearean examples, are thus introductions to the anglophone audience of the character of the 'machiavel', a supposedly new type of character on the stage, one who demonstrates the powers and seductions of ruthlessness, a ruthlessness often exposed in and directed at the exacting of a revenge. Here, then, the machiavel is one who responds to a perceived violation of negative freedom, taking his revenge against the perpetrator of that violation in order to reestablish what the machiavel asserts as his own freedom. In this mode, interestingly, the machiavel shades into Berlinian 'positive freedom', the freedom that Berlin associated with a certain German Romanticism and its legacies, seen first in the Genevan Rousseau but more firmly realised or concretised in Hegel or (for Berlin, worse) Marx, or 'illiberals' (for Berlin, 'totalitarians').[2] This positive freedom is seen in the ostensibly unmotivated actions, the gratuitous evil, of the character such as Iago or Aaron; the very gratuitousness of the act being testimony to the character's 'self-mastery', his assumption of a control (he thinks) over his own history. Again, this crude image is subject to all sorts of refinements and modifications, but the general picture still holds.

We have, therefore, two takes on Machiavelli within literary critical understanding of the European Renaissance and its culture, the culture that forms and informs our contemporary drive for endless modernisation: ruthless character type, or realistic political strategist. Interestingly, however, the two takes offer what seems to be that contradiction or lack of internal coherence that my invocation of Berlin's positive and negative freedoms suggests. Machiavelli seems to be at once an advocate of negative and also of positive freedom, the former (negative) if you want to cite him to support your sociopolitical views, the latter (positive) if your interest lies in seeing him as an influence on the great European public art form of the theatre; and from this implicit shortcoming in our understanding of his importance, I shall explore more fully what it is that he offers to the project of European politics, and more specifically to that cultural aspect of politics that I shall identify as the drive to 'modernisation'; and to do this, I shall focus attention on the *Discourses on Livy*, which seems to straddle what some might see as the divide between a political Machiavelli and a literary Machiavelli. The name for the relation between these two, of course, is the *cultural* Machiavelli; and the exploration of the relation will allow us to find a mode of relating aesthetics to a modernisation associated not, as we might initially expect, with republicanism, but actually with an emergent form of democracy.

The argument here falls into three parts. In the first, I shall claim that, for all his lauding of the ancients, Machiavelli is interested in establishing a major distance between his own contemporary state and that of the Roman republic that figures so much as a model in his writing; and, further, I shall claim that this is an integral part of establishing a version of Italy as a foundational instance of that great modern and modernising political entity, the nation-state.[3] Second, this nation (let us call it that, however anachronistic the term may be) is built on a specific understanding of the position and power of rhetoric in which the philosophical demand for truth gives way to a second great characteristic of the modern, authenticity. Third, I claim that Machiavelli shows us that the trouble with modernising, however necessary the demand for such modernisation may be, is, in fact (and to borrow the phrase from Stanley Fish), 'the trouble with principle'.[4] In brief, the argument traces the shift between 'the trouble with princes' to 'the trouble with principles'.

Nations

Quoted alike—that is, in highly approving fashion—by both Mussolini and Gramsci in the twentieth century, Machiavelli's political position or legacy is, as I suggest above, not always entirely clear. However, there are certain elements in his work that were abundantly clear in his own time; and central to the view of him then is the clear perception of his overt republicanism. Part of the problem in understanding Machiavelli in our own time is due to our confounding of political issues with literary and, more especially, moral issues (most especially and visibly, of course, in recent 'theoreticist' approaches to criticism). Given that some (especially those who would style themselves emancipatory critics) in our time find that he is morally disreputable, it has been difficult to see, amongst those interested in criticism as a form of liberation, anything that can be salvaged in his writings.

Yet, yet: how about this as a good starting place: before stating explicitly, in *Discourses on Livy*, 1:58, that 'governments by peoples are better than governments by princes', he offers a nice description of the nobility as a class:

> To explain more clearly what this title of nobleman means, I will say that men are called noble who, in a state of idleness, live luxuriously off the revenue of their properties without paying any attention whatsoever either to the cultivation of the land or to any other exertion necessary to make a living. Such men as these are pernicious in every republic and in every province, but the most pernicious are those who, besides the aforementioned fortunes, also have castles at their command and subjects who obey them . . . men of this kind are completely hostile to any form of civil life.[5]

The attack on the class of the nobility is clearly an attack on a particular conception of the private ownership of land and of what also follows from that: the ownership of people as 'subjected'. The paragraph cited here does not attack ownership as such, but it attacks that kind of ownership in which there is an established and legitimised formal distance between the owner of the land and its cultivation, a distance bridged by those subjected to the will or demands of the owner as they, the subjects, work the land and bring forth its produce, its riches, its wealth to be enjoyed by the distanced, luxuriating owners. The hostility to civil life of such owners arises from precisely this distancing, in which they themselves do not live but rather have their servants do their living for them. As a consequence, they live 'in a state of idleness' or a condition of luxury that we would nowadays more readily identify as corruption. Another way of putting this would be to declare that their ownership of the land was purely 'formal', that it was an ownership 'without content' as it were: they do not inhabit the land in the sense that they do not have a direct ecological investment in it, but only an economic one; and in that difference between economy and ecology, we can see that they may own it in law but not in reason, in *nomos* but not in *logos*. On the other hand, those who work the land, the servants, inhabit the land ecologically (or by reason) but do not inhabit it economically (or legally).

What is of interest here, however, is not so much the obvious line of argument that sees Machiavelli as a forerunner of both Hegel and Marx, those whose philosophies owe so much to the dialectic of 'master-slave' and to the deconstruction of that dialectic, but rather the insistence on land and its distribution, and, yet more fundamentally, its inhabiting, as something fundamental to the political and to 'civil life' as such. The very possibility of there being such a thing as civil life is threatened immediately there is this split between economy and ecology, immediately there is established this formal distance from the land by idle ownership of it. Accordingly, and to save the possibility of civil life as such, Machiavelli sees the necessity for some kinds of land reform, or, as we might put it, a rationalisation of land ownership, for a successful civil life. Yet more precisely, he sees that the successful establishment of a civil life will require a rationalisation of the way in which people inhabit land, a rationalisation of the required distance from the land or intimacy with it.

In contemporary culture, we might know this question of the inhabiting of land or of place most directly through those poetries or literatures that have taken as their subject the neo-Georgic form of the question of how intimate we might be with a land that is and is not 'ours'. In such a formulation, I am obviously inviting the consideration of poets such as, most obviously, Heaney, but also Walcott, Macdiarmid, Narayan; and, behind these names, offered here simply as exemplars, there is a whole field of literature of postcolonialisation that is fundamentally concerned to reconsider the link of person to place, that local habitation and name that the imagination might construe in political terms in the reestablishment of nations in places that have been formerly colonised. Machiavelli's time might have come to know such a question primarily through the talismanic figure of Dante, say, whose legitimisation of a vernacular was instrumental in the establishment of a national consciousness and, by eventual extension, of the nation of Italy itself; but that time in Europe would also come to know this question, to feel its force and purchase, in that public art of the theatre that was so concerned with precisely the issue of the ownership of land, not only the history plays of Shakespeare but also texts such as *King Lear*, a play not so much about devolution as about the Jamesian myth of the united kingdom, and *Macbeth*, a play about who will rule Scotland.

The argument that Machiavelli deploys here is based less directly on Livy than on Plutarch. In section 1:37 of the *Discourses*, Machiavelli considers the law of agrarian reform proposed by Licinius in 367 B.C., according to which there would be a strict limit on the amount of land that a citizen might own (the limit was to be 500 *jugera*, or yokes); and in the law proposed, families that owned more than this would have their surplus land taken from them and redistributed to others, without compensation. Further, the law would have retrospective applicability. It is this law, in an updated form and in another geographical and geopolitical location (and one that allows us to see how controversial it could become), that Robert Mugabe enacted in Zimbabwe in 1999–2000; and it is a law that has been at the root of many postcolonial struggles between the nation-states of Europe and their former colonies, especially colonies located at the borders or edges of a geographical 'Europe', such as Algeria, or Ireland, or Bosnia. Here is Machiavelli on the law in question:

This law . . . harmed the nobility . . . in two respects: those who possessed more land than the law allowed (and the greatest number of these were nobles) had to be deprived of this surplus, and dividing lands taken from the enemy among the plebeians deprived the nobles of the means of enriching themselves. Thus, as these laws came to offend powerful men who considered opposing them to be defending the public interest, whenever this issue was brought up the entire city . . . was thrown into turmoil and the nobles with patience and skill delayed action on it.[6]

It is here that we find a key central aspect of Machiavelli's thinking: the public interest, and how to act in or on behalf of it. That is to say, what is at stake and in question is how closely one identifies oneself with a public space, here identified not as some conceptual *agora* but rather and more explicitly in terms of land. If I identify myself with this land, then in one sense, when I act, I am acting on behalf of those who also identify themselves with this land. This is the key to most modern understanding of democracy, in which there is a synecdochic relation between the one and the many, based on a logic of representation according to which the differences between individuals are subsumed in their identification with each other through their common ownership of land. As we have seen, however, the question of such ownership occludes the more pressing question of habitation. Thus Machiavelli allows us to see that although we may establish economic (or legal) forms of democracy, it does not follow that we thereby establish ecological (or rational) forms; we can thus have a legalism of democracy without a legitimacy of democracy. Machiavelli's interest for us lies in the distinction that he allows us to make between these forms of democracy; further, it lies in the recipe that he offers as a solution to the problem that might arise in a state based on purely legal democratic principles. That recipe, of course, is one whose ingredients lie within the republican tradition, one concerned with the inhabiting of the public space; and within this, Machiavelli is interested in a reasonable, rather than a purely legalistic, inhabiting of the land of that public space.

Here I am driving a wedge between democracy and republicanism; but this should be understood precisely. Pettit expresses the condition most aptly when he writes that

while the republican tradition finds value and importance in democratic participation, it does not treat it as a bedrock value. Democratic participation may be essential to the republic, but that is because it is necessary for promoting the enjoyment of freedom as non-domination, not because of its independent attractions: not because freedom, as a positive conception would suggest, is nothing more or less than the right of democratic participation.[7]

Machiavelli's interests are ecological rather than economic, in the sense that I have lent to these two terms. The key term would thus not be 'participation', but rather 'inhabiting', in the precise sense that I have given to that term, its ecological sense, as defining an intimacy with a public space or public sphere. In that turn to ecology, Machiavelli opens for us, in a new way, a way that is novel for his moment in Europe, the question of political autonomy and legitimacy for the citizen, the human subject who inhabits the land, but who does not inhabit it in the mode of ownership as its sole occupant. This is the meaning of his republicanism: the inhabiting of a shared public space and the establishment of reasonable legitimacy for human agency in which the individual exists in and through her or his relations with all other citizens in that same space. That ecological sharing is the meaning of the word 'citizen' for Machiavelli.

That Machiavelli was interested in the political effects of the owner-ship of land was not, in his day, a new political issue. What makes Machi-avelli original in this regard is his tying of the ownership of land to issues of political legitimacy and, yet more centrally, to the autonomy of the citi-zen. This, I contend, is the key to the understanding of his republicanism: it depends on our seeing that political legitimacy depends on the identifi-cation of citizen with place, and in ecological terms, that means the tying of individual and community through a shared intimacy with the public place; it is that shared intimacy that establishes the possibility of a public interest, a public domain, a public sphere as we would now term it. That this is a 'modernising' move within Europe's history is, in terms of po-litical theory, largely indisputable (and critics as diverse as Said, Gellner, Hobsbawm, Todorov, and Kristeva would all find some measure of accord with it). I shall now try to show that it is tied to a specific kind of nation-alism.

The simplest way to do this will be by reading history backwards, as it were. In 1741, the Scot David Hume, having lived in France but not yet in Italy, argued that 'You will never convince a man, who is not accus-tomed to ITALIAN music, and has not an ear to follow its intricacies, that a SCOTCH tune is not preferable'.[8] In this, he is making a move that devel-ops into an argument validating the conception of a 'national character'. In his essay 'On Civil Liberty', he offers precisely such a series of short-hand caricatures of the national characters of the European nations.[9] This elaboration of the diversity of national characters, in which individuals are being identified with places, is further developed and theorised in his essay 'On National Character'; but there, the argument takes an extraordinary turn, for Hume states that there is one major exception to his rule: the na-tion of England. The argument is that the characters of political govern-ments determine the typical behaviour or the national character of their populations, with republican governments yielding different nations and different national characters than those established under monarchies, for instance. Yet, argues Hume, the case of England is a special case, for the English government is rather indeterminate in kind, being 'a mixture of monarchy, aristocracy, and democracy'.[10] It follows from this diversity, this hybridity, that 'the ENGLISH, of any people in the universe, have the least of a national character, unless this very singularity may pass for such'.[11] Thus, the English have no national character and, at the same time, their national character is precisely given by the fact that they alone of all nationalities have no national character. The English thus become the neutral, degree-zero standard against which all deviation can now be measured; and such deviations, into 'being French', or 'being typically Italian', or 'what can you expect from a South African' can now be explained and legitimised by reference to the 'naturalness' of being English,[12] alongside which all other people are marked by their national character. The argument is akin to that which sees only nonwhite people as 'raced', only women as 'gendered', only homosexual people as 'having a sexuality' and so on: the attempt is to make some kind of government, in this case that of eighteenth-century England, with its supposed mixture of aristocracy, monarchy, and democracy, appear to be 'natural' and thus unquestionable.

There is a similar kind of structure in some of Machiavelli's thinking. Machiavelli argues that there are three types of republic, each of which is liable to fall into its own specific and particular forms of corruption. Thus, a principality can degenerate into a tyranny; an aristocracy can degenerate into a government of the few; a democracy can fall into its own intrinsic corrupt form of anarchy. He advocates, therefore, a mixed form:

Let me say, therefore, that all the forms of government mentioned above are defective, because of the brief duration of the three good ones [principality, aristocracy, democracy] and because of the evil nature of the three bad ones [tyranny, oligarchy, anarchy]. Thus, since those men who were prudent in establishing laws recognized this defect, they avoided each of these forms by itself alone and chose a form of government that combined them all, judging such a government steadier and more stable, for when in the same city there is a principality, an aristocracy, and a democracy, one keeps watch over the other.[13]

The most natural form, tacitly equated here with the most enduring political form, is the mixed or hybrid, bastard form in which regulation of one system by another becomes the central plank of organisation. Machiavelli, in proposing this, is proposing it as something that will endure, and that, through such endurance, will appear to be natural, eternal, as 'original' as the classical form of that Roman republic that he so admired. Yet the fundamental issue here is that he is establishing the conditions for a

'degree zero' of national citizenship: the identity of the citizen of this bastard form is exactly that of the 'natural' and therefore uncontestable human condition. If this can be established for Italy, then Italy becomes as
'eternal' as the Roman republic that lies latent within it, silently awaiting
its rebirthing, its renaissance, through the body that is a maternal Italy.
Moreover, there is now also that profound identification of citizen, of civil
life itself, with place: it is here, in Italy as it is being construed and constructed by Machiavelli, that these conditions are to be found. This, then,
is the very condition of the possibility of the nation-state as such. It is
founded on a principle of autonomous citizenship given here its formulation by Machiavelli. To look for the influence of the cultural Machiavelli,
then, we might turn to those plays that concern themselves with national
rule or with devolution, say (and it is this that dominates the histories of
Shakespeare as well as his *King Lear*), or to those plays that concern themselves with the establishment of relations of identification between kin and
king (*Hamlet, Macbeth, King Lear* again).

Machiavelli lies, then, at the root of a cultural formation of a specific
version of the nation-state, conceived in republican terms and identified
with the space of an inhabited Italy, that cradle of the modern European
polities.

Rhetoric

This nation-state is built on specific laws. It depends on the legal organisation of the polis, certainly; but equally important, given what I have
argued above concerning mere legalism, are the laws of grammar and of
rhetoric. For the republican, laws are not restrictive of freedom. Rather,
they establish the conditions under which freedom can be articulated. Although most commentators or political theorists have seen this contention
purely in terms of state laws, I extend it here to cover the logic of laws, and
in so doing, I draw attention to the laws governing the possibility of human communication in the public space.

Good speaking, euphemism, and, further, good literature are at the
core of the state as such for Machiavelli; in this, he opens a trajectory
that will be followed by philosophers such as Vico in Naples, Richelieu in
France, Blair in Edinburgh, Schiller, Hegel and others in Germany, New-

man in Dublin, and Arnold, Leavis, and others in England.[14] Machiavelli writes *The Prince* for specific purposes: he is a pragmatic writer in the sense that his writing is concerned to deploy the laws of rhetoric in order to persuade, to effect things, to bring about a better state of affairs in the newly emergent nation-states of Europe whose birth he is witnessing, he in some ways the midwife to that new dispensation and disposition of European political and civil life. To do such a thing, says modern thought, requires that we have access to the truth, to a truth towards which one persuades one's audience. Yet this is not the case for Machiavelli: what is required instead is that an audience can come to inhabit the same civil and public space as the writer. Although he has often been considered to be one of the most significant forerunners of the scientific—even the empirical—mentality, he is not really concerned to establish a truth universally acknowledged or even acknowledgeable. Rather, like his own great precursor and source, Cicero, he organises his work around the principles and the determining forces of rhetoric, in which legitimation is attained not by some supposedly available objective or transpositional truth, but rather by effectiveness, by praxis rather than by gnosis.[15]

For Montaigne, writing in Bordeaux after his own European tour—and writing, more importantly, in the wake of Machiavelli—'le monde n'est qu'une branloire perenne. Toutes choses y branlent sans cesse' (the world is nothing but an everlasting turmoil-machine. All things in it change ceaselessly).[16] The world is shaped by not being shaped, by a constant mutability. The Renaissance sometimes thought of that as fickleness and gendered it as specifically female; but the Renaissance was also beginning to think of such mutability as the very condition of secular historicity itself. The world was a little like some recalcitrant matter that had to be shaped; and history therefore becomes, among many other things, an aesthetic project; one's existence becomes the sculpting of a life, the sculpting and care of a self. For Machiavelli, the state could also usefully be considered as just such a work of art; and therefore an analogy becomes available between the crafts required for making an artifact, for envisioning the possibility of a form that could be hewn from the rough materials of some crude matter, and the guile required for making a political state or nation. It was Jacob Burkhardt, of course, who first outlined the terms of the aesthetics of the state as it existed for the Renaissance. And Machiavelli, although he seemed to have few interests that we today might consider as purely 'aesthetic' or 'arty', nonetheless is at the centre of this way of thinking about the pertinence of a relation between art and politics. The link between these two realms is rhetoric: a city is built on words, on acts of persuasion, on the guile of a war that is, among other things, a mediatic conflict, a conflict of interpretations, a drive for the primacy of one's own speech.[17] Burkhardt helps explain this.

The conditions of war in the Renaissance are new, changed from all that has gone before. No more are wars simply the contests between nobles over lands that they can inhabit only economically; rather, the Renaissance sees the emergence of a new class of soldier, a mercenary class that is not itself aligned with the nobility. As Burkhardt puts it,

Italy . . . was the first country to adopt the system of mercenary troops, which demanded a wholly different [military] organization; and the early introduction of firearms did its part in making war a democratic pursuit not only because the strongest castles were unable to withstand a bombardment, but because the skill of the engineer, of the gun-founder, and of the artillerist—men belonging to another class than the nobility—was now of the first importance in a campaign. . . . [Thus] In Italy, earlier than elsewhere, there existed a comprehensive science and art of military affairs; here, for the first time, that impartial delight is taken in able generalship for its own sake, which might, indeed, be expected from the frequent change of party and from the wholly unsentimental mode of action of the *condottieri*.[18]

This simple fact leads to that state of affairs in which the military general has to learn general rules that can be applied to particular instances—that is, the general has to learn what we now call military tactics. The military general might be regarded as the first theorist, able to construe the particular in terms of more universalisable laws; and war becomes a more theoretical activity, one whose practitioners could be judged, as we might judge works of art, according to their effects, to their ability to win over not just bodies and places but also hearts and minds in such a way that the places that they win over are inhabited and habitable spaces.

This is important in relation to the establishment of the identity between citizen and polity. As I suggested at the outset of this section, what is at the core of this is the emerging notion of autonomy, and, behind that, the modernising tendency par excellence, the drive towards an authenticity whose legitimacy will replace the impossible demand for a transpositional and absolute truth. Now, autonomy and authenticity go hand in hand; and these are obviously important for a writer who is taken, in all the standard readings, as one who advocates fraud, hypocritical activity, and inauthentic presentation of the self in the interests of gaining one's own ends. My case here is that Machiavelli is one of the reasons why we take authenticity to be central to modernity in fact. Modernity exists (together with all that we have learnt to associate with it: empiricism, the drive for reasoned debate in the pursuit of commonly agreed ends, authentic being, and so on), so to speak, in order to deal with the problem given us by the thought of Machiavelli.

To state this briefly: in authentic behaviour, we suppose there to be a seamless continuity between an inner self and an exterior self, between a private sphere and the presentation of that privacy in a public domain. Obviously, for this to happen, we need to subscribe to the belief that there are two such spheres in existence, that they are separate, and that they can be relinked. Machiavelli, however, proposed no such thing; and, indeed, for him, it is only public being that is possible: a private life, in the sense of an inner life, is one that by definition cannot be civil (it is the 'life' of the indolent nobleman), and, precisely to the extent that it cannot be civil, it cannot also be life. Private life has a mere formal existence, a merely conceptual or imaginary substance. As Isaiah Berlin put it, 'For Machiavelli there is no conflict' between the rival demands of private and public spheres; 'public life has its own morality, to which Christian principle (or any absolute personal values) tend to be a gratuitous obstacle'.[19] The world of private morality is so self-contradictory for Machiavelli—in it, there can be no civility and thus no life at all—that the only sphere possible in fact is that of public sociality, the 'civil life' that is lived ecologically and not merely economically. Let us be clear: it is not that there is available here a conflict between personal morals and public being—what we might term the 'Antony and Cleopatra' motif of the clash between private desire and public duty; rather, it is the case that a dramatist such as Shakespeare constructs that kind of motif in an effort to deal with the scandalous and difficult-to-accept view (deriving from Machiavelli) that it is only public being that has any currency or any substantive reality at all. The famous advice of Polonius, taken as a foundational axiom of modern being, 'To thine own self be true', would have had no meaning for Machiavelli, who saw truth as something external, public, established only in the public domain, through civility, and not in any meaningful sense given to the interiority of a self or a private being. 'To thine own self be true' is the desperate attempt of the Renaissance to construct a notion of truth as interiority, as a spurious 'felt life' or desire, and to hang onto the idea that truth is somehow to be felt, to be given eventually as 'self-evident', capable of evidencing itself in the heart and pulse of a human subject alert to itself and conscious of no existence beyond that. Machiavelli is opposed to this noble Renaissance, for in its nobility, it is vacuous, having only a formal, legal, economic existence and not a legitimate, autonomous content such as can be enjoyed by the civil subject, the citizen in the public domain, enjoying an ecological engagement with the polis.

Hence, Machiavelli provides a problem for what modernity is trying to establish. Modernity tries to establish a self based in autonomous agency whose legitimacy lies in the truth that is felt to be interior to this self, as its guiding principle, and a self-evident truth that is one and total. For Machiavelli, however, truth is not like this. As in rhetoric, and as in the mutable *branloire perenne* that is the contemporary world (as in what we might call secular historicity itself), truth is variable. To phrase this yet more accurately and precisely, truth exists only in the mode of the potential. The truth of a state of affairs is not given by 'character', we might say; that is, it is not something established at the individual level and grounded in psychology. Rather, it is established only at the public and communal level. Truth is a *res publica*, its substantiality based on its ability to realise a specific potential for truth. The entire theatrical output of the anglophone Renaissance, then, insofar as it is based upon the sudden and extremely speedy development of 'character', is a defence mechanism against the predations of Machiavelli. England is under attack from Italy, so to speak; and its defence is the establishment of 'character'. Machiavelli, a real Aristotelian in this, places plot instead at the centre of truth; and plots, in theatre just as on land, are sites of culture, of development, of growth, change, or, better, of potential.

To accuse Machiavelli of something like hypocrisy, then, is not only similar to accusing the pope of being a Catholic; it is also to miss something fundamental about his work. Hypocrisy is the inevitable condition of human being for Machiavelli, in a very specific sense. Any action under-taken by an individual is legitimised as an action only by the fact and to the extent that it is undertaken as on behalf of the community as a whole. This is how we ought to make sense of the famous misreading of Machi-avelli according to which he advocates as a fundamental axiomatic truth that the end justifies the means. This, of course, is not what he says at all. When he considers ostensibly evil political action, his question is always: in what interests, in whose interests, was the action carried out? History itself, or the mere passing of time, will show what the action effects; and the action is good if that end is the establishment of political security and stability. Thus, when Romulus kills his brother, the action, although os-tensibly evil in itself, is excused on the grounds of its effects. This is the meaning of the only truth that matters for Machiavelli, what he calls *ver-ità effetuale*. Truth, in these terms, is what happens, what is effected; and so the legitimate action is that which is judged not in accordance with a character's ability to identify an inner soul or essence with an external ac-tion (for that would be simply private morality, which is, strictly speaking, a contradiction in terms for Machiavelli); but rather that which, as in acts of rhetoric, does not give a truth whose validity is given by the identifica-tion of the speaker with what is spoken, of writer with text, but rather one that brings about good—political good. Hypocrisy thus—or acting in a way that is inconsistent with the desires of the individual self—is the only good for the modern republic.

Power and Potentiality

Berlin, writing in 1969, pointed out that Machiavelli produces a ma-jor problem for the modern world. Until Machiavelli's writing (and for many people since that time) it was taken as understood that, no mat-ter how unstable the world, it could all eventually be unified as one grand 'project'. As Berlin put it, 'One of the deepest assumptions of Western po-litical thought is the doctrine, scarcely questioned during its long ascen-dancy, that there exists some single principle which not only regulates the course of the sun and the stars, but prescribes their proper behaviour to all animate creatures'. And yet: 'what reason have we for supposing that jus-tice and mercy, humility and *virtu*, happiness and knowledge, glory and liberty, magnificence and sanctity, will always coincide, or indeed be compatible at all'.[20]

There is a problem here related to what we have learned to call, after Lyotard, a differend. It is the realisation that it may well be the case that not all ultimate values are genuinely mutually compatible with each other, that we might finally and fundamentally have to choose between competing claims for ultimate value—and worse still, that there can be no overarching criteria that will justify choosing one case over the other. We must, as in the famous phrase, judge without criteria. Within modernity itself, some have learned to call this situation existentialism, and to associate its fundamental experience with angst. It should be noted, briefly and in passing, that angst requires character; and so, properly speaking, existentialism itself might also be seen as a philosophy corollary to modernity's need to defend itself against the scandal of Machiavelli. To Machiavelli, judging without criteria appears to pose no problem: he chooses, and what he chooses is the public life. Yet he might—like those who would defend themselves against the terrors posed by his thought—have chosen the other, the route of 'character', private versus public, individual versus society, and so on: Freud, as it were. The fact that he chose at all is what leads to the emergence of the final issue that I address here: the relation of criticism or of critical consciousness (and most specifically that of a republican critical consciousness) with potentiality as opposed to the more normative relation that we are expected to establish between criticism and agency in modernity. It is in this potentiality that we shall also see the importance of an emergent democracy that ghosts Machiavellian republicanism. Here, I shall advert to some more recent critical theory, where we will see, with varying degrees of explicitness, the continuing importance of Machiavelli.

It is interesting to note that Stanley Fish, an eminent Renaissance scholar as well as theorist, is able, in his book *The Trouble with Principle*, to identify his own current project with that of Machiavelli. 'Pragmatism', he writes (and this, of course, is the position that he now adopts) 'may have emerged under democratic conditions (although its basic tenets were long ago articulated by Cicero and Machiavelli), but it neither produces nor necessarily accompanies democracy'.[21] He claims as his own real antecedent the opening of *The Prince*:

In the first paragraph, Machiavelli promises not to stuff his book 'with pompous phrases or elaborate, magnificent words' or to decorate it 'with any form of extrinsic rhetorical embroidery'. In the long tradition in which rhetoric is the negative pole of a binary opposition, the other position is always occupied by Truth or the Real or the Transparent or the Essential or the Normative or some other supra-contextual universal. Rhetoric, on the other hand, is stigmatised as the realm of appearances, of surfaces, of fashion, of flux, of the local, of the parochial, of the contingent, of the 'merely' historical, of language on holiday from its responsibilities, of everything that obscures and threatens to usurp the realm of pure forms and principles.

Machiavelli simply turns this on its head. . . . If you are after the 'real truth of the matter', he counsels, you should study and observe everything that utopian thought disdains and flees.[22]

This is interesting not just because it reveals that there is an intrinsic link still between the European Renaissance and the contemporary world, but also because it reveals and stresses the image of Machiavelli as a proto-deconstructor, one able to prioritise appearance over truth in such a way as to destabilise the value of both those terms. This is of more importance than might be suggested by any simplistic comparison between Machiavelli and, say, a contemporary thinker often taken for a nihilist, Baudrillard.[23]

What is at stake here is what I earlier called, following Agamben, the condition of 'potentiality'. For the ancient Greeks, according to Agamben, there is a distinction to be made between two words for life: *zoe* is basic and biological being (and Agamben translates it as 'bare life'), whereas *bios* is a way of being, a manner of organising *zoe*, so to speak. Agamben argues that 'the entry of *zoe* into the sphere of the polis—the politicisation of bare life as such—[that is, biopolitics] constitutes the decisive event of modernity'. He goes on to argue that 'If anything characterizes modern democracy as opposed to classical democracy, it is that modern democracy presents itself from the beginning as a vindication and liberation of *zoe*, and that it is constantly trying to transform its own bare life into a way of life and to find, so to speak, the *bios* of *zoe*'.[24]

Avoiding the technical terms here, one might express something close to this by saying that modern democracy has tried to base itself on the elision between the bare facts of our existence and our modes of being. Thus, modern democracy demands that there be a seamless continuity between, for example, my gendered being and my politics, between my 'raced' being and my social life. It is thus that modern democracy will find that I can legitimately and adequately represent myself: my vote being one of the 'black vote', or the 'woman's vote'.

The possibility that there might be such a seamless continuity is, for the logic of Machiavelli's thought, a problem; but it is one that he bypasses when he makes his choice for the public sphere as the only reality, accepting thereby that the private sphere is intrinsically self-contradictory. For Machiavelli, there is no *zoe* that was not always already *bios*, so to speak. *Zoe* depends on *bios* for any imaginary existence that it might have. To put it another way, the fiction of human 'character' (and with it that entire economy that structures our purely legal identity) depends on 'civil life' that is transpersonal, public (the ecology that legitimises the very possibility of life itself). Machiavelli thus politicises 'bare life'; but he does so in the mode of a pure potentiality of such life. Such bare life has no meaningful existence, other than a potential existence; and the potential becomes available only through the ecology of the public domain and civil life.

On the question of potentiality, which is also a question of latent power, Agamben follows Aristotle closely and explicitly; but my case is that he is also following Machiavelli, silently if yet more intimately. As Agamben points out, Aristotle was always careful to stress the autonomous existence of potentiality. This requires a brief clarification. We typically think of potentiality, as in some hard sciences, as a kind of latent power: it is the as-yet-unrealised possibility of being, the not-yet-realised capacity to bring something about, to effect a new state of affairs. Once effected or brought into being, the potential is, as it were, used up, deployed, exhausted. Potential here is the ground of kinesis, but a ground that effaces itself or exhausts itself in direct proportion as it brings something into being. However, in contrast to this, consider the musician: she still has her ability to make music even when she is not playing; and therefore, potentiality in this case is not simply a not-yet-realised actuality; rather, it is both the power to be and the power not-to-be (this latter being impotentiality of *adynamia* in Aristotle). This would be the real sense of that most famous of all literary conundrums: 'to be or not to be', now seen for what it is, an expression of Hamlet as the figure of pure potentiality. As Agamben explains this point, 'What is potential can pass over into actuality only at the point at which it sets aside its own potential not to be. . . . To set im-potentiality aside is not to destroy it but, on the contrary, to fulfil it, to turn potentiality back upon itself in order to give it to itself'.[25]

This, as Hamlet would have known only too well, is the paradox that governs the notion of sovereignty. The sovereign is that protector of the law who remains herself exempt from the prescriptions of the law; and Agamben will generalise this to state that 'an act is sovereign when it realizes itself by simply taking away its own potentiality not to be, letting itself be, giving itself to itself'.[26] An action thus is autonomous—sovereign, an enactment or presentation of a self—if and only if it has already made its own happening inevitable by removing the possibility of its not occurring. Paradoxically, then, autonomy in this mode requires that a self fulfil a necessity; and this at precisely the same moment as she defines autonomy in terms of contingency, of a motivation that originates in the self by the self for the self, acting according to a law that the self gives to itself.

Machiavelli knew this paradox; and he also knew that the real issue facing the European Renaissance was what we in modernity have come to know as the problem of autonomy, a problem known most intimately at the time of the emergence of the modern nation-states as the problem of sovereignty, a problem identified directly with monarchy and its (il)legitimacy or (il)legality. If modernisation has anything to do with autonomy, as it certainly has, then the key to understanding this is best expressed by the simple question that ghosts Machiavelli's entire writings: can any human self be or become sovereign? or, is sovereignty the sole preserve of a 'leader'? That is to say, of course, that the question governing Machiavelli is precisely that which we now identify as democracy.

As I indicated above, Machiavelli provides us with an early formulation of the Lyotardian differend, the problem concerning the incommensurability of apparently universal values. For a modern liberal (such as Berlin), the way to deal with the impasse of such a differend would be through a fundamentally monological ethos: acknowledge the difference of the Other, and tolerate her in that difference. Such respect for the Other is not to be found in Machiavelli, however; and Berlin's response to the question of alterity—tolerance—is yet another instance of a defence mechanism being constructed against the power of Machiavelli's thinking.

The shocking thing, in the end, is that in the logic of Machiavelli, every act that is proposed as a good must contain within itself the power to be bad. To be good at all (as Milton knew), one must be able to be bad; evil must lurk potentially and as a potentiality within every good. The name that Renaissance theatre gave to this troubling and unsettling thought is, of course, Iago: the man known and respected for his unsurpassed honesty who yet contains within himself the possibility of depraved dishonesty—and, in the end, vice versa.

By political analogy with this 'Iago condition', we might also say that the sovereign is sovereign precisely insofar as he can be subjected. In stating this, we are stating that the Renaissance is republican through and through; and it is perhaps for this reason that the rebirthing it signifies—that extraordinary potential for a life, for the inhabiting of a public space—is taking place not in Europe at all, haunted as Europe is by the ghosts of its dead and dying kings, but rather in the postcolonial context (including in the America of pragmatists such as Fish or Rorty). By contrast, European 'modernity', cast as an endless process of self-modernisation and of self-fashioning, is a rear-guard action against the power and potentiality of republicanism as such. The identification of modernisation with autonomy has led to a condition in which a fictitious model of 'democracy' (a legal rather than a legitimate mode, an economic rather than an ecological mode) has become the question for Europe instead of the question of the republic, the public space that we might inhabit, whether we were born in and to that space or not. It is time, then, to revive Machiavelli, to give him place, to find a local habitation and a name for Europe that will be organised on ecological rather than purely economic grounds. In that, the 'principles' governing our economic being must give way.

And, of course, we can now recast the question of democracy under the more promising and more accurate sign of a new 'democratic sovereignty', to which I shall turn in my next and closing chapter.

CHAPTER 9

Aesthetic Democracy

In this book, I have reconfigured the way we think of the relations between the arts and politics. More specifically, my concern has been to raise the issue of our critical priorities: does our political condition determine our arts (broadly, the neo-Marxist position); or do the aesthetic events in life condition the possibility of our having political relations or a society at all? The preceding chapters have driven us towards the latter conclusion; and in this concluding chapter, I want to explore the consequences of such a position more fully.

Democracy as a Beyond of Europe

One way of proceeding here is to ask an ostensibly simple question: is it possible to be 'beyond Europe'? I have already described Europe as a condition rather than a place; and I characterised that condition as the 'impossible possibility' that is democracy-as-potential. The question of going 'beyond' Europe, and by implication into the actualisation of such potential, has been asked by many others. In the first instance, it is asked by the great European explorers, those who initiated the very colonial situation whose overcoming I described, at the opening of this book, as a *fons et origo* of the critical consciousness as such. It is asked by their literary contemporary, Shakespeare (as I shall show below). It is asked, very directly and more recently, by Richard Rorty. In the essays in his *Philosophy and Social Hope*, Rorty laments what he sees as Heidegger's ill-informed view of America. Heidegger's problem, for Rorty, is essentially an aesthetic one: Heidegger never read Whitman. 'Had he done so,' Rorty argues, 'he might conceivably have come to see America as Hegel (if only briefly) did: as the further westering of the spirit, the next evolutionary stage beyond Europe'.[1]

Yet Rorty himself here is not actually following Hegel, but rather the philosopher whose work so informs Rorty in its obsessive returns to the questions of democracy and America: John Dewey. In exploring the relations of America, democracy, and pragmatism, Rorty's basic contention is that there does not need to be a seamless continuity between one's philosophy and one's politics, that the relation between these is pretty loose, and that 'Your opinion of pragmatism can, and should, be independent of your opinion of either democracy or America'.[2] However, there is a clear drive in Rorty that does indeed link pragmatism with a mentality that he identifies as a kind of 'going beyond', an exploratory inventiveness that drives the pragmatist beyond herself or himself; and here that 'beyond' is explicitly beyond the Europe that I have identified as the potential for democracy.

In Rorty's reading of Dewey, pragmatism shares with the ever-developing 'America' the kind of mentality that is apparent also in Whitman. Both the philosophy and the poetry are fundamentally different expressions or representations of the same underlying political idea: both are 'expressions of a hopeful, melioristic, experimental frame of mind'.[3] Here, for Rorty, is their democratic impulse, an impulse that can be characterised as future-oriented, inventive, grounded in hope rather than in established principle, and thereby open to novelty, to change, and even to history itself.[4]

We should rid ourselves here of the cruder polemical arguments associated with the Rortean position. To defend Rorty against his leftist detractors, we might see that his position can be clearly aligned with a neo-Marxist desire for the amelioration of the social conditions of our human being, that it is determined to allow people to express themselves fully and uninhibitedly, that it aims to facilitate the fullest possible realisation by an individual of her hopes and potential. These are undeniably good things, and they are all consistent with and served by the position that Rorty argues. Against him, however, we can see that to view history as the endless invention of more and more novelty can play directly into the hands of that very conservative capitalism that drives 'America'; that the very capitalism that is the cause of our misery would renew itself precisely by the tactic of constantly offering novel versions of the fundamentally unchanging old and established stories; that he offers no principled objection to the commodifications of culture in the form of the new-made; that the position is complicit with an ideology of consumerism that would reduce human freedom to a simple matter of market choice, in which the illusions of choice occlude precisely the lack of the very freedom that the enactment of such choice is supposed to illustrate and celebrate.

Rorty has been difficult for the political left precisely because his thought seems to be available to both positions here, even if he would certainly identify himself with the left-liberal position.[5] The task proposed for us by his work is, effectively, to discover the forms of novelty that will allow us to move 'beyond' ourselves, beyond who and where we are, beyond where we're from; and the name that Rorty gives to that process of discovery is variously 'America', 'pragmatism', or 'democracy', or some amalgam of all three.

The influence of Dewey here is pervasive. According to Rorty, Dewey looked at 'old Europe' (not the same 'old Europe' as that identified by Donald Rumsfeld for the purposes of advancing the cause of war against Iraq in 2003) and saw there a series of dualisms. Those dualisms, argued Dewey, were shaped around a fundamental and grounding dualistic opposition between appearance and reality. The problem with this, for Dewey and then also for Rorty, is that it subscribes, at least tacitly, to the view that there is a real-as-such, a real that is independent of its appearance; and further, that this real is unamenable to our views of it, impervious to how we might see or describe it. This would be a reality against which one could not argue, a reality with which one can do nothing except strive to cohabit, a reality that determines the very possibilities (or, better, limits) of our being. This is close to the position argued by Fredric Jameson, who argues that

History is . . . the experience of Necessity. . . . History is what hurts, it is what refuses desire and sets inexorable limits to individual as well as collective praxis . . . . But this History can be apprehended only through its effects, and never directly as some reified force. This is indeed the ultimate sense in which History as ground and untranscendable horizon needs no particular theoretical justification: we may be sure that its alienating necessities will not forget us, however much we might prefer to ignore them.[6]

For Dewey, as for Rorty, these inherently limiting views would deny us the very possibility of ever going beyond ourselves, of ever accepting that we ourselves might change. Indeed, in the limit-form of a subscription to some eternal and unchanging quasi-theological version of Necessity as nature, such positions deny the possibility of human autonomy, preferring to advance an image of the human as, at best, an instrument of nature and, at worst, as its servant or victim. In more recent times, of course, such Necessity/nature has been elided into an amorphous and homogeneous form of 'Power'.

In his analysis of this state of affairs, Dewey sees a Europe that is traditional in the strict sense of being governed entirely by its past, and therefore unable to look forward with excitement, novelty, and freshness, unable to establish a historicity based on the principles of human mutability, change, or experience. For Dewey, if democracy can be established at all, its symptomatic signs will be precisely discovered in the fact of change and of change based in experience. As Rorty has it:

Dewey was convinced that everything that was wrong with traditional European philosophy was the result of clinging to a world picture which arose within, and met the needs of, an inegalitarian society. He saw all the baneful dualisms of the philosophical tradition as remnants and figurations of the social division between contemplators and doers, between a leisure class and a productive class. . . . Dewey argues that so far the thrust of philosophy has been conservative; it has typically been on the side of the leisure class, favouring stability over change. Philosophy has been an attempt to lend the past the prestige of the eternal.[7]

This is interesting in that it translates the basic dualism between mind and body, between reality and mere physical appearance, into a political dualism between two classes: a leisured and aristocratic class of thinkers who are oriented around the life of the mind, and a class of practical doers whose existence is reduced to the physical. What makes this interesting in the present context is that it is a structure whose roots lie in an aesthetic form: it is a mapping, in philosophical terms, of the European comic tradition in which conflict and drama is organised around the contest between leisured masters and working servants.

I suggested above that Shakespeare had already investigated the question of going beyond Europe. The conventional and expected way to exemplify this would be through an examination of *The Tempest*. However, given what I have argued about the structure of comedy, its relation to history-as-necessity, and to pragmatism, we will see that there is a better, if unexpected, play in which to ground our arguments.

The Tempest effectively revisits some old Shakespearean questions—questions about aesthetics—and relocates those questions in a situation whose politics is now effectively foregrounded for us in postcolonial terms. The play establishes a contest between bookish aesthetic life (the life and magic of Prospero, who preferred his books to the running of his dukedom) and a more brutish life of the body (that of Caliban); and it figures the relation between these in terms of the mediation of a working spirit who has aspirations towards a genuine freedom (Ariel). Yet here, in this late play, Shakespeare is effectively reworking a theme that he began to investigate in the very early *Love's Labour's Lost*, another text staging the contest between the academy (the formation of a 'University of Navarre', with its three-year programmes of literary study, divorced from the world of food, the body, and women) and the world of politics (the relations between Navarre and France). The dominant question throughout the comedies is that concerning autonomy: who is in control, and who is able to shape her own history? In many plays this becomes the master-servant trope (*The Comedy of Errors* establishes the template for this); but what makes it interesting in the present argument is that the real question concerning autonomy is whether we can control our environment, whether we can shape it to our needs.

The text that dramatises this most forcefully is the troubling *Taming of the Shrew*. Although *The Comedy of Errors* might have taken for granted the power or class structure in which there is always a contest between the interests of masters and those of servants, *The Taming of the Shrew* sets a rather different, if related, task. Shakespeare uses this play to examine the question of how it is that the master-servant relation can be established in the first place. In short, the plot of this play is one in which Petruchio effectively has to make a servant for himself, in the figure of Kate; and the comic question that shapes the text is how, and even whether, he will succeed. Here, then, the formal comic structure, an aesthetic device, is deployed to political ends, in asking fundamental questions about the nature of the marriage bond and its relation to a social organisation based on an emergent capitalism (here, the ownership of land).

The view that Dewey and Rorty both resist is the hopeless view that there is a real-as-such, unamenable to our descriptions and redescriptions of it. In this sense, Petruchio is the ideal pragmatist. His major weapon is rhetoric; his major power is the capacity to redescribe the world in ways that suit his needs. He has arrived in Padua a wealthy man, having just inherited; and his single intention is to establish himself in society, for which he needs a wife: 'I come to wive it wealthily in Padua; / If wealthily, then happily in Padua' (1.2). Awaiting the arrival of Kate, the woman who will enable this particular wish, he promises to woo her in terms that are, fundamentally if crudely, pragmatic:

> I'll attend her here
> And woo her with some spirit when she comes.
> Say that she rail, why then I'll tell her plain
> She sings as sweetly as a nightingale.
> Say that she frown, I'll say she looks as clear
> As morning roses newly washed with dew.
> Say she be mute and will not speak a word,
> Then I'll commend her volubility
> And say she uttereth piercing eloquence. (2.1)

This is simply a redescription of Kate, a redescription that Petruchio wishes to make the dominant description of her—and thus the 'reality' of her.

By the time we reach a play such as *The Tempest*, Shakespeare's presiding interests have become clear: can books, as modes of redescription of the world, make any real political difference to the world? Where rhetoric was instrumental for Petruchio, aesthetics is precisely the magic that will reconfigure the world for Prospero. By the close of this play, thanks to his magic, Prospero has reconfigured the power relations that shape the relation of Milan to Naples and has effectively 'freed' Milan from the yoke of subjugation—even if friendly and accepted subjugation—to Naples. All, it seems, has changed. Yet there is a larger political reality that remains at the end of the play. Although much attention has been paid to the relation between Milanese Prospero and Algerian Caliban (fundamentally yet another reworking of the master-servant trope), less has been paid to the other colonial relation that frames the play. The very occasion of the play's action is determined by the fact that Ferdinand, Gonzalo, Alonso, Antonio, and the rest are shipwrecked on their way home from the marriage of Ferdinand's sister, Claribel, to the unnamed King of Tunis. When they are shipwrecked, with Ferdinand being separated and presumed lost, Sebastian interrupts Alonso's self-pitying lament for Ferdinand thus:

> Sir, you may thank yourself for this great loss,
> That would not bless our Europe with your daughter,
> But rather loose her to an African,
> Where she, at least, is banished from your eye
> Who has cause to wet the grief on't.
>
> . . .
>
> You were kneeled to and importuned otherwise
> By all of us; and the fair soul herself
> Weighed, between loathness and obedience, at
> Which end o'th'beam should bow. (2.1)

Claribel, as one of the only daughters in Shakespeare who seems prepared to do her father's bidding in erotic matters, has certainly gone 'beyond Europe'; yet she is not entirely forgotten at the end. In trying to sum up the events, Gonzalo recalls her to mind:

> Was Milan thrust from Milan that his issue
> Should become kings of Naples? O, rejoice
> Beyond a common joy, and set it down
> With gold on lasting pillars. In one voyage
> Did Claribel her husband find at Tunis,
> And Ferdinand her brother found a wife
> Where he himself was lost; Prospero his dukedom
> In a poor isle; and all of us ourselves
> When no man was his own. (5.1)

The secret of this speech lies in the fact that, by the end of the play, we do not stand where we once did. Claribel is effectively the model in which we find ourselves by going beyond ourselves: Milan goes beyond Milan to find who he is; Ferdinand, a brother, loses himself in order to become a husband; and we find ourselves 'not our own', not in determining control of our identity, for our identity is that which is always shared, lying 'beyond' ourselves. Africa (Tunis) here is the sign of that beyond; and, as we all know, beyond ourselves lies the self that is Caliban, slave, unfree, physical.

One thing that *The Tempest* dramatises is the relativisation of value. Caliban, in searching for his freedom or autonomy, is willing to change one form of servitude for another. He wants to leave Prospero to serve the drunken Stephano, for from Caliban's point of view, such servitude looks like freedom. Likewise, at the end of the play, when Miranda has become attached to Ferdinand, she suddenly sees a world full of men, and, from a position in which she has thought of Ferdinand as an absolute beauty, she now finds 'How many goodly creatures are there here! / How beauteous mankind is! O brave new world / That has such people in't'. In both these cases, absolute values become relativised; and the logic of the play determines that we are now in a position where we have to live without certainty and without what might pass for a transcendental Truth. *The Tempest* becomes a kind of paradigm of pragmatism, in that it dramatises the fact that values have to be worked out and practised. The play becomes a kind of paradigm of a certain postmodern as well, in that it dramatises the necessity of making judgements in the absence of any legitimising and grounding criteria. This play, we might say, establishes the necessity of critique without foundations; and it does so by raising the question of sovereignty. What is at stake in *The Tempest* is the question of how and whether we can establish a sovereign control of our own history. The play is important not only for this, but also because it raises this issue through the issues of coloniality and of a being 'beyond Europe' that I have shown to be at the very root of our modern critical consciousness.

The great modern question, then, turns out not to be simply the question of autonomy (for which Hamlet is usually taken as the paradigm) but rather the question of sovereignty over the self (for which, I now claim, Claribel is the key). To phrase this question in terms that are more immediately pertinent to the contemporary cultural predicament, we might ask it thus: how can something be brought about; and how might an I bring it about? How do we make things happen? Further, if it is the case that democracy is something of the nature of an event, and not a permanent state of affairs or condition, then how can we make the event that would be 'democratic' happen?

Democracy as a Singular Event

When Eliot made his great argument in 'Tradition and the Individual Talent', he found himself in a philosophical difficulty. The new, he argues, has to rewrite the past: 'what happens when a new work of art is created is something that happens simultaneously to all the works of art that preceded it'.[8] We move, as it were, from one state of perfect wholeness and order to another—different—state of perfect wholeness and order. In this essay, Eliot gets at an abiding question not only for aesthetics, but also for politics: how can we get from one state of affairs to another? How does anything ever happen at all? Why, in short, is there something rather than nothing?

To change a constitution is always unconstitutional. To bring something about is always, in principle, difficult. A puzzled King Lear addresses this problem when he tells Cordelia to mend her words, for, as everyone knows, 'Nothing will come of nothing'. For Hegel, to make something come of nothing was, in some ways, the very mark of freedom; the model was an aesthetic one. In the introduction to his *Aesthetics*, Hegel argues that there is a distinction to be made between a naturally occurring beauty and an artificially made beauty. The latter is infinitely superior because it is entirely unnecessary, purely contingent, and more importantly still, the symptom of a human consciousness exceeding or going beyond itself: 'We may . . . begin at once by asserting that artistic beauty stands higher than nature. For the beauty of art is the beauty that is born—born again, that is—of the mind; and by as much as the mind and its products are higher than nature and its appearances, by so much the beauty of art is higher than the beauty of nature'.[9] This difference is produced by the simple fact that the naturally occurring is indifferent, whereas that which is made or brought about is characterised by intellectual being, spirituality, and (essentially, for our purposes) freedom.[10] Bringing something about—fundamentally an act of transformation—is always an act of inauguration. When Blanchot considers this in explicit relation to writing, he argues (as I laid out in some detail above) that the transformation is double: one transforms an object or raw materials, for example in order to make a stove; but in that very act one also transforms oneself, by making oneself warm instead of cold, say. Writing is such an act of making the self free, but making the self free essentially and fundamentally by changing the self, by altering the self in some way.[11] Yet the question is how we can write at all, or how we can act at all: how does change happen, and how do we get from one state of affairs to another? If it is the case that democracy has something to do with the cultural growth of the self that is marked by such change, by the kind of altering of the self that is grounded in hope and expectation rather than in principle, then the question becomes yet more fundamental: how is democracy possible, especially if we now construe democracy properly as that condition in which we can go from one state of affairs to another?

The answer to this lies within one of the fundamental questions governing democracy: representation. Representation is basically a trope that regulates the relations between the particular and the general, between the one and the many: one stands for many; or one is a 'type' whose characteristics are shared by many. In one early formulation of modern aesthetics, in the work of Francis Hutcheson, we have a refrain that speaks directly to this condition: 'The figures which excite in us the ideas of beauty seem to be those in which there is uniformity amidst variety'[12]; or, in other words, beauty is tied to representation as such. For Hutcheson, beauty was to be found and to be evaluated precisely in terms of the regulation of the general and the particular, and it is from this that we shall now be able to derive a specific understanding of the emergence of 'aesthetic democracy', in which democracy can be characterised not only as an event, but more precisely as an event that is predicated upon beauty and as an event that signals a predicament in representation. Further, this event, insofar as it is democratic, signals not the identification of the self, not the consolidation of a preexisting and predetermining identity, but rather the altering of the self, such that the self that exists after the event must of necessity differ from the self that inaugurated it. In aesthetic democracy, Claribel initiates a series of events, through which she becomes our African queen, even as she remains firmly European; and in those events, she opens for us Europeans the question of what it might be to be beyond Europe.

Aesthetic democracy, then, is based upon the potentiality of democracy. Further, it is linked to the metaphysics of a 'going beyond' (which I have characterised here as a beyond of Europe). Finally, it requires an act of representation whose function is not to identify the self but to alter it; and such a representation, therefore, is akin to that characterisation of the postmodern as a moment when representation becomes a predicament. In aesthetic democracy—which is now the only genuine democracy that is possible—representation becomes an event and not a condition or a state of affairs.

What is the nature of this 'aesthetic-democratic' event? It is best considered as an event that marks a singularity and that enacts a sovereignty. The more usual way of considering democracy has been in terms of the establishment of the autonomy of an individual within an identifiable group that we can call 'the people'. The problem with that is that it takes representation for granted and assumes that somewhere, somehow, there exists a hypothetical individual authority—a particular, in Hutcheson's terms— that is so great that it can stand for the whole—the general. The name that we had given to this in the past was, of course, monarchy; and Hobbes was its great advocate. That is to say, any notion of democracy that sees it as a state of affairs in which there is such a hypothetical ideal position of authority (be it called the king, the elected representative of a bourgeois parliament, the president, the people) is precisely anathema to any genuine democracy, any 'eventful' or really happening democracy.

How, then, might we explain this sovereignty that I put at the core of aesthetic democracy? Agamben, it will be recalled from my arguments earlier in this book, explains sovereignty as that condition that stands outside the law in order to establish the law as such. It is characterised in terms of 'exceptionality'. Yet what is the logic of the exception if not an explication of the very possibility of art and of the aesthetic as such? The basic point about art, about the bringing into existence of something that is contingent, is not only a neo-Hegelian freedom, but also the establishment of something that exempts itself from rules or from the law. Aesthetics, indeed, might even be renamed exceptionality in precisely this sense that aesthetics draws attention to a rule precisely in and through the presence of that which breaks the rule, the artwork itself. The aesthetic democrat is she or he who makes precisely such an exception of herself or himself in the event that we call representation, that altering of the self that marks change, growth, even living itself.

And another word for aesthetic democracy, therefore, is nothing other than history itself. Aesthetics makes possible history as the experience of altering the self; and it is democratic precisely to the extent that such history can never be mine or mine alone, for an altered self knows no I.

Notes

INTRODUCTION

1. See Jean Baudrillard, *La Société de consommation* (Paris: Denoël, 1970). For a fuller explanation of the political stakes here, see my *After Theory*, revised and expanded 2nd ed. (Edinburgh: Edinburgh University Press, 1996), 247–59.

2. See Jean-François Lyotard, *The Postmodern Condition* (1979), trans. Geoff Bennington and Brian Massumi (Manchester: Manchester University Press, 1984), 4, 76.

3. See Hans Blumenberg, *The Legitimacy of the Modern Age*, trans. Robert M. Wallace (Cambridge, MA: MIT Press, 1983).

4. See David Simpson, *Situatedness* (Durham, NC: Duke University Press, 2002).

5. Plato, *Republic*, book 3, §398, trans. Desmond Lee (Harmondsworth: Penguin, 1976), 157.

CHAPTER I

1. The genuinely critical is thus in a sense always 'metacritical'—'theoretical', in an old sense of that term.

2. Jacques Derrida, *Of Grammatology*, trans. Gayatri Chakravorty Spivak (Baltimore: Johns Hopkins University Press, 1976), 266. The year 1967 can be regarded as a kind of beginning for deconstruction, in that it was during that year that the impact of Derrida's writings began to be felt, for the first time in a major fashion, in the anglophone and literary (i.e., nonphilosophically specialist) world.

3. Derrida, *Of Grammatology*, 266–67.

4. Jonathan Culler, *On Deconstruction* (London: Routledge and Kegan Paul, 1983), 87.

5. Paul de Man, *Allegories of Reading* (New Haven, CT: Yale University Press, 1979), 17.

6. Ibid.

7. Ibid., 78. In relation to this, see also Paul Ricoeur, *De l'interprétation* (Paris: Seuil, 1965), 35–36; and cf. my commentary on this in my study, *After Theory*,

revised and expanded 2nd ed. (Edinburgh: Edinburgh University Press, 1996), 43 ff.

8. Paul de Man, *Blindness and Insight*, 2nd ed. (London: Methuen, 1983), 222; but cf. my extended commentary on this essay in *After Theory*, 115–41.

9. Jean-François Lyotard, *La Confession d'Augustin* (Paris: Galilée, 1998), 96.

10. In much earlier work, I characterised this point of conversion as a 'revolutionary moment' in a mode that was perhaps overexcitedly political. This present work offers a more measured reading of autonomy or of beginnings, carried out in a less politicised fashion. For the earlier reading, see my *John Donne, Undone* (London: Methuen, 1986). For a much more sustained inquiry into beginnings, see Edward Said, *Beginnings* (New York: Columbia University Press, 1985).

11. Geoffrey Bennington and Jacques Derrida, *Jacques Derrida* (Paris: Seuil, 1991). It is structurally important that 'Circonfession' is 'presided over' by Bennington's own text, 'Derridabase', part of whose presumption is that there should be no surprise, that it is possible to construct a 'programme' that will have always already foretold what it is possible for Derrida to propose. Yet surprises there are.

12. In fact, Georgette Derrida outlasted the completion of 'Circonfession' by some eighteen months.

13. Bennington and Derrida, *Jacques Derrida*, 3.

14. The fact that Tiresias 'unites' the two sexes is important here, for 'Circonfession' is, as is well known, largely about Derrida's penis and its mutilation through circumcision. That mutilation is one that can be related to symbolic castration, as in John D. Caputo's reading in *The Prayers and Tears of Jacques Derrida* (Bloomington: Indiana University Press, 1997), esp. 239–40; but it also relates to Derrida's 'secret name', Elie or Elijah, the name of the prophet who faces down Jezebel in 1 Kings 18 ff.

15. Augustine, *Confessions*, trans. R. S. Pine-Coffin (Harmondsworth: Penguin, 1961), 208–9.

16. Derrida, 'Circonfession', 30.

17. Ibid., 263.

18. Bennington and Derrida, *Jacques Derrida*, 277: 'je ne voyais même pas mes yeux, pas plus que jadis la main qui leva le couteau sur moi' (I couldn't even see my eyes, much less the hand that wielded the knife over me); cf. 67 for the image of just such a knife.

19. In what follows, I shall leave aside a third parallel between the writers: their passion for playing football.

20. Albert Camus, *L'Etranger* (Paris: Gallimard, 1957), 89–90. On the importance of 'tears', another aspect of the parallels, see Caputo, *Prayers and Tears*.

21. Derrida, 'Circonfession', 38.

22. Camus, *L'Etranger*, 7.

23. Derrida, 'Circonfession', 155.

24. Augustine, *City of God*, trans. Henry Bettenson (Harmondsworth: Penguin, 1972), 38–39 (book 1, chap. 27).

25. Camus, *Le Mythe de Sisyphe* (Paris: Gallimard, 1942), 15. Interestingly, his analysis of death itself strikingly resembles that of Wittgenstein in the *Tractatus Logico-Philosophicus*, proposition 6.4311. There Wittgenstein writes, 'Death is not an event of life. Death is not lived through'. Cf. Camus in *Le Mythe*, 30: 'en réalité, il n'y a pas d'expérience de la mort. Au sens propre, n'est expérimenté que ce qui a été vécu et rendu conscient'.

26. Derrida, 'Circonfession', 263.

27. Ibid., 175.

28. Ibid., 167.

29. Derrida, 'Circonfession', 160; Derrida as a kind of doubting Thomas, therefore.

30. Derrida, 'Circonfession', 263; cf. 39, 'j'ai envie de me tuer'.

31. Ibid, 103; cf. 109 for the direct relation of this to 'the Jews'; and cf. 126 for its direct relation to circumcision.

32. For the fuller political dimension of this, see Chapter 7 below.

33. Giorgio Agamben, *Homo Sacer*, trans. Daniel Heller-Roazen (Stanford, CA: Stanford University Press, 1998), 136.

34. Derrida, 'Circonfession', 84.

35. Augustine, *City of God*, 26 (book 1, chap. 16).

36. Derrida, 'Circonfession', 66, 164.

37. Bennington and Derrida, *Jacques Derrida*, 301.

38. John Milton, *Paradise Lost*, ed. Christopher Ricks (Harmondsworth: Penguin, 1989), 60 (book 3, line 99, lines 103–19).

CHAPTER 2

1. Simon Critchley, *The Ethics of Deconstruction*, 2nd ed. (Edinburgh: Edinburgh University Press, 1999), 189.

2. Ibid.

3. Geoffrey Bennington, 'Frontiers: Of Literature and Philosophy', professorial lecture delivered 4 June 1996, available at http://www.sussex.ac.uk/Users/sffc4/inaug.doc.

4. For my own exploration of this, different from Bennington's, see my recent books: *Alterities: Criticism, History, Representation* (Oxford: Oxford University Press, 1996); *After Theory*, revised and expanded 2nd ed. (Edinburgh: Edinburgh University Press, 1996); and *Criticism and Modernity: Aesthetics, Literature and Nations in Europe and Its Academies* (Oxford: Oxford University Press, 1999).

5. See Bennington's amused but irritated footnote 11 to chap. 2 of *Interrupting Derrida* (London: Routledge, 2000), 199: 'That *Spectres of Marx* always might be

taken to maintain rather than dissipate Derrida's silence about Marx was illustrat-ed at the 1995 "Applied Derrida" conference in Luton, where, in a general discus-sion with Derrida, an irritated participant demanded that Derrida say "what he really thought" about Marx; when politely pointed by Derrida to *Spectres of Marx*, the now angry participant replied that he'd read that, but wanted to know what Derrida *really thought* about Marx'.

6. To some extent, this statement must be read as part of a polemic. There is no such thing as *the* left: it is not a unified, homogeneous whole. However, what I want to indicate here is the dissatisfaction felt among many critics—of divergent leftist positions—regarding the alleged political inefficacy of deconstruction. This became something of a theme in the 1980s: Said preferred Foucault; Eagleton sati-rized Derrida as 'politically evasive' and again preferred Foucault; Arac et al., in the volume on *The Yale Critics: Deconstruction in America*, in 1983, saw the 'decon-structors' as essentially rather conservative. Such views helped New Historicism rise into a brief ascendancy; and, when Derrida eventually produced his study of Marx, it turned out for some to be a book about ghosts, thus seeming to recon-firm that early 1980s view.

7. That is to say, I am contesting the by now conventional and truistic view that our criticism is always and always has been 'political'. The individual who has probably been most responsible for establishing the simplistic 'validity' of such an identification of the critical with the political is doubtless Terry Eagleton: 'There is, in fact, no need to drag politics into literary theory: as with South African sport, it has been there from the beginning' (*Literary Theory* [Oxford: Blackwell, 1983], 194). It is also equally true that, whenever Eagleton tries to clarify what this might actually mean, he is forced into what seems to be the weaker statements (with which I can easily agree) that criticism exists in relation to political states of affairs; thus, for examples, 'the history of modern literary theory *is part of* the po-litical and ideological history of our epoch' (emphasis added); 'literary theory has been indissolubly *bound up* with political *beliefs* and ideological *values*' (empha-sis added); 'any body of theory concerned with human meaning, value, language, feeling and experience will inevitably *engage with* broader, deeper beliefs about the nature of human individuals and societies' (again, emphasis added) (all passages 194–95; but many more punctuating Eagleton's work can be found at random). It is not this weak case that Eagleton claims; rather, although the weak case is all that is warranted, he always claims the stronger case of an identification of the critical with the political; and it is this that I contest.

8. This, of course, after what was felt to be the 'disappointment' of 1968, espe-cially in France, and the consequent rise of the *nouveaux philosophes*, with the re-confirmation in power, at that time, of de Gaulle.

9. This is only the European dimension of this historical moment. Clearly, matters were different in the United States (and, to a lesser extent, Australia),

where the focus of the question was on criticism as a form of protest, and specifically of anti–Vietnam War protest; and they were different again in Asia and Africa. For a more thorough and wide-ranging history, see David Caute, *'68: The Year of the Barricades* (London: Paladin, 1988); and for an engaging, if more personal, history of this period, see Tariq Ali, *Street Fighting Years* (London: Collins, 1987).

10. A more formative moment for Derrida was surely 1962 and the Franco-Algerian situation, about which his views underwent significant modifications and disillusionment.

11. See Imre Salusinzsky, *Criticism in Society* (London: Methuen, 1987), 167; and cf. Michael Ryan, *Marxism and Deconstruction* (Baltimore: Johns Hopkins University Press, Baltimore, 1982).

12. For a good example of such uncertainties in the British context, see the work of Eagleton between about 1980 and 1984, especially *Walter Benjamin; or Towards a Revolutionary Criticism* (London: Verso, 1981), 193; 'Frère Jacques: the Politics of Deconstruction', written in 1984 and republished in *Against the Grain* (London: Verso, 1986); *The Function of Criticism* (London: Verso, 1984), 98; and the first edition of *Literary Theory* (1983). In these, Eagleton certainly makes (sometimes enthusiastic) use of Derrida, but he tries to remain detached (and usually ends up attacking the very criticism that he uses). These vacillations help reveal that what was at stake in his books in this period was more the destabilising of the Oxford English faculty than the Thatcher government—a 'local' and even parochial politics of which his Cambridge forerunner, Leavis, offers a good example.

13. Although related to Homi Bhabha's notions of a colonial time lag, I intend something different here.

14. Gianni Vattimo, *The Transparent Society*, trans. David Webb (Cambridge: Polity, 1989), 6.

15. Ibid., 17.

16. Ibid.

17. Giorgio Agamben, *Potentialities*, ed., trans., intro. Daniel Heller-Roazen (Stanford, CA: Stanford University Press, 1999), 38.

18. See, for examples, Stanley Fish, *Professional Correctness* (Oxford: Oxford University Press, 1995); and *The Trouble with Principle* (Cambridge, MA: Harvard University Press, 1999).

19. Geoffrey Bennington, *Legislations* (London: Verso, 1994), 2. I hope I have understood this; but the point is not that I should simply 'receive' it, but rather that I can transform it through my 'stupid' deployment of it here, stupid because used for purposes other than those intended by Bennington.

20. For the Lyotard adverted to here, see Lyotard and Richard Rorty, 'Discussion', *Critique* 41 (May 1985): 581–84; and cf. Jean Baudrillard and Marc Guillaume, *Figures de l'altérité* (Paris: Descartes & Cie, 1994), 10. See also my discussion of this in *After Theory*, 235–36; and in *Criticism and Modernity*, 32–34; and *Alterities*, 170–96.

21. See Sylviane Agacinski, *Critique de l'egocentrisme* (Paris: Galilee, 1996). A true anecdote: On the 'What is Literature?' panel of the 1998 Cambridge conference on 'The Value of Literature', both Margaret Anne Doody and Wlad Godzich argued a well-worn case attacking canonicity that suggested that anything could become literature. I took the different line that precisely the people that this stance was supposed to help politically were in fact betrayed by it, in that they could be reassured of their literacy even if they were less than literate, and that the stance actually conspired to deny the availability of culture (by which I meant 'high culture') to many people. I spoke of my own mother, whose problems with literacy helped to ensure that she remained, in financial and social terms, relatively impoverished, whereas my own education in classical high literature enabled me to be in a position where I was now addressing an august audience as a professor of English. Doody pounced on this, remarking on how typical it was to ascribe the position of illiteracy to women as usual. She reduced the singularity of a specific woman to the merest sign of woman-as-such. This, I argued—and still maintain here—is the great betrayal: pretending to make a positive political statement (in this instance, a profeminist one) while actually refusing to see the singularity of a specific person in question.

22. Paul de Man, *The Resistance to Theory* (Manchester: Manchester University Press, 1986), 11.

23. Emmanuel Levinas, *La mort et le temps* (Paris: Editions de l'Herne, 1991), 13.

24. Ibid., 14.

25. Ibid.

26. Ibid., 15. It is perhaps worth noting here the intrinsic similarity between this mode of thinking and that, from a different tradition almost entirely, proposed by Lionel Trilling, who, in his *Sincerity and Authenticity* (New Haven, CT: Harvard University Press, 1972) tracked the etymological root of 'authenticity' back to 'authenteo', which means, among other things, 'I kill'.

27. Jacques Derrida, *The Gift of Death*, trans. David Wills (Chicago: University of Chicago Press, 1995), 25.

28. Levinas, *La mort et le temps*, 13.

29. Derrida, *Gift of Death*, 41.

30. Giorgio Agamben, *Il linguaggio e la morte*, 3rd ed. (Turin: Einaudi, 1982), 7.

31. Ibid., 75. It is impossible to do justice to the full complexity of Agamben's argumentation in this place; but I lift from the argument those passages most pertinent to the present argument only.

32. Ibid., 76.

33. Maurice Blanchot, *The Work of Fire*, trans. Charlotte Mandell (Stanford: Stanford University Press, 1995), 301.

34. Ibid., 308.

35. Ibid., 310.

36. Ibid.

37. Ibid., 303.

38. Lyotard, *The Postmodern Condition*, trans. Geoffrey Bennington and Brian Massumi (Manchester: Manchester University Press, 1984), 81.

39. I see this as a specifically 'modern' trope; for its early modern manifestations, see my *John Donne, Undone* (London: Methuen, 1986). The greatest early modern examination of the figure is and remains Montaigne, throughout his *Essais*.

40. Blanchot, *Work of Fire*, 313.

41. Ibid.

42. This was noted years ago by Barthes, of course.

43. Alasdair MacIntyre, *Three Rival Versions of Moral Enquiry* (London: Duckworth, 1990), 82.

44. Blanchot, *Work of Fire*, 318.

45. Ibid., 319

46. Ibid., 307; and we might compare here Lyotard's injunction that the artist ignore the audience.

47. Jacques Derrida, *Cosmopolites de tous les pays, encore un effort!* (Paris: Galilée, 1997), 42: 'L'hospitalité, c'est la culture même et ce n'est pas une éthique parmi d'autres' (Hospitality is culture itself, and is not just one ethos among others).

48. For a fuller investigation of the stakes of this, although in work that is at a slight tangent to this present piece, see my comments on the place of love in criticism in *Criticism and Modernity* and in *Alterities*; and see especially the relation of love to a question concerning Europe in *Criticism and Modernity*.

49. Anne Fourmantelle and Jacques Derrida, *De l'hospitalité* (Paris: Calmann-Levy, 1997), 29.

50. See Sylviane Agacinski, *Critique de l'égocentrisme* (Paris: Galilée, 1996), esp. chap. 5; and cf. Agamben, *Idea della prosa* (Milan: Feltrinelli, 1985), 'idea dell'amore'.

CHAPTER 3

This chapter was initially presented as a keynote lecture in the Sixth International Symposium on Comparative Literature, held in the University of Cairo, 21–23 November 2000. I am extremely grateful to the organisers of the conference, to the offices of the British Council in London and in Cairo who made my trip possible, to Nairy Avedissian who organised my trip, and to the participants in the conference, particularly Hoda Gindi, who made it an extraordinarily productive meeting and a most hospitable encounter between east and west.

1. I owe this term to David Simpson, *Situatedness; or, Why We Keep Saying Where We're Coming From* (Durham, NC: Duke University Press, 2002).

2. See, for example, the essays collected in *Place/Culture/Representation*, ed. James Duncan and David Ley (London: Routledge, 1993); or the work of Derek Gregory, *Geographical Imaginations* (Oxford: Blackwell, 1994); and the extremely influential work of David Harvey, such as his *Justice, Nature and the Geography of Difference* (Oxford: Blackwell, 1996).

3. It should be clear from my opening chapters that 'prejudice' does not denote a moral position, but rather a temporal predicament: that of a judgement or criticism that somehow is out of temporal step with itself—premature, we might say. The present chapter deepens this analysis.

4. George Herbert, *The English Poems of George Herbert*, ed. C. A. Patrides (London: Dent, 1974), 57. Cf. a similar use of the term in Shakespeare, *Twelfth Night*, 3.1.80, when Viola and Toby talk about entering the house and Viola says, 'I will answer you with gait and entrance. But we are prevented', as Olivia opens the door from the other side.

5. On this, see those images deployed by Derrida, first in *La Carte postale* (Paris: Flammarion, 1980) and then parodied by Geoffrey Bennington and Derrida in *Jacques Derrida* (Paris: Seuil, 1991), in which, first, Plato stands behind Socrates and then, second, Bennington stands behind Derrida. We should compare also here two other motifs that will be important in subsequent arguments in this book: first, Derrida's comments on the temporality of love or friendship in his *Politiques de l'amitié* (Paris: Galilée, 1994), 25–27; and second, Augustine's attitude to teaching as explicated by Alasdair MacIntyre, in his *Three Rival Versions of Moral Enquiry* (London: Duckworth, 1990), 82.

6. See Laurence Sterne, *The Life and Opinions of Tristram Shandy* (1759–1767; Harmondsworth: Penguin, 1975), 286.

7. Homi Bhabha, *The Location of Culture* (London: Routledge, 1994), 7.

8. John Donne, 'The Good Morrow', in *Donne: Poetical Works*, ed. Herbert J. C. Grierson (Oxford: Oxford University Press, 1929; repr. 1979), 7. For many, it might appear to be controversial to begin a meditation on the modern/postmodern in the seventeenth century; but, as I have argued before, following Lyotard in this, the postmodern is characterised as a mood or attitude rather than as a chronologically bracketed period. For a fuller explanation of this, see the introduction to my *Postmodernism* (New York: Harvester-Wheatsheaf/Columbia University Press, 1993).

9. For a profound meditation on the odd temporality of this, see the work of Maurice Blanchot, in particular his *The Instant of My Death*, which is published alongside Derrida's commentary, *Demeure*, in *The Instant of My Death*, trans. Elizabeth Rottenberg (Stanford: Stanford University Press, 2000).

10. The reader, seeing me open this argument on the relations of east to west with a reference to Donne and his erotic mappings, might have expected me to refer to the famous lines from Elegy 18, in which Donne refers to woman as 'my

America, my new-found land'; but I suggest that a more appropriate reference here might be to that fuller mapping of the female body that is given in Elegy 19, 'Love's Progress', where the body is shaped by an 'east/west' set of oppositions.

11. Jean-François Lyotard, *The Differend*, trans. Georges van den Abbeele (Manchester: Manchester University Press, 1990), xi.

12. For a fuller explication, see my *Postmodernism*; and cf. my studies *Alterities: Criticism, History, Representation* (Oxford: Oxford University Press, 1996); and *After Theory*, revised and expanded 2nd ed. (Edinburgh: Edinburgh University Press, 1996).

13. Edward Said, *Culture and Imperialism* (London: Chatto and Windus, 1993), 6.

14. Aijaz Ahmad, *In Theory* (London: Verso, 1994), 167.

15. Oswald Spengler, *The Decline of the West* (1918), trans. Charles Francis Atkinson (London: Allen & Unwin, 1926), 1:16, n. 1.

16. It is worth noting, in passing, the coincidence of this prioritisation of narrative cause-and-effect structure in history with the rise to prominence of the European novel. The kinds of narrative that are produced in both cases suggest the centrality of *Bildung*, and also the centrality of the single great individual hero figure in both novel (protagonist/character) and history ('great man'/hero). History is thus reduced to the stories of 'characters', and politics to morality.

17. Spengler, *Decline of the West*, 1, 14.

18. Ibid., 1, 17. In relation to this, we might compare Michel Serres, who questions such an optimistic view of history in his *Eclaircissements: Entretiens avec Bruno Latour* (Paris: Garnier-Flammarion, 1994), 76. There, Serres calls into question the 'theological' view that regards the history of philosophy as a series of errors, there to be 'corrected' by we moderns, as we gradually purge ourselves of one error after another. He satisfies this as a mode of thought that can say: 'Ouf! Nous sommes enfin entrés dans le vrai'—truth is as it is for no better reason than that we are pronouncing it here, now. A literary comparison is available in Swift's satirical attack on the modern author in *A Tale of a Tub* (1704), who proclaims himself the most truthful because the latest writer.

19. See Geoffrey Bennington, professorial lecture delivered 4 June 1996, available at http://www.sussex.ac.uk/Users/sffc4/inaug.doc.

20. Samuel Beckett, *The Unnamable* in *Molloy; Malone Dies; The Unnamable* (London: John Calder, 1979), 386.

21. Spengler, *Decline of the West*, 1, 13.

22. Michael North, *Reading 1922* (Oxford: Oxford University Press, 1999), 19–20.

23. Said, *Culture and Imperialism*, 155.

24. Said, *Orientalism* (London: Routledge, 1978), 84; cf. Spengler, *Decline of the West*, 1, 12, on the mummy as 'a symbol of the first importance. The body of the dead man was made everlasting'.

CHAPTER 4

1. Walter Benjamin, *Selected Writings, Volume 1: 1913–1926*, ed. Marcus Bullock and Michael W. Jennings (Cambridge, MA: Harvard University Press, 1996), 3–5. See also Immanuel Kant, *Critique of Pure Reason*, 2nd ed., 1787, trans. J. M. D. Meiklejohn (London: Dent, 1946), 30.

2. Kant, *Critique*, 31.

3. Ibid., 30.

4. Benjamin, 'Experience', *Selected Writings*, 1:3. I suggest the alignment with modernism so that we can see the emergence of these new forms for what they might have been: the revolt of youth against its immediate forebears, or 'modernism as adolescence'.

5. Ibid., 1:4

6. Benjamin, *Selected Writings, Volume 2: 1927–1934*, ed. Michael W. Jennings, Howard Eiland, and Gary Smith (Cambridge, MA: Harvard University Press, 1999), 266; cf. Charles Baudelaire, *Critique d'art*, ed. Claude Pichois (Paris: Gallimard, 1992), 355.

7. For Benjamin, 'philistine' is an ambivalent term. On one hand, it is the slang term (*Philister*) for the townfolk in a university town, to distinguish them from educated students; on the other, Benjamin knew the Philistines as a tribe from the Old Testament, those occupying the land we now identify as Palestine.

8. Walter Benjamin, 'The Work of Art in the Age of Mechanical Reproduction', in *Illuminations*, ed. Hannah Arendt, trans. Harry Zohn (London: Fontana, 1973), 243.

9. See Momme Brodersen, *Walter Benjamin: A Biography*, trans. Malcolm R. Green and Ingrida Ligers (London: Verso, 1997), 49.

10. Cited in Brodersen, *Walter Benjamin*, 48.

11. See F. R. Leavis, *Mass Civilisation and Minority Culture* (Cambridge: Minority Press, 1930), 3–4, 8, and passim. The views here expressed are variously reiterated throughout Leavis's career, especially in those essays dealing with the sociology of culture, as in *For Continuity* (Cambridge: Minority Press, 1933); *Education and the University* (London: Chatto & Windus, 1943); *The Living Principle* (London: Chatto & Windus, 1975); and in the posthumously collected papers in *The Critic as Anti-Philosopher*, ed. G. Singh (London: Chatto & Windus, 1982). The leftist criticism of the past thirty years, suspicious of Leavis and of his emphasis on experience, now paradoxically finds itself validating experience—specifically, the experience of the oppressed.

12. John Dewey, 'The Basic Values and Loyalties of Democracy', in *The Political Writings*, ed. Debra Morris and Ian Shapiro (Indianapolis, IN: Hackett, 1993), 208, 209.

13. For a different take on this, see my essay 'On Critical Humility', in Paul

Sheehan, ed., *Becoming Human* (Westport, CT: Praeger, 2003), 165–80.

14. For more on this, see my *Criticism and Modernity: Aesthetics, Literature and Nations in Europe and its Academies* (Oxford: Oxford University Press, 1999).

15. Montesquieu, *Essai sur le goût* (Paris: Ed. Payot & Rivages, 1994), 17 (my translation).

16. Let one phrase stand as synecdoche for the whole tendency: Catherine Belsey opens her book on desire with this question and answer: 'What are the materials of this study? Experience? Perish the thought!'. Belsey, *Desire* (Oxford: Blackwell, 1994), 10.

17. Fredric Jameson, *The Political Unconscious* (London: Methuen, 1981), 9.

18. Giorgio Agamben, *Infancy and History* (1978), trans. Liz Heron (London: Verso, 1993), 13–14.

19. Gianni Vattimo, *The Transparent Society* (1989), trans. David Webb (Cambridge: Polity, 1992), 17.

20. Paul Zweig, *The Adventurer* (London: Dent, 1974), 3–4.

21. Benjamin, *Illuminations*, 258.

22. Augustine, *City of God*, trans. Henry Bettenson (Harmondsworth: Penguin, 1972), 512. Samuel Johnson uses a similar tactic, attacking Optimism, in his review of Soame Jenyns's *Free Inquiry*. For my commentary on how this relates to deconstruction as a 'modern, Optimistic' thinking, see my *On Modern Authority* (Brighton: Harvester, 1987), 235.

23. Jacques Derrida, *On Cosmopolitanism and Forgiveness*, trans. Mark Dooley (London: Routledge, 2001), 16.

24. A useful analogy here is in Sheldon Wolin's 'Fugitive Democracy', in *Democracy and Difference*, ed. Seyla Benhabib (Princeton, NJ: Princeton University Press, 1996), 31–45. There, Wolin distinguishes 'politics' ('continuous, ceaseless, endless') from 'the political' ('episodic, rare'): culture, I contend, is not politics, but rather political, in this sense. See my *Criticism and Modernity*, 113, on this.

25. John Keats, *Selected Poetry and Letters*, ed. R. H. Fogle (San Francisco: Rinehart, 1951), 305.

26. Michel de Montaigne, *Essais* (Paris: Garnier-Flammarion, 1969), 1:143 (my translation).

27. W. B. Yeats, *Collected Poems*, 2nd ed. (London: Macmillan, 1950), 393; W. H. Auden, *Collected Poems*, ed. Edward Mendelson (London: Faber and Faber, 1976), 197.

28. Friedrich Schiller, *On the Aesthetic Education of Man*, ed. Elizabeth M. Wilkinson and L. A. Willoughby (Oxford: Clarendon, 1967), 97.

29. Isobel Armstrong, *The Radical Aesthetic* (Oxford: Blackwell, 2000), 37; cf. Leavis's insistence that a literary-critical education is one that trains 'intelligence and sensibility together' in *Education and the University*, 34, 38, 67–68, 70. For a fuller examination of the effects of this, see my essay 'On Reading', *Critical Quar-*

terly 45 (2003): 6–21, esp. 10–12, where I am able to compare contemporary educational policy in the advanced societies with a British nineteenth-century decision, attacked by Arnold, among others, to pay schools 'by results', as Robert Lowe put it.

30. Charles Dickens, *Hard Times* (1854), ed. Terry Eagleton (London: Methuen, 1987), 16.

31. Theodor Adorno and Max Horkheimer, *Dialectic of Enlightenment*, trans. John Cumming (London: Verso, 1979), 6.

32. Armstrong, *Radical Aesthetic*, 38.

33. Note that this does not imply a 'two cultures' mentality: I stress that the latter mode here is *not* to be identified with the mode of the hard sciences, for these too require the inhabiting of potentiality that is culture: these too are aesthetic. If an opposition is required, let it be 'business studies' that has no place in a university.

34. Paul Ricoeur, 'The Metaphorical Process as Cognition, Imagination, and Feeling', in *On Metaphor*, ed. Sheldon Sacks (Chicago: Chicago University Press, 1979), 141–57.

35. Alain Badiou, *Petit manuel d'inesthétique* (Paris: Seuil, 1998), 92 (my translation).

36. Ibid., 97 (my translation).

37. Ibid., 98.

38. Montesquieu, *Essai*, 31.

39. Paul Valéry, *Morceaux choisis* (Paris: Gallimard, 1930), 250–51.

40. See Wayne C. Booth, *The Company We Keep* (Berkeley: California University Press, 1988).

41. See Leavis, *Living Principle*, 33–35.

42. Plato, *Symposium*, trans. Christopher Gill (London: Penguin, 1999), 38.

43. Benjamin, *Selected Writings*, 2:262.

CHAPTER 5

1. John Dewey, *Political Writings*, ed. Debra Morris and Ian Shapiro (Indianapolis, IN: Hackett, 1993), 208.

2. For a somewhat satirical, yet still useful and informative, attack on the premature utopianism of this, see Terry Eagleton, *Literary Theory* (Oxford: Blackwell, 1983), 44–46.

3. I. A. Richards, *The Principles of Literary Criticism* (London: Routledge, 1924; repr. 1967), 193.

4. S. T. Coleridge, *Biographia Literaria*, ed. George Watson (1817; repr. London: Dent, 1975), 173–74.

5. For a useful gloss on this, see Franco Moretti, *The Way of the World*, trans. Albert Sbraggia (London: Verso, 1987).

6. See W. K. Wimsatt, *The Verbal Icon* (New York: Noonday Press, 1958); William Empson, *Seven Types of Ambiguity*, 3rd ed. (Harmondsworth: Penguin, 1972), 274; Terry Eagleton, *Literary Theory* (Oxford: Blackwell, 1983), 6–7; Søren Kierkegaard, *Either/Or* (1843), trans. Alastair Hannay (Harmondsworth: Penguin, 1992), 50.

7. John Keats, *Selected Poetry and Letters*, ed. Richard Harter Fogle (San Francisco: Rinehart, 1969), 308.

8. Edward W. Said, *The World, the Text, the Critic* (London: Faber and Faber, 1983), 28.

9. Kierkegaard, *Either/Or*, 56.

10. Giorgio Agamben, *Potentialities*, trans. Daniel Heller-Roazen (Stanford: Stanford University Press, 1999), 179.

CHAPTER 6

1. Ludwig Wittgenstein, *Tractatus Logico-Philosophicus*, trans. C. K. Ogden (London: Routledge, 1922), 185.

2. See Augustine, *City of God*, trans. Henry Bettenson (Harmondsworth: Penguin, 1972), book 13, chap. 11, 519–20; and cf. my commentary on this in my *Criticism and Modernity: Aesthetics, Literature and Nations in Europe and Its Academies* (Oxford: Oxford University Press, 1999), 200–204.

3. See John Donne, *The Complete English Poems*, ed. A. J. Smith (Harmondsworth: Penguin, 1971), 313; T. S. Eliot, *Complete Poems and Plays* (London: Faber, 1969), 195.

4. Maurice Blanchot, *The Work of Fire*, trans. Charlotte Mandell (Stanford: Stanford University Press, 1995), 337.

5. Giorgio Agamben, *Moyens sans fin* (Paris: Bibliothèque Rivages, 1995), 103. The English version in my text is my translation from the French edition. Unless otherwise stated in my footnotes, translations from Italian or French editions of Agamben's works are my own.

6. Sylviane Agacinski, *Le Passeur du temps: Modernité et nostalgie* (Paris: Seuil, 2000), 152 (my translation).

7. See Walter Benjamin, *Illuminations*, ed. Hannah Arendt, trans. Harry Zohn (London: Fontana, 1973), 243–44.

8. Charles Baudelaire, *Critique d'art*, ed. Claude Pichois (Paris: Gallimard, 1992), 345 (my translation).

9. Ibid., 355 (my translation).

10. John Macmurray, *Creative Society* (London: Student Christian Movement Press, 1935), 93.

11. Agamben, *Infancy and History*, trans. Liz Heron (London: Verso, 1993), 13.

12. Ibid., 13–14.

13. Ibid., 14.

14. It is worth recalling here that Descartes explicitly warns his reader against following his own 'dangerous' example. See René Descartes, *Philosophical Works*, trans. Elizabeth S. Haldane and G. R. T. Ross (Cambridge: Cambridge University Press, 1969), 1:90–91; and cf. my commentary on this in relation to the issue of representation in modernity in *Criticism and Modernity*, 16–21.

15. Agamben, *Infancy and History*, 19 (intercalated comment mine).

16. Ibid., 14.

17. Ibid., 22; for the importance of this precision in reading Descartes, see my *Reading (Absent) Character* (Oxford: Oxford University Press, 1983), esp. 34–36, 87–123.

18. Agamben, *Infancy and History*, 23.

19. See Francis Hutcheson, *Philosophical Writings*, ed. R. S. Downie (London: Everyman, 1994), 15 and passim. For the argument that places Hutcheson at the root of modern aesthetics, and for the consequences of that refocusing of European aesthetic philosophy, see section 2, 'The Subject of Democracy', of my *Criticism and Modernity*.

20. Agamben, *La communità che viene* (Turin: Einaudi, 1990), 4; cf. my *Criticism and Modernity*, chap. 2, 'Love as the European Humour', esp. 57–59.

21. Agamben, *Communità*, 3.

22. Ibid., 4. It is perhaps worth pointing out that this singularity is not the Scotist *haecceitas*, such as we might see it reflected in Joyce's *Portrait of the Artist of a Young Man*, where Stephen 'explains' Thomist aesthetics by isolating a butcher's boy's basket in all its *integritas, consonantia, claritas*. See James Joyce, *A Portrait of the Artist as a Young Man*, in *The Essential James Joyce*, ed. Harry Levin (Harmondsworth: Penguin, 1963), 218 ff.

23. Jacques Derrida, *The Gift of Death*, trans. David Wills (University of Chicago Press, 1995), 41.

24. Montaigne, *Essais* (Paris: Garnier-Flammarion, 1969), chap. 6, 2:41 (my translation).

25. Ibid, 2:6, 2:47.

26. See Agamben, *Infancy and History*, 39–41.

27. Ibid., 40.

28. Ibid., 41. For the relevant passage in Rousseau, see J. J. Rousseau, *Les Rêveries du promeneur solitaire* (Manchester: Editions de l'Université de Manchester, 1946; repr. 1968), 13–14 (the 'deuxième promenade').

29. Agamben, *Infancy and History*, 50. For the relevant Wordsworth text, see William Wordsworth, *Poetical Works*, ed. Thomas Hutchinson, rev. Ernest de Selincourt (Oxford: Oxford University Press, 1969), 460. See especially stanza 5 of the *Immortality Ode* here, beginning: 'Our birth is but a sleep and a forgetting', and stanza 7, on the infant coming into language.

30. This is, in its brevity, a crude formulation here; for more precise argu-

ment, see my *Alterities: Criticism, History, Representation* (Oxford: Oxford University Press, 1996).

31. Tzvetan Todorov, *Le jardin imparfait* (Paris: Grasset, 1998), 74 (my translation).

32. Marx, *The Eighteenth Brumaire of Louis Bonaparte* (Peking: Foreign Languages Press, 1978), 9.

33. Agamben, *Homo Sacer*, trans. Daniel Heller-Roazen (Stanford: Stanford University Press, 1998), 15.

34. Badiou, *Petit manuel d'inesthétique* (Paris: Seuil, 1998), 29.

35. Agamben, *Infancy and History*, 104.

36. Ibid., 86.

37. The by now classic formulation of this in sociology is Pierre Bourdieu, *Distinction*, trans. Richard Nice (London: Routledge, 1984).

38. Agamben, *The Man Without Content*, trans. Georgia Albert (Stanford: Stanford University Press, 1999), 19.

39. Ibid., 8. See also Wayne C. Booth, *The Company We Keep* (Berkeley: University of California Press, 1988), for that entirely different—more conventional—approach to literary ethics. On writing and 'Terror', see also Maurice Blanchot, 'Literature and the Right to Death', in *The Work of Fire*, 319–22.

40. Agamben, *Man Without Content*, 16.

41. G. W. F. Hegel, *Introductory Lectures on Aesthetics*, trans. Michael Inwood (Harmondsworth: Penguin, 1993), 4; but cf. also Hegel, *Aesthetics*, trans. T. M. Knox (Oxford: Oxford University Press, 1975), 1:2, for a slightly more precise translation, but one whose precision, paradoxically, renders back the initial indeterminacy—even obscurity—to the Hegel text.

42. Agamben, *Homo Sacer*, 124.

43. Ibid, 9–10.

44. Agamben, *Moyens sans fin*, 51.

45. Ibid., 52.

46. Agamben, *Homo Sacer*, 134.

47. For the full clarification of this, see Agamben, *Potentialities*, trans. Daniel Heller-Roazen (Stanford: Stanford University Press, 1999), 179–80.

CHAPTER 7

1. Leszek Kolakowsi, *Freedom, Fame, Lying and Betrayal: Essays on Everyday Life*, trans. Agnieszka Kolakowska (Harmondsworth: Penguin, 1999), 25.

2. Roman Frister, *The Cap, or The Price of a Life* (London: Weidenfeld, 1999). This autobiographical example, taken from the facts of a life, clearly has demanded a treatment within fictional literature in the past, most obviously in Ovid and in Shakespeare.

3. See Jacques Derrida, *The Gift of Death* (1992), trans. David Wills (Chicago: University of Chicago Press, 1995), 41: 'Now to have the experience of responsibility on the basis of the law that is given, that is, to have the experience of one's absolute singularity and apprehend one's own death, amounts to the same thing. Death is very much that which nobody else can undergo or confront in my place. . . . It is from the site of death as the place of my irreplaceability, that is, of my singularity, that I feel called to responsibility'. For a fuller exploration of this argument in relation specifically to the case of Molière's *Le misanthrope*, see my study of *Criticism and Modernity* (Oxford: Oxford University Press, 1999), especially chap. 2, 'Love as the European Humour'.

4. The reference to Lyotard here is to his arguments in *Le Différend* (Paris: Minuit, 1983).

5. See James Beattie, *An Essay on the Nature and Immutability of Truth* (Edinburgh: Kincaid and Bell, 1777; facsimile repr., New York: Garland, 1983).

6. Hannah Arendt, *The Human Condition*, 2nd ed. (Chicago: University of Chicago Press, 1998), 50.

7. This is also consistent with, for examples, the work of Lennard J. Davis, in *Resisting Novels* (London: Methuen, 1987), or of Franco Moretti, in *The Way of the World*, trans. Albert Sbraggia (London: Verso, 1987). In these studies, there is a convincing argument that part of the function of the novel (and, in Moretti's case, specifically of the Bildungsroman) is the establishment of an ideological community. It is worth noting that these texts appear broadly at the same moment that Stanley Fish is modifying his early reader-response theories in order to allow him to speak of 'communities of interpreters'. My claim here is that such a community gets its identity precisely through the ways in which it establishes and validates fiction: that is, through the particular ethical stance that is established, dialectically, between texts and readers to organise communities, however these latter may be described (e.g., communities of scholars, linguistic communities, nations, regions, historical moments or complexes, critical 'schools'). Arendt, in *The Human Condition*, argues that the specific inflection given to the 'public realm' in these terms is entirely consistent with the development of the modern nation-state, in explicit opposition to the ancient city-state, where the public was defined as the *political* and as the realm of freedom. It may be worth considering that current critical confusions of the social with the political have much to do with the reestablishment, in the face of globalisation, of regional identities and city-states.

8. Tzvetan Todorov, *Les morales de l'histoire* (Paris: Hachette; Grasset & Fasquelle, 1991), 168.

9. See Richard Rorty, *Philosophy and Social Hope* (Harmondsworth: Penguin, 1999).

10. The case for this supposed relativism of truth and its consequence is easily trounced in much of the work of Christopher Norris, who admittedly takes the

case against which he argues rather too seriously. See, for example, Norris, *What's Wrong with Postmodernism* (Hemel Hempstead: Harvester-Wheatsheaf, 1990); and *Truth and the Ethics of Criticism* (Manchester: Manchester University Press, 1994). See also, more recently, Terry Eagleton, *After Theory* (London: Allen Lane, 2003), a book which bears no resemblance to Thomas Docherty, *After Theory* (1990), revised and expanded 2nd ed. (Edinburgh: Edinburgh University Press, 1996).

11. I shall have more to say on the seeming paradox or circularity of this later in this chapter. For the moment, all that it is important to note is that I am claiming that fictions exist primarily for themselves: their purpose, in being read, is to constitute a reader through that act of reading who will be capable of reading them in the first place. My presentation of such a paradox is indebted to the work of Alain Badiou and to that of Alasdair MacIntyre on Augustine, as will become clear.

12. For a fuller exploration of the relation of reading to autonomy, see my piece 'On Reading' in *Critical Quarterly* 45 (2003): 6–19.

13. For the classic and seminal work on this conflict of interpretations within the hermeneutic tradition, see, for examples, Paul Ricoeur, *De l'interprétation: Essai sur Freud* (Paris: Seuil, 1976); and Ricoeur, *Hermeneutics and the Human Sciences*, trans. John B. Thompson (Cambridge: Cambridge University Press, 1981).

14. For a fuller explication of his attitude to secularisation, which is taken from Arnold Gehlen, see Gianni Vattimo, *The End of Modernity*, trans. Jon R. Snyder (Cambridge: Polity, 1988); and, more thoroughly, *Credere di credere* (Milan: Garzanti, 1996).

15. In Augustine, as we have repeatedly seen, the closest we come to a reconciliation of such a contest of epistemology with ontology is in that specific present moment characterised by death. See Augustine, *City of God*, trans. Henry Bettenson (Harmondsworth: Penguin, 1972), 519–20. See also my commentary on this in my *Criticism and Modernity*, 200 and passim.

16. Jean-Jacques Rousseau, *Ecrits politiques*, ed. Gérard Mairet (Paris: Livre de Poche, 1992), 27. In relation to this, further, see Gianni Vattimo's explorations of such 'transparency' in the contemporary electronic media age in his *The Tranparent Society*, trans. David Webb (Cambridge: Polity, 1992).

17. Recall here Arendt's propositions: it is not the case that there is to be some match between the private and the public spheres; rather, the public sphere functions to give reality to the private realm itself. She writes on this that 'The decisive historical fact is that modern privacy in its most relevant function, to shelter the intimate, was discovered as the opposite not of the political sphere but of the social'; and it is Rousseau whom she credits as the 'first articulate explorer and to an extent even theorist of [this] intimacy' (*Human Condition*, 38).

18. Rousseau, *Ecrits politiques*, 93.

19. See Francis Hutcheson, *Philosophical Writings*, ed. R. S. Downie (London: Everyman, 1994).

20. Jean Ricardou, *Nouveaux problèmes du roman* (Paris: Seuil, 1976), 106.

21. The state of nature, in this regard, is what Clément Rosset would regard as 'idiotic', marked by a pure singularity; but for Rosset, such a singularity is precisely the condition of what he calls reality. The real is that which cannot be duplicated, that which evades representation, according to Rosset; and it is just such a reality that Rousseau is the first to articulate and legitimise. See Rosset, *L'objet singulier* (Paris: Minuit, 1979).

22. The references here are to Luigi Pirandello's *Sei personaggi in cerca d'autore*, and to T. S. Eliot's 'The Waste Land'. For the idea of 'posthumous people' that I have in mind here, see Massimo Cacciari, *Posthumous People*, trans. Rodger Friedman (Stanford: Stanford University Press, 1996), but related to Jacques Derrida's musings on ghosts, death, and the spectral in, for examples, his *Spectres de Marx* (Paris: Galilée, 1993), *The Gift of Death*, and *Adieu, à Emmanuel Levinas* (Paris: Galilée, 1997). As 'posthumous people', we find ourselves in a set of social relations where our focus (our centre, that which we gather around to form the social) is vacuous; and more importantly, we find that this social is also an empty moment as well as an empty space. It is thus that we have only 'inauthenticity' in our social relatedness.

23. Rousseau, *Ecrits politiques*, 66–67.

24. Arendt, *Human Condition*, 53; for Arendt's views on *caritas* in more detail, and specifically in relation to love and *cupiditas*, see her *Love and Saint Augustine*, ed. Joanna Vecchiarelli Scott and Judith Chelius Stark (Chicago: University of Chicago Press, 1996), esp. 18 ff. and 77 ff.

25. Arendt, *Human Condition*, 53. For the more overtly ideological argument here, according to which the novel exists partly to ensure that its readership subscribes to ideological norms, see Franco Moretti, *The Way of the World*, in which Moretti argues that it is most especially in the Bildungsroman—that paradigmatic fiction of change, education, formation—that we see precisely the denial of change. Moretti's compelling argument is that in these great novels, the temporal dimension (in which history and change might be seen as possible) is eventually circumscribed under the spatial relation, according to which it is the network of already-existing relations among characters that triumphs over the protagonist; so the lesson of the fiction is that as we grow up, as we learn, we find that the route to our legitimate and valid social being lies in conformity to the already established values of a society that preexists us.

26. See Wayne C. Booth, *The Company We Keep* (Berkeley: University of California Press, 1988); and cf. the precursor of this kind of work in John Bayley, *The Characters of Love* (Constable, 1960). For work that takes the significantly different angle, in which such relations are simply aspects of the wider question of community formation, see, for examples, Leo Bersani, *A Future for Astyanax* (Boston: Little, Brown, 1976); Tobin Siebers, *The Ethics of Criticism* (Ithaca, NY: Cornell

University Press, 1988); and Thomas Docherty, *Reading (Absent) Character* (Oxford: Oxford University Press, 1983).

27. Michel de Montaigne, *Essais* (Paris: Garnier-Flammarion, 1969), 1:232; Aristotle, *Ethics*, trans. J. A. K. Thomson (Harmondsworth: Penguin, 1953), revised trans. by High Tredennick (1976), 258.

28. Aristotle, *Ethics*, 259.

29. Montaigne, *Essais*, 1:236.

30. I take my sense of 'event' here from the philosophies of Lyotard, Deleuze, and Badiou. In oversimplified terms, an event is something that happens whose outcome is not clear in the instant of its occurring; by contrast, an 'action' would be that which happens in accordance with a pregiven programme (or that which is undertaken with a clear end in view). The event is unpredictable, the actions epistemologically and teleologically guaranteed.

31. Jacques Derrida, *Politiques de l'amitié* (Paris: Galilée, 1994), 26.

32. Alain Badiou, *Petit manuel d'inesthétique* (Paris: Seuil, 1998), chap. 1, 'Art et philosophie'. In what follows here, I offer a much abbreviated and simplified version of the argument.

33. In this vital distinction between event and action, we also see the basis for a distinction between ethics and morality. A critic such as Leavis, for whom morality was central to criticism, is unable to arrive at a properly ethical criticism on the grounds that he has no conception of the ethical as event, but grasps only the moral as action. It would follow from this that I am claiming that moralism is unethical.

34. Alasdair MacIntyre, *Three Rival Versions of Moral Enquiry* (London: Duckworth, 1990), 82.

CHAPTER 8

1. See Isaiah Berlin, *Two Concepts of Liberty* (Oxford: Oxford University Press, 1958). The distinction of positive and negative liberties has its roots in the eighteenth century. Berlin remodelled it to suit his arguments for a certain contemporary liberalism.

2. I am hinting at an opposition, then, between French Enlightenment liberalism and German totalitarianism; and this partly to suggest the limitations of Berlin's arguments, arguments that are shaped partly by his contemporary and personal conditioning. In doing so, I am also outlining a set of parameters within which, I shall claim, modern Europe has been constructed. On this, see also Larry Siedentop, *Democracy in Europe* (Harmondsworth: Penguin, 2000), where Siedentop argues that in one way, Europe is hinged between two possible developmental models, the bureaucratic French model and the federalist German model.

3. Philip Pettit, in *Republicanism* (Oxford: Oxford University Press, 1997), 19,

describes the northern Italian republics of this early modern period as 'the first modern European polities'.

4. Stanley Fish, *The Trouble with Principle* (Cambridge: Harvard University Press, 1999).

5. Niccolò Machiavelli, *Discourses on Livy* (1531), trans. Julia Conaway Bondanella and Peter Bondanella (Oxford: Oxford University Press, 1997), 136. The passage just before the long quotation comes from 144.

6. Machiavelli, *Discourses*, 100.

7. Pettit, *Republicanism*, 8.

8. David Hume, 'The Sceptic', in *Selected Essays*, ed. Stephen Copley and Andrew Edgar (Oxford: Oxford University Press, 1993), 98.

9. Ibid., 51–52.

10. Ibid., 119.

11. Ibid. For a fuller development of the argument that I make here regarding Hume and national character, see my *Criticism and Modernity: Aesthetics, Literature and Nations in Europe and its Academies* (Oxford: Oxford University Press, 1999), chap. 5, 'The Politics of Singularity', esp. 132–39.

12. I have been stressing Hume's Scottishness throughout here. Hugh Macdiarmid, in *The Man of (Almost) Independent Mind* (privately published by Giles Gordon, 1962), described Hume as 'undoubtedly the greatest Scotsman of them all'; but my argument here should be placed alongside Macdiarmid's, and also, perhaps more pertinently, alongside Alasdair MacIntyre's chapter on Hume in *Whose Justice? Which Rationality?* (London: Duckworth, 1988), 281–99, 'Hume's Anglicizing Subversion', for a fuller exploration of the extent of Hume's commitments to Scotland and to England.

13. Machiavelli, *Discourses*, 26.

14. For an argument exploring this in more detail, see my *Criticism and Modernity*, chap. 7.

15. For more on this, see my comments on the philosophy of Alain Badiou in my *Alterities: Criticism, History, Representation* (Oxford: Oxford University Press, 1996), 197–207.

16. Michel de Montaigne, 'Du repentir', in *Essais* (Paris: Garnier-Flammarion, 1969), 3:20.

17. Let it be noted that I am far from endorsing the simplistic view, much trumpeted in the academy in the 1980s, that everything in the material world, especially those violent matters concerning war and other conflicts, both domestic and international, are 'essentially' about signification, or that they are fundamentally wars fought between discourses. Staring down the barrel of a gun is a constitutively different matter from staring at a report that inflects the narrative of that situation in particular ideological ways.

18. Jacob Burkhardt, *The Civilization of the Renaissance in Italy* (1860; repr. New York: Harper-Colophon, 1958), 1:115–17.

19. Isaiah Berlin, 'The Originality of Machiavelli,' in *Studies on Machiavelli*, ed. Myron P. Gilmore (Florence: Sansoni, 1972), 192.

20. Ibid., 193, 198.

21. Fish, *Trouble with Principle*, 301.

22. Ibid., 13.

23. It is worth considering the possibility that the real heir of the European Renaissance is contemporary, pragmatic 'America'. In this case, the real scandal would be that this 'America' proposes itself as the home of democracy as such precisely as it simultaneously depletes the public sphere of any substantive meaning. It is, of course, Baudrillard who is the scourge of an 'America' that might want to retain some principle of reality as its ground; Baudrillard in his work from the 1980s onwards has been at pains to show that America (this time without the scare-quotes) is the home not of democracy but of the simulations of such a politics. I make no statement here regarding the outcome of the U.S. elections in 2000; but I invite contemplation of it in the present context.

24. Giorgio Agamben, *Homo Sacer*, trans. Daniel Heller-Roazen (Stanford: Stanford University Press, 1998), 4, 9.

25. Ibid., 46.

26. Ibid.

CHAPTER 9

1. Richard Rorty, *Philosophy and Social Hope* (Harmondsworth: Penguin, 1999), 28.

2. Ibid., 24.

3. Ibid.

4. In thinking about Dewey as a philosopher who enables Rorty to consider pragmatism, America, and democracy all in one breath, it is always worth remembering his sheer longevity. Born in 1859, he entered a world of an America that was still expanding (Texas, New Mexico, and California having all been annexed in 1848); and he was but a six-year-old boy when the Civil War effectively ended slavery and established a new and fundamental ethic—beyond the Eurocentric, as we might put it—for the United States. When he died in 1952, he was still active and still feeling the need to advocate democracy. Although it would be foolish to see the early formation as entirely determining of his mature attitudes, it would be equally foolish to ignore it entirely.

5. See Rorty's *Philosophy and Social Hope*, 6: 'I grew up knowing that all decent people were, if not Trotskyites, at least socialists', a position that he has moved on from, certainly—but not always so very far away.

6. See Fredric Jameson, *The Political Unconscious* (London: Methuen, 1981), 102. It is interesting to note, however, that here Jameson considers Necessity pure-

ly and explicitly as 'the *form* of events' (emphasis Jameson's) and not as something marked or characterised by content. For my own argumentation heretofore, such a Necessity—Necessity as form—would be precisely anathema to any actual history.

7. Rorty, *Philosophy and Social Hope*, 29.

8. T. S. Eliot, 'Tradition and the Individual Talent', in *Selected Essays*, 3rd enlarged ed. (London: Faber and Faber, 1951), 15.

9. G. W. F. Hegel, *Introductory Lectures on Aesthetics*, ed. Michael Inwood, trans. Bernard Bosanquet (Harmondsworth: Penguin, 1993), 4; cf. Hegel, *Aesthetics*, trans. T. M. Knox (Oxford: Oxford University Press, 1975), 1:2.

10. See Hegel, *Introductory Lectures*. Bosanquet gives 'intellectual being' where Knox gives 'spirituality'.

11. Maurice Blanchot, *The Work of Fire*, trans. Charlotte Mandell (Stanford: Stanford University Press, 1995), 313. See also chapter 4 above.

12. Francis Hutcheson, *Philosophical Writings*, ed. R. S. Downie (London: Dent, 1994), 15 and passim.

Index